CHILD ABUSE

BETRAYING A TRUST

ISSN 1534-1607

CHILD ABUSE
BETRAYING A TRUST

Mei Ling Rein

INFORMATION PLUS® REFERENCE SERIES
Formerly published by Information Plus, Wylie, Texas

THOMSON
★
GALE

Detroit • New York • San Francisco • San Diego • New Haven, Conn. • Waterville, Maine • London • Munich

THOMSON
—★—
GALE
™

Child Abuse: Betraying a Trust

Mei Ling Rein

Paula Kepos, Series Editor

Project Editor
John McCoy

Permissions
Margaret Abendroth, Edna Hedblad, Emma Hull

Composition and Electronic Prepress
Evi Seoud

Manufacturing
Drew Kalasky

LIBRARY OF CONGRESS CATALOGING-IN-PUBLICATION DATA

ISBN 0-7876-5103-6 (set)
ISBN 0-7876-9068-6
ISSN 1534-1607

Printed in the United States of America
10 9 8 7 6 5 4 3 2 1

TABLE OF CONTENTS

PREFACE

Child Abuse: Betraying a Trust is part of the *Information Plus Reference Series*. The purpose of each volume of the series is to present the latest facts on a topic of pressing concern in modern American life. These topics include today's most controversial and most studied social issues: abortion, capital punishment, care for the elderly, child abuse, crime, health care, the environment, immigration, minorities, social welfare, women, youth, and many more. Although written especially for the high school and undergraduate student, this series is an excellent resource for anyone in need of factual information on current affairs.

By presenting the facts, it is Thomson Gale's intention to provide its readers with everything they need to reach an informed opinion on current issues. To that end, there is a particular emphasis in this series on the presentation of scientific studies, surveys, and statistics. These data are generally presented in the form of tables, charts, and other graphics placed within the text of each book. Every graphic is directly referred to and carefully explained in the text. The source of each graphic is presented within the graphic itself. The data used in these graphics are drawn from the most reputable and reliable sources, in particular from the various branches of the U.S. government and from major independent polling organizations. Every effort was made to secure the most recent information available. The reader should bear in mind that many major studies take years to conduct, and that additional years often pass before the data from these studies are made available to the public. Therefore, in many cases the most recent information available in 2005 dated from 2002 or 2003. Older statistics are sometimes presented as well, if they are of particular interest and no more-recent information exists.

Although statistics are a major focus of the *Information Plus Reference Series* they are by no means its only content. Each book also presents the widely held positions and important ideas that shape how the book's subject is discussed in the United States. These positions are explained in detail and, where possible, in the words of those who support them. Some of the other material to be found in these books includes: historical background; descriptions of major events related to the subject; relevant laws and court cases; and examples of how these issues play out in American life. Some books also feature primary documents, or have pro and con debate sections giving the words and opinions of prominent Americans on both sides of a controversial topic. All material is presented in an even-handed and unbiased manner; the reader will never be encouraged to accept one view of an issue over another.

HOW TO USE THIS BOOK

The abuse of children is one of America's most tragic social problems. The effects of abuse on a child, be it verbal, physical, sexual, or neglect, can be considerable. Thousands of children die each year as a direct result of abuse, and countless others develop psychological and emotional problems that may well last a lifetime. The causes of abusive behavior in adults and their effects on children are therefore a matter of great concern. The latest scientific studies and theories on these issues are covered in this book. Dealing with child abuse also raises complicated and controversial legal questions, which this book presents and addresses.

Child Abuse: Betraying a Trust consists of eight chapters and three appendices. Each chapter is devoted to a particular aspect of the problem of child abuse in the United States. For a summary of the information covered in each chapter, please see the synopses provided in the Table of Contents at the front of the book. Chapters generally begin with an overview of the basic facts and background information on the chapter's topic, then proceed to examine subtopics of particular interest. For example, Chapter 5: Causes and Effects of Child Abuse begins with a discussion of how the normal pressures of caring for children can sometimes overwhelm people and lead to abuse. It then examines the factors that have been linked to an increased likelihood of abuse, such as living in a single-parent family, young first-time parents, a history of drug abuse by the parents, and other characteristics. Later, the chapter addresses the effects of child abuse on a child's intelligence and behavior over the short and long term. Other topics covered in the chapter include the relationships between child abuse and spousal abuse and controversies surrounding corporal punishment and its impact on children. Readers can find their way through a chapter by looking for the section and subsection headings, which are clearly set off from the text. Or, they can refer to the book's extensive index, if they already know what they are looking for.

Statistical Information

The tables and figures featured throughout *Child Abuse: Betraying a Trust* will be of particular use to the reader in learning about this issue. These tables and figures represent an extensive collection of the most recent and important statistics on child abuse and related issues. For example, reports include statistics on child maltreatment, childhood victimization and later criminality, and the percentage of teenagers polled in 2003 who personally knew someone who had been physically or sexually abused. Thomson Gale believes that making this information available to the reader is the most important way in which we fulfill the goal of this book: To help readers understand the issues and controversies surrounding child abuse in the United States and reach their own conclusions about them.

Each table or figure has a unique identifier appearing above it, for ease of identification and reference. Titles for the tables and figures explain their purpose. At the end of each table or figure, the original source of the data is provided.

In order to help readers understand these often complicated statistics, all tables and figures are explained in the text. References in the text direct the reader to the relevant statistics. Furthermore, the contents of all tables and figures are fully indexed. Please see the opening section of the index at the back of this volume for a description of how to find tables and figures within it.

Appendices

In addition to the main body text and images, *Child Abuse: Betraying a Trust* has three appendices. The first is

the Important Names and Addresses directory. Here the reader will find contact information for a number of organizations that study child abuse, fight child abuse, or that advocate influential opinions and policies on child abuse. The second appendix is the Resources section, which is provided to assist the reader in conducting his or her own research. In this section, the author and editors of *Child Abuse: Betraying a Trust* describe some of the sources that were most useful during the compilation of this book. The final appendix is this book's index.

ADVISORY BOARD CONTRIBUTIONS

The staff of Information Plus would like to extend their heartfelt appreciation to the Information Plus Advisory Board. This dedicated group of media professionals provides feedback on the series on an ongoing basis. Their comments allow the editorial staff who work on the project to make the series better and more user-friendly. Our top priorities are to produce the highest-quality and most useful books possible, and the Advisory Board's contributions to this process are invaluable.

The members of the Information Plus Advisory Board are:

- Kathleen R. Bonn, Librarian, Newbury Park High School, Newbury Park, California

- Madelyn Garner, Librarian, San Jacinto College— North Campus, Houston, Texas

- Anne Oxenrider, Media Specialist, Dundee High School, Dundee, Michigan

- Charles R. Rodgers, Director of Libraries, Pasco-Hernando Community College, Dade City, Florida

- James N. Zitzelsberger, Library Media Department Chairman, Oshkosh West High School, Oshkosh, Wisconsin

COMMENTS AND SUGGESTIONS

The editors of the *Information Plus Reference Series* welcome your feedback on *Child Abuse: Betraying a Trust*. Please direct all correspondence to:

Editors
Information Plus Reference Series
27500 Drake Rd.
Farmington Hills, MI, 48331-3535

CHAPTER 1
CHILD ABUSE—A HISTORY

OVERVIEW

The recognition of child abuse in its multiple forms (physical abuse, sexual abuse, emotional abuse, and neglect) came to the forefront in the twentieth century. Child abuse continues to be more likely recognized in economically developed countries than in developing countries. Children, however, have been beaten and abandoned for many thousands of years, based primarily on the belief that children are the property of their parents.

Early civilizations regularly abandoned deformed or unwanted children, and the ritual sacrifice of children to appease the gods took place in the Egyptian, Carthaginian, Roman, Greek, and Aztec societies. In Roman society the father had complete control over the family, even to the extent that he could kill his children for disobedience. Sexual abuse of children was common in both Greek and Roman societies. Children were also sold as prostitutes. Women often participated in abuse. Petronius (c. 27–c. 66), a Roman writer, recorded the rape of a seven-year-old girl witnessed by a line of clapping women.

During the Middle Ages (c. 350–c. 1450) in Europe, healthy but unwanted children were apprenticed to work or offered to convents and monasteries. Infanticide, or the murder of babies, was also common. The Roman Catholic Church contributed to infanticide when it declared that deformed infants were omens of evil and the product of relations between women and demons or animals. In another example of religious support for what would now be considered child abuse, the archbishop of Canterbury in the seventh century ruled that a man could sell his son into slavery until the child reached the age of seven.

In thirteenth-century England the law read, "If one beats a child until it bleeds, it will remember, but if one beats it to death, the law applies" (Albrecht Peiper, *Chronik der Kinderheilkunde,* Leipzig, Germany: Georg Thieme, 1966). By the child's fourth year, harsh discipline played a major role in his or her socialization. Children and parents were taught that beatings were in the child's best interest. In *The Babees' Book: Medieval Manners for the Young,* a primer on manners used first in the eleventh century in France to educate the upper classes, a verse in "How the Good Wife Taught Her Daughter" instructed future mothers, "But take a smart rod and beat them in a row/Till they cry mercy and their guilt well know/Dear child by this lore/They will love thee ever more" (York University, http://www.yorku.ca/inpar/babees_rickert.pdf [accessed November 2, 2004]).

Children were beaten not only by their parents but also by their teachers. In a poem written around 1500, a schoolboy admitted that he would gladly become a clerk, but learning was such strange work because the birch twigs used for beating were so sharp. The children at an Oxford school must have felt justice was served when their schoolmaster, out early one morning to cut willow twigs for a switch to beat them, slipped, fell into the river, and drowned.

The late Middle Ages and the Renaissance (roughly the fourteenth through sixteenth centuries) saw changes in how society viewed children, but abuse was still common. Neil Postman, in *The Disappearance of Childhood* (New York: Delacorte Press, 1982), noted that the idea that children were small adults had started to change by that time. Among the upper classes children began to receive a long, formal education, increasingly separated from adults and kept with their peers. It was becoming apparent that children were not really that similar to adults after all, but rather like mounds of clay to be molded.

In sixteenth- and seventeenth-century Europe fathers commonly placed their children in apprenticeships to provide inexpensive labor. The apprentice system was the major job training method of pre-industrial Western society. The apprentice who trained with a master frequently worked under conditions that, by today's standards, would be considered severely abusive.

The practice of paternal control was brought to the American colonies, and the father ruled his wife and children. The mother, however, was also expected to discipline her children, inflicting corporal punishment as she saw fit. A child was little more than the property of the parents. At the same time, the child was an asset that could be used to perform work on the farm.

Parental discipline was typically severe, and parents, teachers, and ministers found support for stern discipline in the Bible. Several verses in Proverbs (Proverbs 22:15, Proverbs 23:13–14, and Proverbs 29:15), summed up in the phrase, "Spare the rod and spoil the child," were cited as justification for beating children. It should be noted that the biblical "rod" referred to was a shepherd's rod, used to guide the sheep in the right direction, not to beat the sheep. Church elders taught that children were born corrupted by original sin, and the only path to salvation was "to beat the Devil out of the child." (In Christian theology, original sin is humankind's inherent tendency to sin as a result of Adam's rebellion against God.) Some colonial legislatures even passed "stubborn children laws," giving parents the legal right to kill unruly children. According to journalist Roger Rosenblatt, Massachusetts enacted a law in 1646 that allowed the death penalty for a rebellious child, though the law was never enforced ("The Society That Pretends to Love Children," *New York Times Magazine,* October 8, 1995).

By their teens, many children were living with other families, bound out as indentured servants or apprentices. It was common for heads of households and masters to brutalize these children without fear of reprisal except in cases involving excessive beatings, massive injury, or death.

Holding a Child Abuser Accountable

The earliest recorded trial for child abuse involved a master and his apprentice. In 1639 in Salem, Massachusetts, Marmaduke Perry was charged in the death of his apprentice. The evidence showed the boy had been ill-treated and subjected to "unreasonable correction." Nevertheless, the boy's allegation that the master had been responsible for his fractured skull (which ultimately killed him) was called into question by testimony that claimed that the boy had told someone else that the injury was a result of falling from a tree. Perry was acquitted.

In 1643 a master was executed for killing his servant. In 1655 in Plymouth, Massachusetts, a master found guilty of slaying a servant was punished by having his hand burned and all his property taken away. Other early records show brutal masters being warned for abusing young servants. In some cases the children were freed because of the harsh treatment. Virginia passed laws protecting servants against mistreatment in 1700.

Most of the early recorded cases of child abuse were specifically related to offenses committed by masters against servants and did not involve protecting children from abusive parents. Society generally tolerated the abuse of family members as a personal matter while condemning abuse by strangers.

The few recorded cases involving family matters were limited to the removal of children from "unsuitable" home environments, which usually meant that parents were not giving their children a good religious upbringing or were refusing to instill the proper work ethic. In two Massachusetts cases, in 1675 and 1678, children were removed from such "unsuitable" homes. In the first case the children were taken from the home because the father refused to send them out to apprentice or work. In the second case the same offense was compounded by the father's refusal to attend church services. Physical abuse was not an issue in either case.

It was during the nineteenth century that the American legal system began to change in favor of protecting children even against their own parents. In 1840, in *Johnson v. State* (21 Tenn. [2 Hum.] 283), a Tennessee parent was prosecuted for excessive punishment of a child. According to the testimony, a mother had hit her daughter with her fists, pushed her head against the wall, whipped her, and tied her to a bedpost. A lower court convicted the abusive parent, but a higher court reversed the conviction, claiming that the jury was improperly instructed, but concluding:

> In chastising a child, the parent must be careful that he does not exceed the bounds of moderation and inflict cruel and merciless punishment; if he do[es], he is a trespasser, and liable to be punished by indictment. It is not, then, the infliction of punishment, but the excess, which constitutes the offence, and what this excess shall be is not a conclusion of law, but a question of fact for the determination of the jury.

ABUSE DURING THE INDUSTRIAL REVOLUTION

With the coming of industrialization in Europe and the United States, the implied right of abuse was transferred to the factory, where orphaned or abandoned children as young as five worked sixteen hours a day. In many cases irons were riveted around their ankles to bind the children to the machines, while overseers with whips ensured productivity. In England the Factory Act of 1802 stopped this pauper-apprentice work system, but the law did not apply to children who had parents. Those youngsters worked in the mills for twelve hours a day at the mercy of often tyrannical supervisors.

Nonworking hours offered little relief to poor, orphaned, or abandoned children. Dependent children such as these were put into deplorable public poorhouses with adult beggars, thieves, and paupers. Not until the beginning of the nineteenth century did the public recognize the terrible abuses that occurred in these almshouses, and major efforts were begun to provide separate housing for children.

During the nineteenth century, middle-class families began to see their children as representative of the family's status. For many of these families, education for the child, rather than labor, became the goal. With this attitude, many of the labor abuses gradually came to an end. Eventually, child labor laws were passed in most industrialized countries to limit the kinds of jobs children could do and the number of hours they could work.

Private Organizations Take Action against Abuse

The first case of child abuse that caught public attention in the United States occurred in 1874. Neighbors of Mary Ellen, a nine-year-old child in New York City, contacted a church social worker, Etta Angell Wheeler, when they heard disturbances from the little girl's tenement ("The Story of Mary Ellen," American Humane Association, http://www.americanhumane.org/site/PageServer? pagename=wh_mission_maryellen_wheeler [accessed November 23, 2004]).

Upon investigating the child's home, the social worker found her suffering from malnutrition, serious physical abuse, and neglect. Mary Ellen was living with Mary and Francis Connolly. The girl, who was said to be the illegitimate daughter of Mrs. Connolly's first husband, was apprenticed to the couple.

At that time there were laws protecting animals, but no local, state, or federal laws protected children. Consequently, Wheeler turned to the American Society for the Prevention of Cruelty to Animals (ASPCA) for help. The case was presented to the court on the theory that the child was a member of the animal kingdom and therefore entitled to the same protection from abuse that the law gave to animals. The court agreed, and the child, because she was considered an animal, was taken from her brutal foster mother.

In court Mary Ellen related how her foster mother beat her daily with a leather whip and cut her face with scissors. She was not allowed to play with other children and was locked in the bedroom whenever her "mamma" left the house. The court placed the child in an orphanage. She was later adopted by the social worker's family.

The court found Mary Connolly guilty of assault and battery for felonious assault with scissors and for beatings that took place during 1873 and 1874. She was sentenced to one year of hard labor in a penitentiary.

Mary Ellen Wilson's case led to the founding of the New York Society for the Prevention of Cruelty to Children (NYSPCC) in 1875. The first child protective agency in the world, the NYSPCC continues in the twenty-first century to work for the best interests of children. Similar societies were soon organized in other U.S. cities. By 1922, fifty-seven societies for the prevention of cruelty to children and 307 other humane societies had been established to tend to the welfare of children. After the federal government began intervening in child welfare, the number of these societies declined.

The Beginnings of Federal Protection for Children

In 1900 the U.S. Census found that about two million American children, representing 18.3% of children ages ten to fifteen, were working in mills, farms, factories, and on city streets all over the country. As a result of this finding, a private organization, the National Child Labor Committee (NCLC), was established in 1904 to work for child labor reforms. The committee hired Lewis Hine (1874–1940) to photograph and write about the working conditions of child laborers, some as young as three years of age, across the country.

It was also during this time that many concerned people lobbied for the creation of a federal agency dedicated solely to promoting the welfare of children. Starting in 1906 and for the next six years, legislators introduced bills proposing such an agency. In 1909 the first White House Conference on the Care of Dependent Children under President Theodore Roosevelt (1858–1919) recommended that Congress pass legislation to create the Children's Bureau. It was not until 1912 that the bill became law under President William Howard Taft (1857–1930).

The Children's Bureau promoted the passage of the Keating-Owen Child Labor Act of 1916 (39 Stat. 675), the first federal law regulating child labor. The act prohibited the interstate sale of products from any mine made by children under the age of sixteen, from any cannery, factory, and shop made by children under the age of fourteen, and from any business employing children under the age of sixteen who worked at night or more than eight hours during the day. The law did not cover youngsters employed in agriculture and domestic work. In 1918, however, the U.S. Supreme Court, in *Hammer v. Dagenhart* (247 U.S. 251), found the law unconstitutional. According to the Court, the law was not about regulating interstate commerce; it was designed to regulate states' manufacturing conditions over which Congress had no right to interfere. It was not until 1938, with the passage of the Fair Labor Standards Act (52 Stat. 1060), that the federal government started regulating child labor, among other provisions. The law established sixteen as the minimum age for child labor and eighteen for hazardous jobs (The Our Documents Initiative, "Keating-Owen Child Labor Act of 1916: Document Info," http://www.ourdocuments.gov/doc.php?flash=false&doc=59# [accessed November 23, 2004]).

MODERN AMERICA

The federal government first provided child welfare services with the passage of the Social Security Act of 1935 (49 Stat. 620). Under Title IV-B (Child Welfare Services Program) of the act, the Children's Bureau received funding for grants to states for "the protection and care of homeless, dependent, and neglected children and children in danger of becoming delinquent." Prior to 1961 Title IV-B was the only source of federal funding for child welfare services.

The 1962 Social Security Amendments (Public Law 87-543) required each state to make child welfare services available to all children. It further required states to provide coordination between child welfare services (under Title IV-B) and social services (under Title IV-A, or the Social Services program), which served families on welfare. The law also revised the definition of "child welfare services" to include the prevention and remedy of child abuse. In 1980 Congress created a separate Foster Care program under Title IV-E.

Title IV-A became Title XX (Social Services Block Grant) in 1981, giving states more options regarding the types of social services to fund. Today child abuse prevention and treatment services have remained an eligible category of service.

State Programs That Help Children at Risk

Under Title IV-B Child Welfare Services (Subpart 1) and Promoting Safe and Stable Families (Subpart 2) programs, families in crisis receive preventive intervention so that children will not have to be removed from their homes. If this cannot be achieved, children are placed in foster care temporarily until they can be reunited with their families. If reunification is not possible, parents' rights are terminated and the children are made available for adoption.

States use the Foster Care (Title IV-E) program funds for the care of foster children and for the training of foster parents, program personnel, and private-agency staff. Title XX funds provide such services as child daycare, child protective services, information and referral, counseling, and employment.

The Battered Child Syndrome and the Development of a Child Abuse Reporting Network

In 1961 Dr. C. Henry Kempe, a pediatric radiologist, and his associates proposed the term "battered child syndrome" at a symposium on the problem of child abuse held under the auspices of the American Academy of Pediatrics. The term refers to the collection of injuries sustained by a child as a result of repeated mistreatment or beatings. The following year *The Journal of the American Medical Association* published the landmark article "The Battered Child Syndrome" (C. Henry Kempe et al., vol. 181, no. 17, July 7, 1962). The term "battered child syndrome" developed into "maltreatment," encompassing not only physical assault but other forms of abuse, such as malnourishment, failure to thrive, medical neglect, and sexual and emotional abuse.

Dr. Kempe had also proposed that physicians be required to report child abuse. According to the National

Association of Counsel for Children, by 1967, after Dr. Kempe's findings had gained general acceptance among health and welfare workers and the public, forty-four states had passed legislation that required the reporting of child abuse to official agencies, and the remaining six states had voluntary reporting laws. This was one of the most rapidly accepted pieces of legislation in American history. Initially only doctors were required to report and then only in cases of "serious physical injury" or "nonaccidental injury." Today all the states have laws that require most professionals who serve children to report all forms of suspected abuse and either require or permit any citizen to report child abuse.

One of the reasons for the lack of prosecution of early child abuse cases was the difficulty in determining whether a physical injury was a case of deliberate assault or an accident. In recent years, however, doctors of pediatric radiology have been able to determine the incidence of repeated child abuse through sophisticated developments in X-ray technology. These advances have allowed radiologists to see more clearly such things as subdural hematomas (blood clots around the brain resulting from blows to the head) and abnormal fractures. This brought about more recognition in the medical community of the widespread incidence of child abuse, along with growing public condemnation of abuse.

Federal Legislation against Child Abuse

In 1974 Congress passed the Child Abuse Prevention and Treatment Act (CAPTA; Public Law 93-247). The law stated:

> [Child abuse and neglect refer to] the physical or mental injury, sexual abuse, negligent treatment or maltreatment of a child under age eighteen, or the age specified by the child protection law of the state in question, by a person who is responsible for the child's welfare under circumstances which indicate the child's health or welfare is harmed or threatened thereby, as determined in accordance with regulations prescribed by the Secretary of Health, Education, and Welfare.

This law created the National Center on Child Abuse and Neglect (NCCAN), which developed standards for handling reports of child maltreatment. NCCAN also established a nationwide network of child protective services and served as a clearinghouse for information and research on child abuse and neglect.

Since 1974 CAPTA has been amended a number of times. (See Figure 1.1.) In 1978 the Child Abuse Prevention and Treatment and Adoption Reform Act (Public Law 95-266) promoted the passage of state laws providing comprehensive adoption assistance. The act provided grants to encourage the adoption of children with special needs and broadened the definition of abuse, adding a specific reference to sexual abuse and exploitation to the basic

FIGURE 1.1

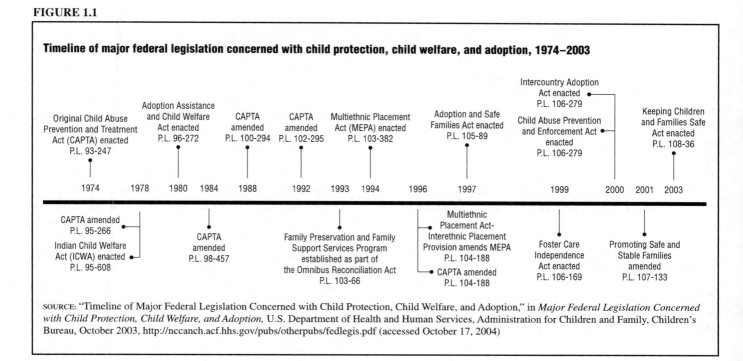

Timeline of major federal legislation concerned with child protection, child welfare, and adoption, 1974–2003

SOURCE: "Timeline of Major Federal Legislation Concerned with Child Protection, Child Welfare, and Adoption," in *Major Federal Legislation Concerned with Child Protection, Child Welfare, and Adoption,* U.S. Department of Health and Human Services, Administration for Children and Family, Children's Bureau, October 2003, http://nccanch.acf.hhs.gov/pubs/otherpubs/fedlegis.pdf (accessed October 17, 2004)

definition. That year the Indian Child Welfare Act (Public Law 95-608) was also enacted to reestablish tribal jurisdiction over the adoption of Native American children.

In response to the public outcry about the placement of an increasing number of children in foster care, Congress passed the Adoption Assistance and Child Welfare Act of 1980 (Public Law 96-272), with the goal of promoting family reunification. In 1988 the Child Abuse Prevention, Adoption and Family Services Act (Public Law 100-294) replaced the original 1974 CAPTA, mandating, among other things, the establishment of a system to collect national data on child maltreatment.

In 1994 Congress passed the Multiethnic Placement Act (Public Law 103-382), directing states to actively recruit adoptive and foster families, especially for minority children waiting a long time for placement in a home. Pursuant to the Child Abuse Prevention and Treatment Act Amendments of 1996 (Public Law 104-235), the National Center on Child Abuse and Neglect (NCCAN) created by the first CAPTA was abolished. Its functions have subsequently been consolidated within the Children's Bureau of the U.S. Department of Health and Human Services.

By 1997 the federal government had realized that reuniting abused children with their families did not always work in the best interests of the children. Congress revisited the "reasonable efforts" for family reunification originally mandated by the 1980 Adoption Assistance and Child Welfare Act. Under the 1997 Adoption and Safe Families Act (Public Law 105-89), "reasonable efforts" was clarified to mean the safety of the child comes first. States were directed to indicate circumstances under which an abused child should not be returned to the parents or caretakers.

The Promoting Safe and Stable Families Amendments of 2001 (Public Law 107-133) was enacted partly to address the rising number of children with incarcerated parents. The law provided a grant program for creating mentoring services for these children. The law also created a new program to assist youth aging out of foster care, helping them pursue an education or vocational training.

In 2003 CAPTA received reauthorization through 2008 under the Keeping Children and Families Safe Act (Public Law 108-36). The law, among other things, directed more comprehensive training of child protective services personnel, including a mandate that they inform alleged abusers, during the first contact, of the nature of complaints against them. The law called for child welfare agencies to coordinate services with other agencies, including public health, mental health, and developmental disabilities agencies. The law also directed the collection of data for the fourth *National Incidence Study of Child Abuse and Neglect.*

Federal Legislation Dealing with the Prosecution of Child Abusers

The Children's Justice and Assistance Act of 1986 (CJA; Public Law 99-401) offers grants to states to improve the investigation and prosecution of cases of child abuse and neglect, especially sexual abuse and exploitation. The program aims to reduce additional trauma to the child by training persons who are involved in child maltreatment cases, such as law enforcement, mental health personnel, prosecutors, and judges. CJA also supports legislation that would allow indirect testimony from children, shorten the time spent in court, and make their courtroom experience less intimidating.

Until 1995 none of the federal child abuse legislation dealt specifically with punishing sex offenders. In December of that year, with growing acknowledgment of and concern about sex crimes against minors, Congress passed the Sex Crimes Against Children Prevention Act of 1995 (Public Law 104-71). The act increased penalties for those who sexually exploit children by engaging in illegal conduct, or for exploitation conducted via the Internet, as well as for those who transport children with the intent to engage in criminal sexual activity.

Three years later Congress enacted the Protection of Children from Sexual Predators Act of 1998 (Public Law 105-314) that, among other things, established the Morgan P. Hardiman Child Abduction and Serial Murder Investigative Resources Center (CASMIRC). The purpose of CASMIRC, as stated in the text of the act, is "to provide investigative support through the coordination and provision of federal law enforcement resources, training, and application of other multidisciplinary expertise, to assist federal, state, and local authorities in matters involving child abductions, mysterious disappearance of children, child homicide, and serial murder across the country."

Congress passed the Prosecutorial Remedies and Other Tools to End the Exploitation of Children Today (PROTECT) Act (Public Law 108-21) on April 30, 2003. Among other things, the act established a national Amber Alert Program for recovering abducted children and provided that there will be no statute of limitations for sex crimes and abduction of children. (Under previous laws, the statute of limitations expired when the child turned twenty-five.) The law also provided for severe penalties for sex tourism and the denial of pretrial release for suspects in federal child rape or kidnap cases. (The Amber Alert program is named after Amber Hagerman of Texas who was abducted and murdered in 1996. She was nine years old. A witness notified police, giving a description of the vehicle and the direction it had gone, but police had no way of alerting the public.)

THE INTERNATIONAL EXPLOITATION OF CHILDREN

Cleric Abuse

Allegations of child abuse have surfaced among several religious denominations. For example, a survey of Roman Catholic dioceses in the United States commissioned by the United States Conference of Catholic Bishops and released in 2004 revealed that 10,667 incidents of alleged sexual abuse occurred between 1950 and 2002 involving 4,392 priests and deacons ("The Nature and Scope of the Problem of Sexual Abuse of Minors by Catholic Priests and Deacons in the United States," http://www.usccb.org/nrb/johnjaystudy [accessed November 1, 2004]). During most of this period, church leaders who knew of the abuse worked to keep it secret, by paying millions of dollars to victims' families and moving the abusive priests from parish to parish. Allegations of sexual abuse by priests have also surfaced in Mexico, Ireland, Canada, Colombia, Venezuela, Italy, Spain, England, Australia, and Hong Kong.

Other religious denominations have also been involved in sexual abuse allegations. Some members of the Jehovah's Witnesses spoke out against their church's policy of handling reports of child sexual abuse. The church follows biblical standards to resolve problems. A group of church elders meet in secret to decide each sexual abuse allegation. The elders require two credible witnesses, including the accuser, to determine whether or not the allegations are true. William Bowen, a former elder and founder of silentlambs, a group that monitors sexual abuse in the Jehovah's Witnesses, claimed that it is usually impossible for a child victim to have a witness to the incident. Without the witnesses to attest to the abuse, the alleged perpetrator is considered innocent and the charges are kept confidential (http://www.silentlambs.org [accessed November 13, 2004]). According to church officials, they do report suspected abuse if the state law requires it.

In June 2000 former Hare Krishna children sued the International Society for Krishna Consciousness (ISKCON), a sect of Hinduism that became popular in the United States during the 1960s. The parents left the children in boarding schools while they went out to recruit new members and to solicit donations. The plaintiffs alleged physical, emotional, and sexual abuse, including being deprived of food and sleep, being severely beaten, being locked up in roach-infested rooms, and being offered in marriage to older men who were patrons of ISKCON. ISKCON officials, while substantiating that the abuse had occurred, denied that hundreds of children were involved.

The lawsuit attempted to use a federal law, Racketeer-Influenced and Corrupt Organizations (RICO) chapter of the Organized Crime Control Act of 1970 (Public Law 91-452), which was originally intended to curb organized crime. The lawsuit sought $400 million in damages from ISKCON congregations and individuals. In September 2001 the U.S. District Court of Dallas, Texas, permanently dismissed the case.

Child Soldiers

In wars past and present throughout the world, government armed forces and opposition groups have forced children to serve as soldiers. According to the *Human Rights Watch World Report 2004: Human Rights and Armed Conflict* (New York, 2004), the number of child soldiers remained constant at about three hundred thousand in at

TABLE 1.1

Definition of "severe forms of trafficking in persons" from the Trafficking Victims' Protection Act

The Act defines "severe form of trafficking in persons" as

(a) sex trafficking in which a commercial sex act is induced by force, fraud, or coercion, or in which the person induced to perform such act has not attained 18 years of age; or (b) the recruitment, harboring, transportation, provision, or obtaining of a person for labor or services, through the use of force, fraud or coercion for the purpose of subjection to involuntary servitude, peonage, debt bondage, or slavery.

Definition of Terms Used in the Term "Severe Forms of Trafficking in Persons":

"Sex trafficking" means the recruitment, harboring, transportation, provision, or obtaining of a person for the purpose of a commercial sex act.

"Commercial sex act" means any sex act on account of which anything of value is given to or received by any person.

"Involuntary servitude" includes a condition of servitude induced by means of (A) any scheme, plan, or pattern intended to cause a person to believe that, if the person did not enter into or continue in such condition that person or another person would suffer serious harm or physical restraint; or (B) the abuse or threatened abuse of the legal process.

"Debt bondage" means the status or condition of a debtor arising from a pledge by the debtor of his or her personal services or of those of a person under his or her control as a security for debt, if the value of those services as reasonably assessed is not applied toward the liquidation of the debt or the length and nature of those services are not respectively limited and defined.

"Coercion" means (A) threats of serious harm to or physical restraint against any person; (B) any scheme, plan or pattern intended to cause a person to believe that failure to perform an act would result in serious harm to or physical restraint against any person; or (C) the abuse or threatened abuse of the legal process.

SOURCE: "Definition of 'Severe Forms of Trafficking in Persons'," in *2004 Trafficking in Persons Report,* U.S. Department of State, June 2004, http://www.state.gov/documents/organization/34158.pdf (accessed October 27, 2004)

least twenty countries in which they were used both by government and nongovernmental forces. As wars ended in such places as Angola and Sierra Leone in 2003, children were recruited, many by abduction, by other countries, including Liberia, Côte d'Ivoire, Burundi, the Democratic Republic of Congo, Myanmar, Sudan, and Uganda.

The Coalition to Stop the Use of Child Soldiers, in *Child Soldier Use 2003: A Briefing for the Fourth UN Security Council Open Debate on Children and Armed Conflict* (London, 2004), reported that the government of Myanmar had an estimated seventy thousand children serving in the armed forces in 2003. Child soldiers in the Democratic Republic of the Congo reportedly were forced to commit atrocities and were raped and beaten. Children in Sri Lanka and northern Uganda continued to be abducted by rebel forces. In Colombia children as young as twelve underwent training in the use of explosives and weapons. Colombian girls also fought on the frontlines. Many served as sexual slaves to military officers.

TRAUMA REPORTED AMONG FORMER CHILD SOLDIERS. Since 1986 children in Uganda have been recruited in an ongoing war. In 2004 child soldiers were used by both the Ugandan People's Defense Forces and the rebel forces, the Lord's Resistance Army. Ilse Derluyn, Eric Broekaert, Gilberte Schuyten, and De Temmerman Els interviewed former child soldiers of the northern Ugandan Lord's Resistance Army (LRA) to determine the nature of trauma the children experienced during abduction by the army. Derluyn et al. also investigated the children's post-traumatic stress symptoms ("Post-Traumatic Stress in Former Ugandan Child Soldiers," *The Lancet,* vol. 363, no. 9412, March 13, 2004). As of 2004 about twenty thousand children had been abducted by the LRA over a period of eighteen years. A total of 301 children who were in contact with a rehabilitation center participated in the study. During the time of abduction the children had a mean age of 12.9 years, with nearly two-thirds (64%) abducted from their homes. They spent a mean period of more than two years with the LRA.

More than three-quarters (77%) of the former child soldiers witnessed someone being killed, with 6% seeing their father, mother, or sibling killed. Nearly two-thirds (65%) were forced into military training, while 64% were forced to participate in combat. About 39% had to kill another person, and 2% had to kill their own father, brother, or another relative. More than half (52%) were seriously beaten, and 48% were injured. Among the female child soldiers, 35% served as wives to the adult soldiers. Nearly one-fifth (18%) reported giving birth to one or more children while in captivity. Of seventy-one children who agreed to be tested for post-traumatic stress disorder, sixty-nine showed clinical symptoms.

Trafficking in Children

Trafficking in women, men, and children is a worldwide problem. The U.S. Department of State reported in the *2004 Trafficking in Persons Report* (Washington, DC, June 2004) that an estimated six hundred thousand to eight hundred thousand men, women, and children were trafficked across international borders in 2003 (trafficking is generally defined as the transport of a person against his or her will, usually for the purpose of exploitation). An estimated 80% of the victims were female, and 70% of those females were trafficked for sexual exploitation. Experts believed that if trafficking within countries were counted, the total would be between two million and four million.

The Trafficking Victims Protection Act (Division A of Public Law 106-386), enacted in 2000, defines "severe forms of trafficking in persons." (See Table 1.1.) In October 2001, as authorized by the act, the Department of State established the Office to Monitor and Combat Trafficking in Persons. The office works with other governments in prosecuting traffickers and in assisting domestic and global victims. According to the *2004 Trafficking in Persons Report,* between 14,500 and 17,500 people were trafficked into the United States in 2003.

Organized criminal groups in many countries work with one another in procuring or abducting young girls for the prostitution business, which makes millions of dollars. Very young children are forced into prostitution because clients mistakenly believe that a nine- or ten-year-old will not be infected with AIDS. In many Asian countries, in what is known as debt bondage, girls are traded for money to brothels by their parents or guardians. Many never leave prostitution because they cannot afford to pay for the additional debt added for food and rent.

Child Labor

In 1989 the United Nations General Assembly adopted the *Convention on the Rights of the Child* as an international human rights treaty. Article 32 of the *Convention* defines child labor as any economic exploitation or "work that is likely to be hazardous or interferes with the child's education, or is harmful to the child's health or physical, mental, spiritual, moral, or social development" (http://www.unhchr.ch/html/menu3/b/k2crc.htm [accessed November 23, 2004]).

In 2003 the International Labour Office (ILO) published global estimates of working children, using data from national household surveys collected from various countries in 2000 and from 2003 surveys. Overall, the data gathered were extrapolated to 152 countries, which were divided into five regions (*Investing in Every Child: An Economic Study of the Costs and Benefits of Eliminating Child Labour,* International Programme on the Elimination of Child Labour (IPEC), Geneva, Switzerland, 2004). The ILO uses "economic activity" and "child labor" to describe children's work. "Economic activity" encompasses paid and unpaid work, including the production of goods in a market-oriented business owned by a relative in the same household. "Child labor" refers to the following:

• Ages five to eleven: Children who are economically active

• Ages twelve to fourteen: Children who are economically active, except those performing light work

• Ages fifteen to seventeen: Children in hazardous work and other worst forms of child labor

The ILO reported that in 2003 about 182 million children ages five to fourteen were engaged in child labor, representing 18.5% of that age group worldwide. Asia (60.6%) had the largest proportion of child laborers, fol-

TABLE 1.2

Percent distribution of child labor and child economic activity, ages 5 to 14, by geographic region, 2003

Region	Child labor	Child economic activity
Transition countries	4.6	1.2
Asia	60.6	61.1
Latin America	9.0	8.3
Sub-Saharan Africa	20.8	23.0
North Africa and Middle East	5.0	6.4
Total*	**100.0**	**100.0**

*Total child economic activity excludes the developed countries.

SOURCE: "Table 3.2. Percentage Distribution of Child Labour and Child Economic Activity, Ages 5 to 14, across Regions," in *Investing in Every Child: An Economic Study of the Costs and Benefits of Eliminating Child Labour,* p. 32, International Labour Office, International Programme on the Elimination of Child Labour (IPEC), Geneva, Switzerland, 2004, http://www.ilo.org/public/english/standards/ipec/publ/download/2003_12_inves tingchild.pdf (accessed October 27, 2004). Copyright © 2004 International Labour Organization.

lowed by Sub-Saharan Africa (20.8%), and Latin America (9%). (See Table 1.2.)

In *Investing in Every Child: An Economic Study of the Costs and Benefits of Eliminating Child Labour,* the ILO categorized labor that exploits children into two types: hazardous work and the unconditional worst forms of child labor. Hazardous work is defined by the ILO as "any activity or occupation which, by its nature or type, has, or leads to, adverse effects on the child's safety, health (physical or mental), and moral development." Hazards can also come from too much work, very long hours, and physical conditions of the job. Hazardous work includes mining, construction, and the work that exposes the children to pesticides or heavy machinery. About 10.8 million children ages five to fourteen were engaged in hazardous work, led by Asia and the Pacific (5.1 million) and Latin America (4.6 million).

Children engaged in forced and bonded labor, armed conflict, prostitution and pornography, and illegal activities (for example, working in poppy farms and trafficking in drugs) are considered in unconditional worst forms of labor. Since these activities are typically carried out in secrecy, the ILO considered the figures provided by fifty-six countries conservative minimum estimates. Table 1.3 shows low, medium, and high estimates of this problem, bringing the number of children ages five to seventeen who were performing unconditional worst forms of labor from 8.2 million on the low end to 20.4 million on the high end. Asia and the Pacific region (80% to 90%) accounted for the largest proportion of children engaged in unconditional worst forms of labor.

CHILDREN AS DOMESTIC WORKERS. In the 1990s public attention became focused on the problem of illegal child labor in such industries as the production of cloth-

TABLE 1.3

Children in the unconditional worst forms of child labor, ages 5 to 17, 2003

(In thousands)

Region	Low	Medium	High
Transitional countries	9	9	9
Asia and Pacific	6,581	12,691	18,450
Latin America	887	952	1,018
Sub-Saharan Africa	689	770	85
North Africa and Middle East	71	71	71
Total	**8,236**	**14,492**	**20,398**

SOURCE: "Table 3.4. Children in the Unconditional Worst Forms of Child Labour, Ages 5 to 17 (in Thousands)," in *Investing in Every Child: An Economic Study of the Costs and Benefits of Eliminating Child Labour,* p. 30, International Labour Office, International Programme on the Elimination of Child Labour (IPEC), Geneva, Switzerland, 2004, http://www.ilo.org/public/english/standards/ipec/publ/download/2003_12_investingchild.pdf (accessed October 27, 2004). Copyright © 2004 International Labour Organization.

ing. However, the largest group of child laborers in the world—domestic workers—had not received much attention at all. The United Nations Children's Fund (UNICEF) refers to these children as the "invisible workforce," because they usually work by themselves in private homes. The majority (approximately 90%) are girls ages twelve to seventeen, but they can be as young as five years old. These children receive very low or no salaries and put in long hours, sometimes seven days a week. In many cases the children's parents or other guardians collect the salaries. Most child domestic workers do not attend school. Those who live with their employers may not have contact with their families and peers.

In 2004 the ILO reported that as many as ten million children or more were engaged in domestic labor globally (Dr. June Kane, *Helping Hands or Shackled Lives? Understanding Child Domestic Labour and Responses to It,* Geneva, Switzerland, 2004). The report gives estimates of child domestic workers in various countries, including 700,000 children in Indonesia, 559,000 in Brazil, 300,000 in Dhaka, Bangladesh, 264,000 in Pakistan, 250,000 in Haiti, 200,000 in Kenya, and 100,000 in Sri Lanka. Many children were very young. About 22% of domestic child workers in Senegal were under fourteen years of age, 70% in Morocco were under twelve, and 10% were under ten in Haiti.

According to Dr. Kane, due to the hidden nature of domestic child labor, children are at risk of physical abuse and violence, as well as sexual abuse. They may be beaten and tortured, not only by the adults in the house but also by the children in the family who consider domestic workers as their inferiors. They may also suffer beatings at the hands of the other domestic workers in the house. Girls are especially at risk for sexual abuse by their male employers, visitors to the house, and other domestic laborers. In addi-

tion, children in domestic service may be exposed to dangers associated with their jobs. They may have to handle hazardous substances, such as cleaning fluids and machinery with which they are not familiar. Poor working conditions, such as rooms lacking in proper ventilation and heating, are also detrimental to their health.

Child Mutilation

Actions considered abusive in some cultures are often celebrated as rites of passage by others. According to the World Health Organization (WHO), female circumcision is practiced by followers of many religions, as well as by animists and nonbelievers. An estimated 100 million to 140 million women and girls have been circumcised worldwide. Each year about two million more girls are at risk of undergoing the procedure ("Female Genital Mutilation," http://www.who.int/mediacentre/factsheets/fs241/en [accessed November 23, 2004]).

Female circumcision was first called female genital mutilation in the international document *Programme of Action,* from the International Conference on Population and Development in 1994 in Cairo, Egypt. Female circumcision may be performed as early as infancy, although the procedure is usually done between the ages of four and twelve. It involves the partial or complete removal of the female genitalia, usually performed without anesthesia. In its most severe form, called infibulation, after the major mutilation of the external genitalia and the joining of the scraped sides of the vulva across the vagina, a small opening that may be as tiny as a matchstick is kept for urination and menstruation. Because of the small vaginal opening, sexual intercourse is quite painful, and the infibulation scar may have to be recut to relieve penetration problems.

Female circumcision is practiced in many African countries, as well as in certain countries in Asia and the Middle East. People who migrate from these regions to the United States, Canada, and Europe bring the practice with them.

Some of the health implications of female circumcision include hemorrhage, shock, injuries to the surrounding tissues, and death. Infections may lead to sterility and chronic pelvic pain. If a woman has been infibulated, she may have to undergo a series of cutting and resewing procedures during her childbearing years. She may also develop cysts, abscesses, and incontinence as a result of damage to the urethra. The risk of being infected with the human immunodeficiency virus (HIV) that leads to acquired immunodeficiency virus (AIDS) is also possible because the circumciser typically uses the same knife for other procedures, thus potentially spreading HIV from patient to patient.

CHAPTER 2
CHILD ABUSE—A PROBLEM OF DEFINITION

WHAT IS ABUSE?

Child abuse is often a secret. Since the 1960s, however, Americans have become increasingly aware of the problems of child abuse and neglect (together referred to as child maltreatment). In 1963 some 150,000 young victims of maltreatment were reported to authorities (*Juvenile Court Statistics,* U.S. Department of Health, Education, and Welfare, Children's Bureau, Washington, DC, 1966). In 2002 state child protective services (CPS) agencies received nearly 2.6 million reports of child maltreatment involving about 4.5 million children (*Child Maltreatment 2002,* U.S. Department of Health and Human Services, Administration for Children and Families, Administration on Children, Youth and Families, Children's Bureau, Washington, DC, 2004).

There is still no agreement on what constitutes child abuse. In August 2002 a mother in Brilliant, Ohio, was charged with three counts of felony child endangerment for allegedly allowing her three children to become seriously sunburned. A sheriff's deputy had arrested the woman after noticing that her three young children had sunburned faces while at the county fair in 95°F weather. The woman spent eight days in jail. Authorities later released the mother after determining that the children were not that badly burned. She was charged with a single count of misdemeanor child endangerment, which the prosecutor dismissed two months later.

In September 2002 a surveillance camera in a store in Mishawaka, Indiana, recorded a mother apparently beating and punching her four-year-old daughter inside her car. The videotape, which aired nationally, caused public outrage. The mother was charged with battery to a child, a felony that could bring her a maximum of three years in jail. The child was put in foster care while the case was under investigation. While extreme cases like the Indiana one are easy to label, less severe cases, such as the sunburned children, are viewed differently by different people.

Federal Definition

Official definitions of child abuse and neglect differ among institutions, government bodies, and experts. According to the Child Abuse Prevention and Treatment Act (CAPTA) Amendments of 1996 (Public Law 104-235), which amended the 1974 CAPTA:

> The term "child abuse and neglect" means, at a minimum, any recent act or failure to act, on the part of a parent or caretaker [including any employee of a residential facility or any staff person providing out-of-home care who is responsible for the child's welfare], which results in death, serious physical or emotional harm, sexual abuse or exploitation, or an act or failure to act which presents an imminent risk of serious harm. [The term "child" means a person under the age of eighteen, unless the child protection law of the state in which the child resides specifies a younger age for cases not involving sexual abuse.]

It should be noted that this definition of child abuse and neglect specifies that only parents and caregivers can be considered perpetrators of child maltreatment. Abusive or negligent behavior by other persons—strangers or persons known to the child—is considered child assault. Both forms of abusive behavior are crimes against children.

Based on a concern that severely disabled newborns may be denied medical care, CAPTA also considers as child abuse and neglect the "withholding of medically indicated treatment," including appropriate nutrition, hydration, and medication, which in the treating physician's medical judgment would most likely help, improve, or correct an infant's life-threatening conditions. This definition, however, does not refer to situations where treatment of an infant, in the physician's medical judgment, would prolong dying, be ineffective in improving or correcting all of the infant's life-threatening conditions, or would be futile in helping the infant to survive. In addition, this definition does not include circumstances where the infant is chronically or irreversibly comatose.

State Definitions

CAPTA provides a foundation for states by identifying a minimum set of acts or behaviors that characterize child abuse and neglect. Each state, based on CAPTA guidelines, has formulated its own definitions of the different types of child maltreatment. State definitions, however, may be unclear. For example, states typically define neglect as the failure to provide adequate food, clothing, shelter, or medical care. About one-fifth of states do not have a separate definition for neglect. Moreover, most child protective services agencies consider recent incidences of neglect instead of patterns of behavior that may constitute chronic, or continuing, neglect.

States define child abuse and neglect in three areas in state statutes: reporting laws for child maltreatment, criminal codes, and juvenile court laws. Most state laws also include exceptions, such as religious exemptions, corporal punishment, cultural practices, and poverty.

CAPTA DEFINES FOUR MAIN TYPES OF CHILD MALTREATMENT

Physical Abuse

Physical abuse is the infliction of physical injury through punching, beating, kicking, biting, burning, shaking, or otherwise harming a child. Physical abuse is generally a willful act. There are cases, however, in which the parent or caretaker may not have intended to hurt the child. In such cases, the injury may have resulted from over-discipline or corporal punishment. Nonetheless, if the child is injured, the act is considered abusive.

Sexual Abuse

Sexual abuse includes fondling a child's genitals, intercourse, incest, rape, sodomy, exhibitionism, and commercial exploitation through prostitution or the production of pornographic materials.

Psychological Abuse (Emotional Abuse, Verbal Abuse, or Mental Injury)

Psychological abuse includes acts or omissions by the parents or by other caregivers that have caused, or could cause, serious behavioral, cognitive, emotional, or mental disorders. In some cases of emotional abuse, the abuser's act alone, without any harm evident in the child's behavior or condition, is enough cause for intervention by child protective services (CPS) agencies. For example, the parent/caregiver may use extreme or bizarre forms of punishment, such as locking a child in a dark room or closet.

Other forms of psychological abuse may involve more subtle acts, such as habitual scapegoating (erroneously blaming the child for things that go wrong), belittling, or rejection of the child. For CPS to intervene, demonstrable harm to the child is often required. Although any of the types of child maltreatment may be found separately, different types of abuse often occur in combination with one another. Emotional abuse is almost always present when other types are identified.

Child Neglect

Child neglect is an act of omission characterized by failure to provide for the child's basic needs. Neglect can be physical, educational, or emotional. Physical neglect includes failure to provide food, clothing, and shelter; refusal of or delay in seeking health care (medical neglect); abandonment; inadequate supervision; and expulsion from the home or refusal to allow a runaway to return home. Educational neglect includes permitting chronic truancy, failure to enroll a child of mandatory school age in school, and failure to take care of a child's special educational needs. Emotional neglect includes substantial inattention to the child's need for affection, failure to provide needed psychological care, spousal abuse in the child's presence, and allowing drug or alcohol use by the child. It is very important to distinguish between willful neglect and a parent's or a caretaker's failure to provide the necessities of life because of poverty or cultural factors.

A DESCRIPTION OF MALTREATED CHILDREN

Perhaps better than a definition of child abuse is a description of the characteristics likely to be exhibited by abused and/or neglected children. The Department of Health and Human Services indicates that, in general, abused or neglected children are likely to have at least several of the following characteristics:

- They appear to be different from other children in physical or emotional makeup, or their parents inappropriately describe them as being "different" or "bad."

- They seem unduly afraid of their parents.

- They may often bear welts, bruises, untreated sores, or other skin injuries.

- Their injuries seem to be inadequately treated.

- They show evidence of overall poor care.

- They are given inappropriate food, drink, or medication.

- They exhibit behavioral extremes—for example, crying often or crying very little and showing no real expectation of being comforted; being excessively fearful or seemingly fearless of adult authority; being unusually aggressive and destructive or extremely passive and withdrawn.

- Some are wary of physical contact, especially when initiated by an adult. They become fearful when an adult approaches another child, particularly one who is crying. Others are inappropriately hungry for affection, yet may have difficulty relating to children and adults. Based on their past experiences, these children cannot risk getting too close to others.

- They may exhibit a sudden change in behavior—for example, displaying regressive behavior, such as pants wetting, thumb sucking, frequent whining, becoming disruptive, or becoming uncommonly shy and passive.

- They take over the role of the parent, being protective or otherwise attempting to take care of the parent's needs.

- They have learning problems that cannot be diagnosed. If a child's academic intelligence quotient (IQ) is average or better and medical tests indicate no abnormalities, but the child still cannot meet normal expectations, the answer may well be problems in the home—one of which may be abuse or neglect. Particular attention should be given to the child whose attention wanders and who easily becomes self-absorbed.

- They are habitually truant or late for school. Frequent or prolonged absences sometimes result when a parent keeps an injured child at home until the evidence of abuse disappears. In other cases, truancy indicates lack of parental concern or inability to regulate the child's schedule.

- In some cases, they arrive at school too early and remain after classes have ended, rather than go home.

- They are always tired and often sleep in class.

- They are inappropriately dressed for the weather. Children who never have coats or shoes in cold weather are receiving less than minimal care. Those who regularly wear long sleeves or high necklines on hot days, however, may be dressed to hide bruises, burns, or other marks of abuse.

Many of the psychological symptoms of abuse can be contradictory. One child may be excessively aggressive, while another may be too compliant. One child may be extremely independent, while another may exhibit a clinging behavior. A child may be overly mature, attending to the emotional needs of a parent who is incapable of meeting his or her own needs. These different behaviors are possible symptoms of abuse. No one behavior on the part of a child, however, is conclusive evidence of abuse.

Victims of Physical Abuse

Victims of physical abuse often display bruises, welts, contusions, cuts, burns, fractures, lacerations, strap marks, swellings, and/or lost teeth. While internal injuries are seldom detectable without a hospital examination, anyone in close contact with children should be alert to multiple injuries, a history of repeated injuries, new injuries added to old ones, and untreated injuries, especially in very young children. Older children may attribute an injury to an improbable cause, lying for fear of parental retaliation. Younger children, however, may be unaware that a severe beating is unacceptable and may admit to having been abused.

Physically abused children frequently have behavior problems. Especially among adolescents, chronic and unexplainable misbehavior should be investigated as possible evidence of abuse. Some children come to expect abusive behavior as the only kind of attention they can receive and so act in a way that invites abuse. Others break the law deliberately in order to come under the jurisdiction of the courts to obtain protection from their parents. According to "Recognizing Signs of Child Abuse" (The Nemours Foundation, http://www.kidshealth.org [accessed December 27, 2004]), children who have been abused may display a wide array of behavioral problems including being aggressive or disruptive; displaying intense anger or rage; being self-abusive or self-destructive; feeling suicidal or depressed; using drugs or alcohol; fearing certain adults; and avoiding being at home.

Parents who inflict physical abuse generally provide necessities, such as adequate food and clean clothes. Nevertheless, they get angry quickly, have unrealistic expectations of their children, and are overly critical and rejecting of their children. "Parents who abuse their children may avoid other parents in the neighborhood, may not participate in school activities, and may be uncomfortable talking about their children's injuries or behavioral problems," according to the Nemours Foundation. While many abusive parents have been mistreated as children themselves and are following a learned behavior, an increasing number who physically abuse their own children do so under the influence of alcohol and drugs.

Victims of Physical Neglect

Physically neglected children are often hungry. They may go without breakfast and have neither food nor money for lunch. Some take the lunch money or food of other children and hoard whatever they obtain. They show signs of malnutrition: paleness, low weight relative to height, lack of body tone, fatigue, inability to participate in physical activities, and lack of normal strength and endurance.

These children are usually irritable. They show evidence of inadequate home management and are unclean and unkempt. Their clothes are often torn and dirty. They may lack proper clothing for different weather conditions, and their school attendance may be irregular. In addition, these children may frequently be ill and may exhibit a generally repressed personality, inattentiveness, and withdrawal. They are in obvious need of medical attention for such correctable conditions as poor eyesight, poor dental care, and lack of immunizations.

A child who suffers physical neglect also generally lacks parental supervision at home. The child, for example, may frequently return from school to an empty house. While the need for adult supervision is, of course, relative to both the situation and the maturity of the child, it is generally held that a child younger than twelve should always be supervised by an adult or at least have immediate access to a concerned adult when necessary.

Parents of neglected children are either unable or unwilling to provide appropriate care. Some neglectful parents are mentally deficient. Most lack knowledge of parenting skills and tend to be discouraged, depressed, and frustrated with their role as parents. Alcohol or drug abuse may also be involved.

Physical neglect can be a result of poverty and/or ignorance and may not be intentional. According to the National Clearinghouse on Child Abuse and Neglect Information (*Acts of Omission: An Overview of Child Neglect,* April 2001), if poor parents fail to feed their children adequately, they would be charged with neglect only if they know of food assistance programs but have failed to use them.

Victims of Emotional Abuse and Neglect

Emotional abuse and neglect are as serious as physical abuse and neglect, although this condition is far more difficult to describe or identify. Emotional maltreatment often involves a parent's lack of love or failure to give direction and encouragement. The parent may either demand far too much from the child in the area of academic, social, or athletic activity or withhold physical or verbal contact, indicating no concern for the child's successes and failures and giving no guidance or praise.

Parents who commit emotional abuse and neglect are often unable to accept their children as fallible human beings. The effects of such abuse can often be far more serious and lasting than those of physical abuse and neglect. Emotionally abused children are often extremely aggressive, disruptive, and demanding in an attempt to gain attention and love. They are rarely able to achieve the success in school that tests indicate they can achieve.

Emotional maltreatment can be hard to determine. Is the child's abnormal behavior the result of maltreatment on the part of the parents, or is it a result of inborn or internal factors? Stuart N. Hart, Marla R. Brassard, Nelson J. Binggeli, and Howard A. Davidson ("Psychological Maltreatment," *The APSAC Handbook on Child Maltreatment,* 2nd ed., Thousand Oaks, CA: Sage Publications, Inc., 2002) have listed problems associated with emotional abuse and neglect, including poor appetite, lying, stealing, enuresis (bed-wetting), encopresis (passing of feces in unacceptable places after bowel control has been achieved), low self-esteem, low emotional responsiveness, failure to thrive, inability to be independent, withdrawal, suicide, and homicide.

Victims of Medical Neglect and Abuse

Medical neglect refers to the parents' failure to provide medical treatment for their children, including immunizations, prescribed medications, recommended surgery, and other intervention in cases of serious disease or injury. Some situations involve a parent's inability to care for a child or lack of access to health care. Other situations involve a parent's refusal to seek professional medical care, particularly because of a belief in spiritual healing.

Thorny legal issues have been raised by cases in which parents' freedom of religion clashes with the recommendations of medical professionals. Medical abuse may also involve the Munchausen syndrome by proxy, in which psychologically disturbed parents create illnesses or injuries in children in order to gain sympathy for themselves.

RELIGIOUS BELIEFS. Religious beliefs sometimes prevent children from getting needed medical care. For example, Christian Scientists believe that God heals the sick and that prayer and perfect faith are the proper responses to illness. Other religions, most notably Jehovah's Witnesses, forbid blood transfusions. Religious exemption laws make it difficult to prosecute parents who do not seek treatment for a sick child because their religion forbids it, although courts generally order the emergency treatment of the children.

Rita Swan, a former Christian Scientist who lost her sixteen-month-old child to untreated meningitis, is the president of Children's Healthcare Is a Legal Duty, Inc. (CHILD, Inc.), an organization that seeks to protect children from abusive cultural and religious practices, especially religion-based medical neglect. CHILD, Inc., reported that as of September 2004, thirty-nine states had religious exemptions from child abuse and neglect charges in the civil code, and thirty-one states had a religious defense to criminal charges. All states except Mississippi and West Virginia had religious exemptions from immunizations.

According to CHILD, Inc., Sec. 113 (42 U.S.C. 5106i) of the CAPTA Amendments of 1996 allows parents to withhold medical care from their children based on religious beliefs. Section 113 states:

Nothing in this Act shall be construed:

1.) as establishing a Federal requirement that a parent or legal guardian provide a child any medical service or treatment against the religious beliefs of the parent or legal guardian; and

2.) to require that a State find, or to prohibit a State from finding, abuse or neglect in cases in which a parent or legal guardian relies solely or partially upon spiritual means rather than medical treatment, in accordance with the religious beliefs of the parent or legal guardian.

MUNCHAUSEN SYNDROME BY PROXY. Munchausen syndrome is a psychiatric disorder in which patients fake illness or make themselves sick in order to get medical attention. In 1977 British physician Roy Meadow wrote a paper describing a condition he called Munchausen syndrome by proxy (MSBP) in which parents, usually mothers, call attention to themselves by inducing illnesses in their children or by hurting them ("Munchausen Syndrome by Proxy: The Hinterland of Child Abuse," *The Lancet,* vol. 310, issue 8033). As a result of Meadow's article, authorities have concluded that some incidents of sudden infant death syndrome (SIDS), or the unexplained death of an infant, are murders attributable to parents, especially mothers, suffering from MSBP. Meadow became an expert witness for prosecutors and child protective services. As a result of his testimony, many parents lost their children to the state, had their parental rights terminated, or were charged with murder.

In MSBP situations, children are usually subjected to endless and often painful diagnostic tests, medications, and even surgery. The abuse is most often perpetrated against infants and toddlers before they can talk. Some older children who have been abused in this way do not reveal the deception, however, because they fear they will be abandoned by their parents if they are no longer sick. Others come to believe that they must truly be ill. According to Dr. Guy E. Brannon in "Munchausen Syndrome by Proxy" (http://www.emedicine.com/med/topic3544.htm [accessed January 6, 2005]), in about 10% of cases, MSBP has led to children's deaths.

Dr. Brannon reported that about six hundred cases of MSBP occur each year. He also noted that mothers are the perpetrators in 95% of the cases. Although there are no specific numbers, some experts believe that many of these mothers themselves have been abused as children. A mother with MSBP may think that by devoting her life to "helping" her sick child, she could be a nurturing parent, unlike her own abusive mother. She not only gets the attention that she craves but also the sympathy of those involved in her child's care.

In June 2000 David E. Hall et al. reported the diagnosis of MSBP in twenty-three out of forty-one suspected cases at Children's Healthcare of Atlanta at Scottish Rite, Atlanta, Georgia ("Evaluation of Covert Video Surveillance in the Diagnosis of Munchausen Syndrome by Proxy: Lessons from 41 Cases," *Pediatrics,* vol. 105, no. 6). For four years the researchers, after notifying law enforcement, monitored the children through hidden video cameras to determine the reasons for their inexplicable illnesses. The video surveillance showed the mothers abusing their children, from suffocation to injection with chemicals. Critics charged that the families' right to privacy had been invaded, but the researchers argued that abused children cannot speak up for themselves and need others to protect them.

FALSE ALLEGATIONS OF MUNCHAUSEN SYNDROME BY PROXY. In 2003 a British high court overturned the conviction of three mothers who had been found guilty of murdering their children based on Meadow's expert testimony. In one case, Meadow testified that the chances of two SIDS deaths in a family were one in seventy-three million. In another case, a jury convicted a mother of murder based on the pediatrician's sole testimony that three SIDS must be murder. Meadow based his testimony on his own theory, Meadow's law, which states that in a single family "one sudden infant death is a tragedy, two is suspicious, and three is murder until proved otherwise." Since then, Meadow's theories have been proven wrong. It was also discovered that Meadow could not produce any peer-reviewed research that would have supported his MSBP findings in 1977. Critics say that Meadow's discovery of the new illness resulted from just two of his cases and that he had not produced any records of his research on these cases. In 2004 British authorities continued to review child abuse cases that used Meadow's expert testimony. The British Medical Council also began an investigation of Meadow.

Physicians and child abuse experts are more cautious in labeling parents who harm their children as suffering from MSBP. Despite the controversies concerning MSBP, many physicians believe that there is such a condition, although it is said to be rare. In 2004 the *British Medical Journal* reported that just a minority of parents who intentionally hurt their children have shown Munchausen syndrome characteristics (Alan W. Craft and David M. B. Hall, "Munchausen Syndrome by Proxy and Sudden Infant Death," vol. 328, May 29, 2004). According to the authors, because "there is no single psychological profile in Munchausen syndrome by proxy," pediatricians replaced the term with Fabricated and/or Induced Illness in Children (FII). They noted, however, that research has shown that some cases of SIDS were later shown to be FII. They added that the occurrence of more than one infant death in a family is more likely to be due to homicide or inherited conditions.

A FAMILY AT RISK FOR MALTREATMENT

While it is impossible to determine whether child maltreatment will occur, generally a family may be at risk if the parent is young, has little education, has had several children born within a few years, and is highly dependent on social welfare. According to the *Field Guide to Child Welfare* (Judith S. Rycus and Ronald C. Hughes, Washington, DC: Child Welfare League of America, 1998), a family at high to moderate risk includes parents who do not understand basic child development and who may discipline inappropriately for the child's age; those who lack the necessary skills for caring for and managing a child; those who use physical punishment harshly and excessively; and those who do not appropriately supervise their children.

Furthermore, families under stress are more likely to produce abusive parents and abused or neglected children, such as during divorce or other problems with adult relationships, death, illness, disability, incarceration, or loss of a job, according to Rycus and Hughes. Small stresses can have a cumulative effect and become explosive with a relatively minor event. For potentially abusive parents, high levels of ongoing stress, coupled with inadequate coping strategies and limited resources, produces an extremely high-risk situation for children involved.

According to the Department of Health and Human Services, a family may also be at risk if the parent:

- is a "loner"—feels isolated with no family to depend on, has no real friends, or does not get along well with the neighbors

- has a poor self-image and feels worthless, with a pervading sense of failure

- feels unloved, unappreciated, and unwanted, with a great fear of rejection

- has severe personal problems, such as ill health, alcoholism, or drug dependency

- feels that violence can often be the solution to life's problems or has not learned to "blow off steam" in a socially acceptable manner

- was abused or neglected as a child

A family may also be at risk if the child:

- is "different"—smaller than average, more sickly, disabled, considered unattractive, or was premature

- resembles or reminds the parent of someone the parent hates, or if the child "takes after" a disappointing spouse or former loved one

- is more demanding or otherwise has more problems than do other children in the family

- is unwanted—seen as a "mistake" or burden, having "ruined things" for the parent

CHAPTER 3
REPORTING CHILD ABUSE

MANDATORY REPORTING

In 1974 Congress enacted the first Child Abuse Prevention and Treatment Act (CAPTA; Public Law 93-247) that set guidelines for the reporting, investigation, and treatment of child maltreatment. States had to meet these requirements in order to receive federal funding to assist child victims of abuse and neglect. Among its many provisions, CAPTA required the states to enact mandatory reporting laws and procedures so that child protective services (CPS) agencies can take action to protect children from further abuse. (The term "CPS" refers to the services provided by an agency authorized to act on behalf of a child when his or her parents are unable or unwilling to do so. CPS is also often used to refer to the agency itself.)

The earliest mandatory reporting laws were directed at medical professionals, particularly physicians, who were considered the most likely to see abused children. Currently each state designates mandatory reporters, including health care workers, mental health professionals, social workers, school personnel, child care providers, and law enforcement officers. Any individual, however, whether or not he or she is a mandatory reporter, may report incidents of abuse or neglect.

Some states also require maltreatment reporting from other individuals, such as firefighters, Christian Science practitioners, battered women's counselors, animal control officers, veterinarians, commercial/private film or photograph processors, and even lawyers. As of June 2003, eighteen states and Puerto Rico required all citizens to report suspected child maltreatment. (See Table 3.1.)

Privileged Communications

Some state statutes include provisions pertaining to the right of confidentiality of communications between professionals and their clients. As of June 2003, twenty-one states, the Northern Mariana Islands, and the Virgin Islands exempted from mandatory reporting the privileged communications between attorneys and clients. Twenty-five states exempted from mandatory reporting the privileged communications between clergy and penitents. Ohio and Wyoming recognize privileged communications between physicians and patients, while Oregon exempts from mandatory reporting privileged communications between mental heath professionals and patients. (See Table 3.1.)

WHO REPORTS CHILD MALTREATMENT?

In 2002 more than half (56.5%) of all reports of alleged child maltreatment came from professional sources—educators (16.1%); legal, law enforcement, and criminal justice personnel (15.7%); social services personnel (12.6%); medical personnel (7.8%); mental health personnel (2.6%); child daycare providers (1%); and foster care providers (0.7%). Friends, neighbors, parents, and other relatives comprised nearly one-fifth (19.6%) of the reporters, while alleged victims and self-identified perpetrators reported abuse in 0.9% of the cases. Another 18.6% of reports came from anonymous and other sources. (See Figure 3.1.)

All states offer immunity to individuals who report incidents of child maltreatment "in good faith," or with sincerity. Besides physical injury and neglect, most states include mental injury, sexual abuse, and the sexual exploitation of minors as cases to be reported.

FAILURE TO REPORT MALTREATMENT

Many states impose penalties, either a fine and/or imprisonment, for failure to report child maltreatment. A mandated reporter, such as a physician, may also be sued for negligence for failing to protect a child from harm. The landmark California case *Landeros v. Flood et al.* (17 Cal. 3d 399, 551 P.2d 389, 1976) illustrates such a case. Eleven-month-old Gita Landeros was brought by her mother to the San Jose Hospital in California for treatment of injuries. Besides a fractured lower leg, the girl had bruises on her back and abrasions on other parts of her body. She also

TABLE 3.1

Mandatory reporting statutes for child abuse and neglect, 2003

State	Professions that must report					Others who must report		Standard for reporting	Privileged communications
	Health care	Mental health	Social work	Education/ child care	Law enforcement	All persons	Other		
Alabama § 26-14-3(a) § 26-14-10	✓	✓	✓	✓	✓		Any other person called upon to give aid or assistance to any child	Known or suspected	Attorney/client
Alaska § 47.17.020(a) § 47.17.023 § 47.17.060	✓	✓	✓	✓	✓		Paid employees of domestic violence and sexual assault programs and drug and alcohol treatment facilities Members of a child fatality review team or multidisciplinary child protection team Commercial or private film or photograph processors	Have reasonable cause to suspect	
American Samoa § 45.2002	✓	✓	✓	✓			Medical examiner or coroner Christian Science practitioner	Have reasonable cause to know or suspect Have observed conditions which would reasonably result	
Arizona § 13-3620(A) § 8-805(B)-(C)	✓	✓	✓	✓	✓		Parents Anyone responsible for care or treatment of children Clergy/Christian Science practitioners Domestic violence victim advocates	Have reasonable grounds to believe	Clergy/penitent Attorney/client
Arkansas § 12-12-507(b)-(c) § 12-12-518(b)(1)	✓	✓	✓	✓	✓		Prosecutors Judges Department of Human Services employees Domestic violence shelter employees and volunteers Foster parents Court Appointed Special Advocates Clergy/Christian Science practitioners	Have reasonable cause to suspect Have observed conditions which would reasonably result	Clergy/penitent Attorney/client
California Penal Code § 11166(a), (c) § 11165.7(a)	✓	✓	✓	✓	✓		Firefighters Animal control officers Commercial film and photographic print processors Clergy Court Appointed Special Advocates	Have knowledge of or observe Know or reasonably suspect	Clergy/penitent
Colorado § 19-3-304(1), (2) (2.5) § 19-3-311	✓	✓	✓	✓	✓		Christian Science practitioners Veterinarians Firefighters Victim advocates Commercial film and photographic print processors Clergy	Have reasonable cause to know or suspect Have observed conditions which would reasonably result	Clergy/penitent
Connecticut § 17a-101(b) § 17a-103(a)	✓	✓	✓	✓	✓		Substance abuse counselors Sexual assault counselors Battered women's Clergy Child advocates	Have reasonable cause to suspect or believe	
Delaware tit. 16, § 903 § 909	✓	✓	✓	✓		✓		Know or in good faith suspect	Attorney/client Clergy/penitent

TABLE 3.1

Mandatory reporting statutes for child abuse and neglect, 2003 [CONTINUED]

State	Professions that must report					Others who must report		Standard for reporting	Privileged communications
	Health care	Mental health	Social work	Education/ child care	Law enforcement	All persons	Other		
District of Columbia § 4-1321.02(a), (b), (d) § 4-1321.05	✓	✓	✓	✓	✓			Know or have reasonable cause to suspect	
Florida § 39.201(1) § 39.204	✓	✓	✓	✓	✓	✓	Judges Religious healers	Know or have reasonable cause to suspect	Attorney/client
Georgia § 19-7-5(c)(1), (g) § 16-12-100(c)	✓	✓	✓	✓	✓		Persons who produce visual or printed matter	Have reasonable cause to believe	
Guam Tit. 19 § 13201	✓	✓	✓	✓	✓		Christian Science practitioners Commercial film and photographic print processors	Have reason to suspect Have knowledge or observe	
Hawaii § 350-1.1(a) § 350-5	✓	✓	✓	✓	✓		Employees of recreational or sports activities	Have reason to believe	
Idaho § 16-1619(a), (c) § 16-1620	✓	✓	✓	✓	✓	✓		Have reason to believe Have observed conditions which would reasonably result	Clergy/penitent Attorney/client
Illinois 325 ILCS § 5/4	✓	✓	✓	✓	✓		Homemakers, substance abuse treatment personnel Christian Science practitioners Funeral home directors Commercial film and photographic print processors Clergy	Have reasonable cause to believe	Clergy/penitent
Indiana § 31-33-5-1 § 31-33-5-2 § 31-32-11-1	✓	✓	✓	✓	✓	✓	Staff member of any public or private institution, school, facility, or agency	Have reason to believe	
Iowa § 232.69(1)(a)-(b) § 728.14(1) § 232.74	✓	✓	✓	✓	✓		Commercial film and photographic print processors Employees of substance abuse programs Coaches	Reasonably believe	
Kansas § 38-1522(a), (b)	✓	✓	✓	✓	✓		Firefighters Juvenile intake and assessment workers	Have reason to suspect	
Kentucky § 620.030(1), (2) § 620.050(2)	✓	✓	✓	✓	✓	✓		Know or have reasonable cause to believe	Attorney/client Clergy/penitent
Louisiana Ch. Code art. § 603(13) § 609(A)(1) § 610(F)	✓	✓	✓	✓	✓		Commercial film or photographic print processors Mediators	Have cause to believe	Clergy, Christian Science practitioner/ penitent
Maine tit. 22, § 4011(1) tit. 22, § 4015	✓	✓	✓	✓	✓		Guardians *ad litem* and Court Appointed Special Advocates Fire inspectors Commercial film processors Homemakers Humane agents Clergy	Know or have reasonable cause to suspect	Clergy/penitent

appeared scared when anyone approached her. At the time Gita was also suffering from a fractured skull, but this was never diagnosed by the attending physician, Dr. A. J. Flood.

Gita returned home with her mother and subsequently suffered further serious abuse at the hands of her mother and the mother's boyfriend. Three months later Gita was brought to another hospital for medical treatment, where the doctor diagnosed "battered child syndrome" and reported the abuse to the proper authorities. ("Battered child syndrome" refers to the collection of injuries sustained by a child as a result of repeated mistreatment or beatings. The term was coined in 1961 by Dr. C. Henry Kempe and his colleagues and includes not only

State	Professions that must report					Others who must report		Standard for reporting	Privileged communications
	Health care	Mental health	Social work	Education/ child care	Law enforcement	All persons	Other		
Maryland Family Law § 5-704(a) § 5-705(a)(1)	✓	✓	✓	✓	✓	✓		Have reason to believe	Attorney/client Clergy/penitent
Massachusetts ch. 119, § 51A ch. 119, § 51B	✓	✓	✓	✓	✓		Drug and alcoholism counselors Probation and parole officers Clerks/magistrates of district courts Firefighters Clergy/Christian Science practitioners	Have reasonable cause to believe	Clergy/penitent
Michigan § 722.623 (1), (8) § 722.631	✓	✓	✓	✓	✓		Clergy	Have reasonable cause to suspect	Attorney/client Clergy/penitent
Minnesota § 626.556 Subd. 3(a), 8	✓	✓	✓	✓	✓			Know or have reason to believe	Clergy/penitent
Mississippi § 43-21-353(1)	✓	✓	✓	✓	✓	✓	Attorneys Ministers	Have reasonable cause to suspect	
Missouri § 210.115(1) § 568.110 § 210.140	✓	✓	✓	✓	✓		Persons with responsibility for care of children Christian Science practitioners Probation/parole officers Commercial film processors Internet service providers Clergy	Have reasonable cause to suspect Have observed conditions which would reasonably result	Attorney/client Clergy/penitent
Montana § 41-3-201 (1)-(2), (4)	✓	✓	✓	✓	✓		Guardians *ad litem* Clergy Religious healers Christian Science practitioners	Know or have reasonable cause to suspect	Clergy/penitent
Nebraska § 28-711(1) § 28-714	✓		✓	✓		✓		Have reasonable cause to believe Have observed conditions which would reasonably result	
Nevada § 432B.220(3), (5) § 432B.250	✓		✓	✓		✓	Religious healers Alcohol/drug abuse counselors Clergy/Christian Science practitioners Probation officers Attorneys Youth shelter workers	Know or have reason to believe	Clergy/penitent Attorney/client
New Hampshire § 169-C:29 § 169-C:32	✓	✓	✓	✓	✓	✓	Christian Science practitioners Clergy	Have reason to suspect	Attorney/client *Clergy/penitent privilege denied*
New Jersey § 9:6-8.10						✓		Have reasonable cause to believe	
New Mexico § 32A-4-3(A) § 32A-4-5(A)	✓	✓	✓	✓	✓	✓	Judges Clergy	Know or have reasonable suspicion	Clergy/penitent
New York Soc. Serv. Law § 413(1)	✓	✓	✓	✓	✓		Alcoholism/substance abuse counselors District attorneys Christian Science practitioners	Have reasonable cause to suspect	

physical assault but other forms of abuse, such as malnourishment, failure to thrive, medical neglect, and sexual and emotional abuse. The term now used is child maltreatment.)

After surgery the child was placed with foster parents. The mother and boyfriend were eventually convicted of the crime of child abuse. The guardian *ad litem* (a court-appointed special advocate) for Gita Landeros filed a malpractice suit against Dr. Flood and the hospital, citing painful permanent physical injury to the plaintiff as a result of the defendants' negligence.

State	Professions that must report					Others who must report		Standard for reporting	Privileged communications
	Health care	Mental health	Social work	Education/ child care	Law enforcement	All persons	Other		
North Carolina § 7B-301 § 7B-310						✓	Any institution	Have cause to suspect	Attorney/client *Clergy/penitent privilege denied*
North Dakota § 50-25.1-03 § 50-25.1-10	✓	✓	✓	✓	✓		Clergy Religious healers Addiction counselors	Have knowledge of or reasonable cause to suspect	Clergy/penitent Attorney/client
Northern Mariana Islands Tit. 6, § 5313(a); § 5316	✓			✓	✓		Medical examiners/ coroners Religious healers	Know or have reasonable cause to suspect	Attorney/client
Ohio § 2151.421(A)(1), (A)(2), (G)(1)(b)	✓	✓	✓	✓			Attorneys Religious healers Agents of humane societies	Know or suspect	Attorney/client Physician/patient
Oklahoma tit. 10, § 7103(A)(1) tit. 10, § 7104 tit. 10, § 7113	✓			✓		✓	Commercial film and photographic print processors	Have reason to believe	
Oregon § 419B.005(3) § 419B.010(1)	✓	✓	✓	✓	✓		Attorneys Clergy Firefighters Court Appointed Special Advocates	Have reasonable cause to believe	Mental health/ patient Clergy/penitent Attorney/client
Pennsylvania 23 Pa. § 6311(a),(b)	✓	✓	✓	✓	✓		Funeral directors Christian Science practitioners Clergy	Have reasonable cause to suspect	Clergy/penitent
Puerto Rico Tit. 8, § 441a; § 411b	✓	✓	✓	✓	✓	✓	Professionals or public officials Processors of film or photographs	Should know or have knowledge of Suspects Observes	
Rhode Island § 40-11-3(a) § 40-11-6(a) § 40-11-11	✓					✓		Have reasonable cause to know or suspect	Attorney/client *Clergy/penitent privilege denied*
South Carolina § 20-7-510(A) § 20-7-550	✓	✓	✓	✓	✓		Judges Funeral home directors and employees Christian Science practitioners Film processors Religious healers Substance abuse treatment staff Computer technicians	Have reason to believe	Attorney/client Clergy/penitent
South Dakota § 26-8A-3 § 26-8A-15	✓	✓	✓	✓	✓		Chemical dependency counselors Religious healers Parole or court services officers Employees of domestic abuse shelters	Have reasonable cause to suspect	
Tennessee § 37-1-403(a) § 37-1-605(a) § 37-1-411	✓	✓	✓	✓	✓	✓	Judges Neighbors Relatives Friends Religious healers	Knowledge of/ reasonably know Have reasonable cause to suspect	
Texas Family Code § 261.101(a)-(c) § 261.102	✓			✓		✓	Juvenile probation or detention officers Employees or clinics that provide reproductive services	Have cause to believe	*Clergy/penitent privilege denied*
Utah § 62A-4a-403(1)-(3) § 62A-4a-412(5)	✓					✓		Have reason to believe Have observed conditions which would reasonably result	Clergy/penitent

TABLE 3.1

Mandatory reporting statutes for child abuse and neglect, 2003 [CONTINUED]

State	Professions that must report					Others who must report		Standard for reporting	Privileged communications
	Health care	Mental health	Social work	Education/ child care	Law enforcement	All persons	Other		
Vermont tit. 33, § 4913(a), (f)-(h)	✓	✓	✓	✓	✓		Camp administrators and counselors Probation officers Clergy	Have reasonable cause to believe	Clergy/penitent
Virgin Islands Tit. 5, § 2533(a) § 2538	✓	✓	✓	✓	✓			Have reasonable cause to suspect Observe conditions which would reasonably result	Attorney/client
Virginia § 63.2-1509(A) § 63.2-1519	✓	✓	✓	✓	✓		Mediators Christian Science practitioners Probation officers Court Appointed Special Advocates	Have reason to suspect	
Washington § 26.44.030 (1), (2) § 26.44.060(3)	✓	✓	✓	✓	✓		Any adult with whom a child resides Responsible living skills program staff	Have reasonable cause to believe	
West Virginia § 49-6A-2 § 49-6A-7	✓	✓	✓	✓	✓		Clergy Religious healers Judges, family law masters or magistrates Christian Science practitioners	Reasonable cause to suspect When believe Have observed	Attorney/client *Clergy/penitent privilege denied*
Wisconsin § 48.981(2), (2m)(c)-(e)	✓	✓	✓	✓	✓		Alcohol or drug abuse counselors Mediators Financial and employment planners Court Appointed Special Advocates	Have reasonable cause to suspect Have reason to believe	
Wyoming § 14-3-205(a) § 14-3-210						✓		Know or have reasonable cause to believe or suspect Have observed conditions which would reasonably result	Attorney/client Physician/patient Clergy/penitent

SOURCE: *2003 Child Abuse and Neglect State Statute Series Statutes-at-a-Glance: Mandatory Reporters of Child Abuse and Neglect,* U.S. Department of Health and Human Service, Administration for Children and Families, National Clearinghouse on Child Abuse and Neglect Information, June 2003, http://nccanch.acf .hhs.gov/general/legal/statutes/manda.pdf (accessed October 27, 2004).

The trial court of Santa Clara County dismissed the Landeros complaint, and the case was appealed to the California Supreme Court. The California Supreme Court agreed that the "battered child syndrome" was a recognized medical condition that Dr. Flood should have been aware of and diagnosed. The court ruled that the doctor's failure to do so contributed to the child's continued suffering, and Dr. Flood and the hospital were liable for this. While this case applied specifically to a medical doctor, the principles reached by the court are applicable to other professionals. Most professionals are familiar with the court's decision in *Landeros.*

State Statutes Vary in Reporting Standards

Although all states have enacted legislation requiring, among other things, the mandatory reporting of child maltreatment by certain professionals, states vary in the standard for reporting. The standard to report child maltreatment varies from, "have reasonable cause to suspect," to "have reason to believe," to "have observed conditions which would reasonably result," to "know or suspect."

EMERGENCY NURSE CHARGED WITH FAILURE TO REPORT. On August 10, 2002, two-year-old Dominic James was brought to Cox South Hospital in Springfield, Missouri. Paramedics told emergency nurse Leslie Ann Brown that the boy, who was having seizure-like symptoms, had bruises on his back and to report this to the attending physician. Told by Dominic's foster parents that the child got bruised by leaning back on a booster seat, Brown did not report the bruises to the physician. Neither did she include the presence of bruises on her medical reports. Dominic was rehospitalized a week later and died soon after.

In February 2003 the state of Missouri charged Brown with failure to report child abuse. In September 2003 Green County Judge Calvin Holden dismissed the

FIGURE 3.1

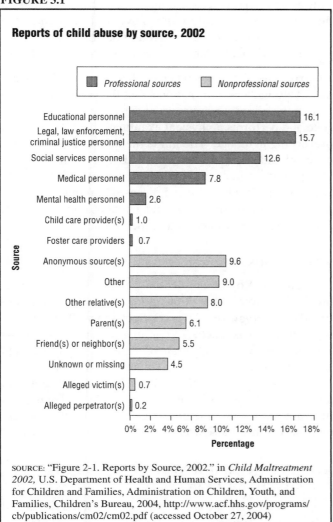

Reports of child abuse by source, 2002

■ *Professional sources*   □ *Nonprofessional sources*

Source	Percentage
Educational personnel	16.1
Legal, law enforcement, criminal justice personnel	15.7
Social services personnel	12.6
Medical personnel	7.8
Mental health personnel	2.6
Child care provider(s)	1.0
Foster care providers	0.7
Anonymous source(s)	9.6
Other	9.0
Other relative(s)	8.0
Parent(s)	6.1
Friend(s) or neighbor(s)	5.5
Unknown or missing	4.5
Alleged victim(s)	0.7
Alleged perpetrator(s)	0.2

SOURCE: "Figure 2-1. Reports by Source, 2002." in *Child Maltreatment 2002*, U.S. Department of Health and Human Services, Administration for Children and Families, Administration on Children, Youth, and Families, Children's Bureau, 2004, http://www.acf.hhs.gov/programs/cb/publications/cm02/cm02.pdf (accessed October 27, 2004)

criminal charges, stating that the Missouri statute with the "reasonable cause to suspect" standard for reporting child abuse was unconstitutionally vague in violation of the U.S. and Missouri Constitutions. The state appealed the case in May 2004. In August 2004 the Missouri Supreme Court reversed Judge Holden's ruling, allowing the case to proceed to trial.

WHY MANDATED REPORTERS FAIL TO REPORT SUSPECTED MALTREATMENT

Gail L. Zellman and C. Christine Fair conducted a national survey to determine why mandated reporters may not report suspected maltreatment ("Preventing and Reporting Abuse," *The APSAC Handbook on Child Maltreatment,* 2nd ed., Thousand Oaks, CA: Sage Publications, Inc., 2002). The researchers surveyed 1,196 general and family practitioners, pediatricians, child psychiatrists, clinical psychologists, social workers, public school principals, and heads of child care centers. Nearly eight of ten (77%) survey participants had made a child maltreatment

report at some time during their professional career. More than nine of ten (92%) elementary school principals reported child maltreatment at some time, followed closely by child psychiatrists (90%) and pediatricians (89%). A lesser proportion of secondary school principals (84%), social workers (70%), and clinical psychologists (63%) reported child maltreatment at some time in their career.

Nearly 40% of the mandated reporters, however, indicated that, at some time in their career, they had failed to report even though they had suspected child maltreatment. Almost 60% failed to report child maltreatment because they did not have enough evidence that the child had been maltreated. One-third of the mandated reporters thought the abuse was not serious enough to warrant reporting. An equal proportion of mandated reporters did not report suspected abuse because they felt they were in a better position to help the child (19.3%) or they did not want to end the treatment (19%) they were giving the child. Almost 16% failed to report because they did not think CPS would do a good job.

PEDIATRICIANS

Pediatricians, typically the first professionals to come into contact with a maltreated child, may hesitate to report suspected abuse because they fear offending the parents who pay the bills and who may spread rumors about their competence, potentially damaging their practice. Some fear the time lost in reporting abuse, the possibility of being sued by an outraged parent, or having to testify in court.

Physicians in the United States and in other countries fear repercussions from reporting child abuse. In Great Britain publicity surrounding the investigations of pediatricians connected with child protection work in the mid-1990s through 2003 resulted in increasing complaints from the public. In March 2004 the Royal College of Paediatrics and Child Health (RCPCH; London, England) released a survey of the country's pediatricians regarding these complaints. Nearly 80% of the 6,072 pediatricians responded to the survey. The survey showed that one of seven (14%) RCPCH members who had participated in child abuse investigations had been the subjects of complaints. Complaints against pediatricians working in child protection rose from less than twenty in 1995 to more than one hundred in 2003. Some pediatricians received hate mail, as well as threats to themselves and their families. Nearly one-third (29%) indicated an unwillingness to take part in child protection work in the future.

Reporting Psychological Maltreatment of Children

According to the American Academy of Pediatrics (AAP), pediatricians play a major role in preventing, recognizing, and reporting psychological, or emotional, maltreatment (Steven W. Kairys, Charles F. Johnson, and the Committee on Child Abuse and Neglect, "The Psychological Maltreatment of Children—Technical Report," *Pediatrics,* vol. 109, no. 4, April 2002). Generally, pediatricians are the only professionals young children see before they attend school. Pediatricians are in a position to observe any abusive interaction between the child and the parent/caregiver. They should be able to identify parental characteristics, such as substance abuse and poor parenting skills, that may predispose parents to abuse their children. Pediatricians should also be able to identify at-risk children, including those who are disabled or whose parents are undergoing a hostile divorce. The consequences of psychological maltreatment may take years to surface; hence, pediatricians are encouraged to report their suspicions so that the child and the caregivers can get help right away.

Pediatricians Intervene in Domestic Abuse to Prevent Child Maltreatment

Researchers Richard A. Wahl, Doris J. Sisk, and Thomas M. Ball reported that an estimated ten million children in the United States are exposed to domestic violence (intimate partner violence) each year ("Clinic-Based Screening for Domestic Violence: Use of a Child Safety Questionnaire," *BMC Medicine,* vol. 2, May 2004). Noting the American Academy of Pediatrics' policy statement about the role of pediatricians in recognizing families experiencing child abuse, the researchers conducted the first study of its kind. The study involved mothers accompanying their children (sixteen thousand patient visits annually) to their pediatricians. Since research has shown that children of battered women are more likely to be abused, Wahl and his associates sought to screen for domestic abuse among their patients' mothers.

The authors found that active screening (having the mothers fill out a questionnaire asking their exposure to domestic violence) increased the odds of identifying families experiencing domestic violence. Prior to the screening, pediatricians identified four cases of domestic violence per one thousand children during a three-month period. Active screening identified fifteen cases per one thousand children during the subsequent three months. The study was conducted for two years, and overall the pediatricians identified nineteen cases of domestic violence per one thousand children the first year and twenty cases per one thousand children the following year. Wahl et al. noted that the numbers of children living with battered women are probably higher. Up to one-third of questionnaires were not returned.

SEXUAL ASSAULT NURSE EXAMINER

A sexual assault nurse examiner (SANE) is a registered nurse trained in forensic (using science to study evidence of a crime) examination of sexual assault victims. The SANE program emerged in the 1990s in response to the need for a more thorough collection of evidence, as well as compassionate care for the victim and better prosecution of the perpetrator. It has been recognized that, in the past, sexual assault victims have been retraumatized during forensic-evidence collection because the hospital personnel may lack training in dealing with such victims.

After the victim has received the proper medical care, the SANE gathers information about the patient and a history of the crime. The nurse evaluates the victim's mental state and performs a physical examination, collecting and preserving evidence. The nurse then documents the evidence obtained, as well as other findings. The SANE may also provide other care, including giving medication to counter sexually transmitted diseases and making referrals for other medical aid and psychological support. SANEs also testify in court as expert witnesses.

EDUCATORS

Felicia F. Romero, in "The Educator's Role in Reporting the Emotional Abuse of Children" (*Journal of Instructional Psychology,* vol. 27, no. 3, September 2000), pointed out that, whereas teachers attending in-service programs learn the behavioral indicators of neglect and physical and sexual abuse, they do not receive much information about emotional, or psychological, abuse. Victims of emotional abuse suffer "injuries" that are not visible, and educators may not realize that the consequences of such abuse are more severe than those from other forms of maltreatment.

A NEED FOR FAMILY VIOLENCE EDUCATION AMONG PHYSICIANS

Although child abuse is a well-documented social and public health problem in the United States, few medical schools and residency training programs include child abuse education and other family violence education in their curricula. The Committee on the Training Needs of Health Professionals to Respond to Family Violence of the Institute of Medicine examined the curricula on family violence for six groups of health professionals: physicians, physician assistants, nurses, psychologists, social workers, and dentists (*Confronting Chronic Neglect: The Education and Training of Health Professionals on Family Violence,* Felicia Cohn, Marla E. Salmon, and John D. Stobo, eds., Washington, DC: National Academies Press, 2002).

The committee noted that as many as one out of four children and adults experience family violence during their lifetimes. Studies have shown that family violence is associated with many problems affecting health, including homelessness, alcohol and substance abuse, and delinquency. Although health professionals are usually the first people to interact with victims of family violence, their lack of education on family violence keeps them from identifying, treating, and helping their patients.

The committee found that most medical schools give instruction regarding at least one form of family violence.

TABLE 3.2

Requirements by accreditation institutions for family violence curriculum

Health care discipline	Accreditation institutions	Requirements related to family violence	Description
Medical schools	Liaison Commission on Medical Education (LCME)	S	"The curriculum should prepare students for their role in addressing the medical consequences of common societal problems, for example, providing instructions in the diagnosis, prevention, appropriate reporting and treatment of violence and abuse." Standards can be found on the LCME web site www.lcme.org.
	Accreditation Council for Graduate Medical Education (ACGME)	X	The institutional requirements of the ACGME are very practical in nature and do not outline any single curriculum requirements including any dealing with family violence.
	American Osteopathic Healthcare Association (AOHA)	NS	Institutions are required to include with the spectrum of "Emergency Procedures" some instruction regarding "abuse and neglect" of children. While these standards are not a requirement unto themselves, they do seem to be somewhat quantifiable.
Physician residencies	Residency Review Committees (RRC) of the ACGME	S	The residency review committees of the ACGME, which accredit programs rather than institutions, do have provisions for family violence in certain fields. Though the genetics area does not mention family violence, the areas of family practice and obstetrics indicate how to identify signs of family violence and the steps to take.
Dental schools	American Dental Association Commission on Dental Accreditation (ADA)	NS	There is no specific mention of family violence in the accreditation commission's standards. Such training is believed to fall under the purview of a provision for "ethical reasoning" and "professional responsibility."
Nursing schools	Commission on Collegiate Nursing Education Accreditation (CCNE)	X	CCNE guidelines are very generic and do not provide for any particular curriculum requirements. The guidelines allow schools to choose their own direction and philosophy and subsequently measures them against the standard they have chosen.
Nurse practitioners	National League for Nursing Accrediting Commission (NLNAC)	NS	"NLNAC does not include specific curriculum content areas within its standards and criteria. When specific curriculum content is designated it is usually from the State Boards of Nursing since NLNAC is voluntary." Standards can be accessed on the website at www.nlnac.org.
	National Association of Pediatric Nurse Associates & Practitioners, Inc. (NAPNAP)	NS	NAPNAP recognizes that there is "substantial scientific evidence that children who are abused physically, sexually, emotionally or who are neglected, are prevented from optimal development." NAPNAP has in place a thorough position statement on child abuse/neglect.
Psychology programs and internship sites	Committee on Accreditation of the American Psychological Association: accredits both school and internship sites (APA)	X	There is no mention of family violence in the APA accreditation guidelines. They take a broad stance on evaluating the goals that institutions set for themselves.
Social work programs	Council on Social Work Education (CSWE)	NS	CSWE has no specific requirements mandating that the issue of family violence be discussed on any level. There is an expectation that a program dealing with social work must at some point address the problem. Should an institution not do this, it would probably be cited.
Physician assistant	Commission on Accreditation of Allied Health Education (CAAHEP) Programs	X	There is no reference to family violence made in the CAAHEP standards or guidelines. Curriculum is the responsibility of the sponsoring institution with the exception of a few general study education requirements.
	Effective January 1, 2001, CAAHEP no longer will be the accreditor of physician assistant education programs. All current accreditations are being transferred from CAAHEP to the Accreditation Review Commission on Education of the Physician Assistant (ARC-PA) http://www.CAAHEP.org/caahep_pa.htm		

Note:
S = specific existing requirements.
NS = nonspecific requirements.
X = no identifiable requirements.

SOURCE: "Requirements by Accreditation Institutions Relating to Family Violence Curriculum," in *Confronting Chronic Neglect: the Education and Training of Health Professionals on Family Violence,* Felicia Cohn, Marla E. Salmon, and John D. Stobo, eds., National Academy Press, 2002

In most cases, education revolves around reporting requirements, patient interviewing skills, screening tools, health conditions related to violence, and service referrals for victims. The teaching sessions vary, ranging from a very brief discussion to several lectures or case discussions. Although about 95% of schools teach material related to child maltreatment, usually during pediatric rotation, the committee found that the curriculum is inadequate. Table 3.2 illustrates the minimal requirements for accreditation, a process that determines whether a medical school or program meets certain established standards. Accreditation is needed for eligibility to participate in federal student loan programs.

Medical residents specializing in fields in which they are most likely to interact with maltreatment victims are required to receive training in family violence. These include pediatricians, internists, obstetricians/gynecologists, geriatricians (specialists who treat the elderly), psychiatrists, and emergency-medicine doctors. The training consists of lectures and case discussions, and the training duration varies from program to program. As for continuing medical education on family violence, the committee found very little information, including lectures and programs on the Internet, for which health professionals can earn credits.

The committee also noted that not much is being done to evaluate the effects of family violence training. So far, evaluations that had been performed concerned short-term effects of the training, such as how the training had increased the health professionals' knowledge of family violence. The committee suggested that more in-depth evaluation of the training programs should measure the effects of training on health professionals' behavior and victims' health.

Primary Care Residency Program in Child Maltreatment

Suzanne P. Starling and Stephen Boos noted that, since 1962, when Dr. C. Henry Kempe wrote of the "battered child syndrome," a term that encompasses all aspects of child abuse, research on the subject has grown. Physicians' knowledge about child abuse, however, has not followed suit ("Core Content for Residency Training in Child Abuse and Neglect," *Child Maltreatment*, vol. 8, no. 4, November 2003). According to the authors, while there are physician specialists in child maltreatment, their numbers are limited. Therefore, primary care physicians are called upon to perform their functions, including monitoring family health, diagnosing abuse, consulting with government agencies, testifying in court, and participating in abuse prevention programs and in multidisciplinary teams that evaluate and manage child maltreatment. Drs. Starling and Boos suggested offering a core curriculum in residency programs that would enable primary care physicians (including pediatricians, family doctors, and emergency-medicine doctors) to recognize, evaluate, and manage cases of child abuse and neglect.

PSYCHOLOGISTS LACK CHILD MALTREATMENT TRAINING

The American Psychological Association (APA) believed that, because psychologists are likely to encounter cases of child maltreatment in their practice, training in this area is very important. In 2003 the APA sought to gain information on the type and amount of training psychologists receive regarding child maltreatment in APA-accredited doctoral programs (Kelly M. Champion, Kimberly Shipman, Barbara L. Bonner, Lisa Hensley, and Allison C. Howe, "Child Maltreatment Training in Doctoral Programs in Clinical, Counseling, and School Psychology: Where Do We Go from Here?" *Child Maltreatment,* vol. 8, no. 3, August 2003). The study examined surveys sent to training directors of doctoral programs in 1992 and 2001. The APA found that doctoral programs had remained the same within those ten years. Few doctoral programs offered specific courses on child maltreatment in 1992 and 2001, just 13% and 11%, respectively. Although 65% of programs in 1992 and 59% in 2001 covered child maltreatment in three or more courses, these courses were rarely required to complete a doctoral program. Twenty percent of programs in 1992 and 22% in 2001 offered training in child maltreatment in clinical settings; most programs, however, reported that students completed just 1% to 10% of such training. Finally, research activities in child maltreatment decreased from 60% in 1992 to 47% in 2001.

CHILD PROTECTIVE SERVICES

Partly funded by the federal government, child protective services (CPS) agencies were first established in response to the 1974 Child Abuse Prevention and Treatment Act (CAPTA; Public Law 93-247), which mandated that all states establish procedures to investigate suspected incidents of child maltreatment. Upon receipt of a report of suspected child maltreatment, CPS screens the case to determine its proper jurisdiction. For example, if it is determined that the alleged perpetrator of sexual abuse is the victim's parent or caretaker, CPS screens in the report and conducts further investigation. If the alleged perpetrator is a stranger or someone who is not the parent or caregiver of the victim, the case is screened out, or referred elsewhere, in this case, to the police because it does not fall within CPS jurisdiction as outlined under federal law.

A state's child welfare system, under which CPS functions, consists of other components designed to ensure a child's well-being and safety. These include foster care, juvenile and family courts, and other child welfare services. Other child welfare services include family reunification, granting custody to a relative, termination of parental rights, and emancipation. Cases of reported child abuse or neglect typically undergo a series of steps through the child welfare system. (See Figure 3.2.)

Court Involvement

The juvenile or family court hears allegations of maltreatment and decides if a child has been abused and/or

FIGURE 3.2

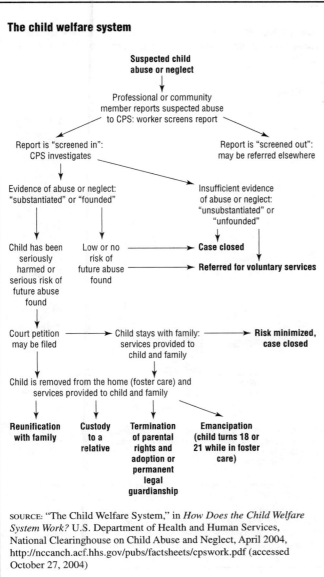

The child welfare system

Suspected child abuse or neglect

Professional or community member reports suspected abuse to CPS: worker screens report

Report is "screened in": CPS investigates

Report is "screened out": may be referred elsewhere

Evidence of abuse or neglect: "substantiated" or "founded"

Insufficient evidence of abuse or neglect: "unsubstantiated" or "unfounded"

Child has been seriously harmed or serious risk of future abuse found

Low or no risk of future abuse found

Case closed

Referred for voluntary services

Court petition may be filed

Child stays with family: services provided to child and family

Risk minimized, case closed

Child is removed from the home (foster care) and services provided to child and family

Reunification with family

Custody to a relative

Termination of parental rights and adoption or permanent legal guardianship

Emancipation (child turns 18 or 21 while in foster care)

SOURCE: "The Child Welfare System," in *How Does the Child Welfare System Work?* U.S. Department of Health and Human Services, National Clearinghouse on Child Abuse and Neglect, April 2004, http://nccanch.acf.hhs.gov/pubs/factsheets/cpswork.pdf (accessed October 27, 2004)

neglected. The court then determines what should be done to protect the child. The child may be left in the parents' home under the supervision of the CPS agency, or the child may be placed in foster care. If the child is removed from the home and it is later determined that the child should never be returned to the parents, the court can begin proceedings to terminate parental rights so that the child can be put up for adoption. The state may also prosecute the abusive parent or caretaker when a crime has allegedly been committed.

Family Preservation

The Adoption Assistance and Child Welfare Act of 1980 (Public Law 96-272) mandated: "In each case, reasonable efforts will be made (A) prior to the placement of a child in foster care, to prevent or eliminate the need for removal of the child from his home, and (B) to make it possible for the child to return to his home." Because the law, however, did not define the term "reasonable efforts," states and courts interpreted the term in different ways. In many cases, child welfare personnel took the "reasonable efforts" of providing family counseling, respite care, and substance abuse treatment, thus preventing the child from being removed from abusive parents.

The law was a reaction to what was seen as zealousness in the 1960s and 1970s, when children, especially African-American children, were taken from their homes because their parents were poor. At the beginning of the twentieth-first century, however, some feel that problems of drug or substance abuse can mean that returning the child to the home is likely a guarantee of further abuse. Others note that some situations exist where a parent's live-in partner, who has no emotional attachment to the child, may also present risks to the child.

FAMILY PRESERVATION DOES NOT WORK. Dr. Richard J. Gelles, a prominent family violence expert, once a vocal advocate of family preservation, had a change of heart after studying the case of fifteen-month-old David Edwards, who was suffocated by his mother after the child welfare system failed to come to his rescue. Although David's parents had lost custody of their first child because of abuse, and despite reports of David's abuse, CPS made "reasonable efforts" to let the parents keep the child. In *The Book of David: How Preserving Families Can Cost Children's Lives* (New York, NY: Basic Books, 1996), Dr. Gelles points out that CPS needs to abandon its blanket solution to child abuse in its attempt to use reasonable efforts to reunite the victims and their perpetrators.

Dr. Gelles found that those parents who seriously abuse their children are incapable of changing their behaviors. On August 2, 2001, testifying before the U.S. House of Representatives during the reauthorization hearing on CAPTA, Dr. Gelles reported:

> A major failing in child abuse and neglect assessments is the crude way behavioral change is conceptualized and measured. Behavioral change is thought to be a two-step process—one simply changes from one form of behavior to another. . . . As yet, there is no empirical evidence to support the effectiveness of child welfare services in general or the newer, more innovative intensive family preservation services. The lack of empirical support for the effectiveness of intensive family preservation services was the finding of the National Academy of Sciences panel on Assessing Family Violence Prevention and Treatment Programs and the United States Department of Health and Human Services national evaluation of family preservation programs.

FAMILY PRESERVATION WORKS. The National Coalition for Child Protection Reform (NCCPR), a nonprofit organization of experts on child abuse and foster care who are committed to the reform of the child welfare system, believes that many allegedly maltreated children are unnecessarily removed from their homes. NCCPR recognizes that, while there are cases in which the only way to save a child is to remove him or her from an abusive home, in many cases providing support services to the family in crisis, while letting the child remain at home, helps ensure child safety.

The NCCPR believes that, with the proper assistance, a family in crisis can change its behavior (*What is "Family Preservation?"* Issue Paper 10, Alexandria, VA, undated). According to the NCCPR, family preservation encompasses intervention procedures based on the Homebuilders program first implemented in 1974 in Tacoma, Washington. Homebuilders services are designed for families with children at risk of an imminent placement in foster care. It starts with an intensive initial intervention lasting four to six weeks in the family's home with provision of counseling and concrete services (for example, buying food, paying rent, providing clothing). The Homebuilders worker is on call twenty-four hours a day during that period, and the amount of counseling he or she gives the family has been compared to a year's worth of conventional counseling. After the period of intensive intervention, aftercare is afforded the family as needed.

CPS SYSTEM UNDER SIEGE

The Child Welfare Workforce

Child welfare caseworkers perform multiple tasks in the course of their job. Among other things, they investigate reports of child maltreatment, coordinate various services (mental health, substance abuse, etc.) to help keep families together, find foster care placements for children if needed, make regular visits to children and families, arrange placement of children in permanent homes when they cannot be safely returned to their parents or caretakers, and document all details pertaining to the case. Caseworker supervisors monitor and support their caseworkers, sometimes taking on some of the cases when there is a staff shortage or heavy caseload. In 2003 the U.S. General Accounting Office (GAO), the investigative arm of Congress, examined the child welfare workforce and how challenges in recruiting and retaining caseworkers affect the children under their care (*Child Welfare: Health and Human Services Could Play a Greater Role in Helping Child Welfare Agencies Recruit and Retain Staff*, Washington, DC, March 2003). Among other things, GAO examined exit interview documents of caseworkers who had left their jobs from seventeen states, forty counties, and nineteen private child welfare agencies. GAO also interviewed child welfare officials and experts and conducted on-site visits to agencies in four states—California, Illinois, Kentucky, and Texas.

GAO found that CPS agencies continued to have difficulty attracting and retaining experienced caseworkers.

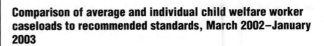

FIGURE 3.3

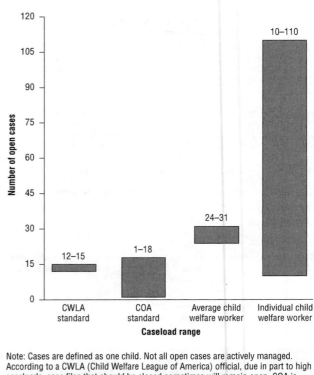

Comparison of average and individual child welfare worker caseloads to recommended standards, March 2002–January 2003

Note: Cases are defined as one child. Not all open cases are actively managed. According to a CWLA (Child Welfare League of America) official, due in part to high caseloads, case files that should be closed sometimes will remain open. COA is Council of Accreditation for Children and Family Services.

SOURCE: "Figure 3. Comparison of Average and Individual Child Welfare Worker Caseloads to Recommended Standards," in *Child Welfare: HHS Could Play a Greater Role in Helping Child Welfare Agencies Recruit and Retain Staff*, U.S. General Accounting Office, March 2003, http://www.gao.gov/new.items/d03357.pdf (accessed October 27, 2004)

The low pay not only made it difficult to attract qualified workers but also contributed to CPS employees leaving for better-paying jobs. Since the federal government has not set any national hiring policies, employees have college degrees that may not necessarily be related to social work. Workers that the GAO interviewed in different states also mentioned risk to personal safety, increased paperwork, lack of supervisory support, and insufficient time to attend training as reasons that affected their job performance and decision to leave.

Heavy Caseloads

In the four states GAO visited, caseworkers spent from 50% to 80% of their time doing paperwork. Staff shortage due to workers quitting their jobs resulted in excessive caseloads. Figure 3.3 shows the GAO's findings for worker caseloads as compared to recommended standards. The Child Welfare League of America (CWLA), a private child welfare organization, recommends a caseload of twelve to fifteen cases per caseworker, while the Council on Accreditation for Children and Family Services (COA), which evaluates organizations against best-practice standards, recommends no more than eighteen cases per worker. GAO found that, in reality, individual caseworkers handled anywhere from ten to 110 cases, with the average being twenty-four to thirty-one cases.

SLIPPING THROUGH THE CRACKS. Some CPS workers at times fail to monitor the children they are supposed to protect. In Florida the Department of Children and Families could not account for the disappearance of a five-year-old foster child, Rilya Wilson, who had been missing for more than a year before the agency noticed her absence in April 2002. At around that time the agency had reportedly lost track of more than 530 children. Rilya's disappearance was only discovered after her caseworker was fired and the new caseworker could not locate the child. The former caseworker had falsely reported that Rilya was fine, although she had not visited the child at her foster home for months. As of November 2004 the Department of Children and Families still could not account for Rilya's disappearance. Authorities, however, discovered that her foster mother continued to receive welfare payments for the girl in her absence. Witnesses had also testified the foster mother and her roommate abused the child prior to her disappearance. The women faced charges of aggravated child abuse, and her foster mother was convicted of fraud and sentenced to three years in jail.

New Jersey's child welfare system had also come to national attention because of its failure to protect adopted and foster children. In October 2003 four brothers of the Jackson family in Collingswood, New Jersey, ages nine, ten, fourteen, and nineteen, were removed from their adoptive parents' home and the couple were arrested. Investigations later revealed the brothers were systematically starved over many years. They weighed no more than forty-five pounds and stood less than four feet tall. The children reportedly subsisted on peanut butter, pancake batter, and wallboard. Authorities admitted two of the boys had fetal alcohol syndrome and two had eating disorders, the reasons the adoptive parents gave to neighbors for the brothers' emaciated appearance. The brothers, however, had put on weight and height since living with other foster families.

Investigations also revealed that Division of Youth and Family Services (DYFS) workers visited the adoptive parents' home thirty-eight times in the past to check on three other foster children but never asked about the brothers. In 1995, when DYFS was notified by the oldest boy's school that he seemed malnourished, DYFS did not require a medical examination and even agreed to the adoptive mother's decision to homeschool the brothers. DYFS poli-

TABLE 3.3

Estimated numbers and percentage of children aged 17 or younger living with one or more parents with past year substance abuse or dependence, 2001

Ages of children (years)	Estimated numbers (in thousands)	Percentage	Standard error
Younger than 3	1,078	9.8	0.81
3 to 5	1,115	9.8	1.10
6 to 11	1,816	7.5	1.28
12 to 17	2,100	9.2	0.81

Notes: Children include biological, step, adoptive, or foster. Children aged 17 or younger who were not living with one or more parents for most of the quarter of the NHSDA interview are excluded from the present analysis. According to the 2000 Current Population Survey, this amounts to approximately 3 million or 4 percent of children aged 17 or younger.

SOURCE: "Table 2. Estimated Numbers (in Thousands) and Percentage of Children Aged 17 or Younger Living with One or More Parents with Past Year Substance Abuse or Dependence: 2001," in *The NHSDA Report: Children Living with Substance-Abusing or Substance-Dependent Parents*, U.S. Department of Health and Human Services, Substance Abuse and Mental Health Services Administration, Office of Applied Studies, June 2, 2003, http://www.oas.samhsa.gov/2k3/children/children.pdf (accessed October 27, 2004)

cies required an annual medical evaluation and interview of each household member, but these never took place. In May 2004 the adoptive parents were indicted on twenty-eight counts of aggravated assault and child endangerment.

In January 2003 Newark, New Jersey, police found two boys, ages four and seven, locked in a basement and the dead body of another seven-year-old, twin brother Faheem Williams, stuffed in a plastic container. The boys' mother had left the children with a cousin before leaving to serve a prison sentence. It was discovered that a DYFS caseworker and a supervisor assigned to the family had closed the file on the boys a year earlier without ever checking on them.

The Problem of Substance Abuse

CPS workers are faced with the growing problem of substance abuse among families involved with the child welfare system. According to the National Household Survey on Drug Abuse, with information from the U.S. Bureau of the Census, in 2001 nearly seventy million children younger than eighteen lived with at least one parent. About 6.1 million children seventeen or younger (comprising 8.7% percent of all children in the nation) lived with one or more parents with past-year substance abuse or dependence. About one-fifth (19.6%) were five years old or younger. (See Table 3.3.) Among these children, about 4.5 million lived with an alcoholic parent, an estimated 953,000 lived with a parent with an illicit drug problem, and approximately 657,000 lived with parents who abused both alcohol and illicit drugs. (See Figure 3.4.) Fathers (7.8%) were more likely than mothers (4%)

FIGURE 3.4

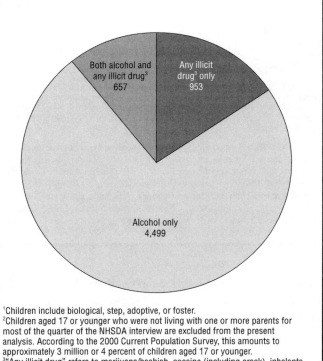

Estimated number of children[1] aged 17 or younger living with one or more parents[2] with past year substance abuse or dependence, 2001

(In thousands)

Both alcohol and any illicit drug[3]
657

Any illicit drug[3] only
953

Alcohol only
4,499

[1]Children include biological, step, adoptive, or foster.
[2]Children aged 17 or younger who were not living with one or more parents for most of the quarter of the NHSDA interview are excluded from the present analysis. According to the 2000 Current Population Survey, this amounts to approximately 3 million or 4 percent of children aged 17 or younger.
[3]"Any illicit drug" refers to marijuana/hashish, cocaine (including crack), inhalants, hallucinogens, heroin, or prescription-type drugs used nonmedically.

SOURCE: "Figure 1. Estimated Numbers (in Thousands) of Children Aged 17 or Younger Living with One or More Parents with Past Year Substance Abuse or Dependence: 2001," in *The NHSDA Report: Children Living with Substance-Abusing or Substance-Dependent Parents,* U.S. Department of Health and Human Services, Substance Abuse and Mental Health Services Administration, Office of Applied Studies, June 2, 2003, http://www.oas.samhsa.gov/2k3/children/children.pdf (accessed November 23, 2004)

FIGURE 3.5

Percentages of fathers and mothers (living with one or more children[1] aged 17 or younger) reporting past year substance abuse or dependence, 2001

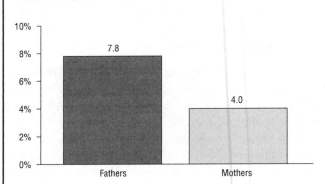

Fathers — 7.8
Mothers — 4.0

[1]Children include biological, step, adoptive, or foster.

SOURCE: "Figure 2. Percentages of Fathers and Mothers (Living with One or More Children Aged 17 or Younger) Reporting Past Year Substance Abuse or Dependence: 2001," in *The NHSDA Report: Children Living with Substance-Abusing or Substance-Dependent Parents,* U.S. Department of Health and Human Services, Substance Abuse and Mental Health Services Administration, Office of Applied Studies, June 2, 2003, http://www.oas.samhsa.gov/2k3/children/children.pdf (accessed November 23, 2004)

to report having had a past-year substance abuse or dependence (*National Household Survey on Drug Abuse (NHSDA) Report: Children Living with Substance Abusing or Substance-Dependent Parents,* U.S. Department of Health and Human Services, Substance Abuse and Mental Health Services Administration, Office of Applied Science, Rockville, MD, June 2003). (See Figure 3.5.)

According to the U.S. Department of Health and Human Services, about one-third to two-thirds of substantiated child maltreatment reports (those having sufficient evidence to support the allegation of maltreatment) involve substance abuse. Younger children, especially infants, are more likely to be victimized by substance-abusing parents, and the maltreatment is more likely to consist of neglect than abuse. Many children experience neglect when a parent is under the influence of alcohol or

is out of the home looking for drugs. Even when the parent is at home, he or she may be psychologically unavailable to the children.

SUBSTANCE ABUSE AMONG PREGNANT WOMEN. Illicit drug use among pregnant women continues to be a national problem. Each year the *National Survey on Drug Use and Health (NSDUH),* formerly known as the *National Household Survey on Drug Abuse,* asked female respondents ages fifteen to forty-four about their pregnancy status and illicit drug use the month prior to the survey. In 2002, 3% of pregnant women, compared to 9% of non-pregnant women, reported using illicit drugs during the past month (*The NSDUH Report: Pregnancy and Substance Use,* U.S. Department of Health and Human Services, Substance Abuse and Mental Health Services Administration, Office of Applied Studies, Rockville, MD, 2004). Nearly 7% of pregnant women fifteen to twenty-five years old reported illicit drug use the previous month, compared to just 0.5% of pregnant women ages twenty-six to forty-four. Among pregnant women, more African-Americans (6.2%) than whites (3.6%) and Hispanics (1.7%) reported using illicit drugs the previous month. (See Figure 3.6.)

CHILDREN AT ILLICIT DRUG LABS. The rapid growth of methamphetamine use in the United States has resulted in the establishment of clandestine methamphetamine laboratories (meth labs) in many places. Traditionally, large-scale operations, particularly in California and Mexico, have produced large quantities of drugs, which are then dis-

FIGURE 3.6

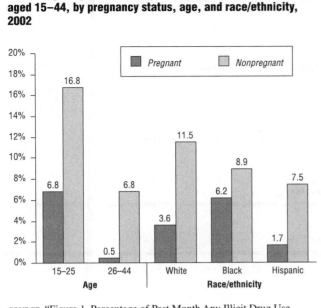

Percentage of past month any illicit drug use among women aged 15–44, by pregnancy status, age, and race/ethnicity, 2002

SOURCE: "Figure 1. Percentage of Past Month Any Illicit Drug Use among Women Aged 15 to 44, by Pregnancy Status, Age, and Race/Ethnicity: 2002," in *The NSDUH Report: Pregnancy and Substance Use,* U.S. Department of Health and Human Services, Substance Abuse and Mental Health Services Administration, Office of Applied Studies, January 2, 2004 (accessed October 27, 2004)

tributed throughout various areas in the country. With more demand for methamphetamines, many small-scale businesses have started operating. Since methamphetamines can be produced almost anywhere, using readily available ingredients, nearly anyone can set up a temporary laboratory, make a batch of drugs, then dismantle the apparatus. Authorities have found makeshift laboratories in places inhabited or visited by children, including houses, apartments, mobile homes, motel rooms, and storage lockers.

As more children are found living in or visiting home-based meth labs, child protection personnel have to deal with those children who have been exposed not only to potentially abusive people associated with the production of methamphetamines, but also to such dangers as fire and explosions. Hazardous living conditions include unsafe electrical equipment, chemical ingredients, syringes, and the presence of firearms and pornography (Karen Swetlow, *OVC Bulletin: Children at Clandestine Methamphetamine Labs: Helping Meth's Youngest Victims,* U.S. Department of Justice, Office of Justice Programs, Office for Victims of Crime, Washington, DC, June 2003). Police have found meth homes with defective plumbing, rodent and insect infestation, and without heating or cooling. The author added that children living in meth labs are likely to be victims of severe neglect and physical and sexual abuse. A report by the El Paso Intelligence Center, a collaborative effort of more than fifteen federal and state agencies that track drug movement and immigration, showed that thousands of children were living in or visiting meth labs that were seized by law enforcement nationwide from 2000 to 2002. In 2002 more than one thousand children, or about half of the children present during lab-related incidents, were taken into protective custody. (See Table 3.4.)

CPS and Domestic Violence

When CPS workers get involved with children who have witnessed domestic violence, their main concern is the interests of the children. Critics have charged that CPS further penalizes battered women by taking away their children when their partners have abused the children. Stephanie Walton, who tracks domestic violence for the National Conference of State Legislatures, observed that experts on domestic violence and child welfare like Jeffrey L. Edleson have noted that "fragmented treatment systems" stand in the way of solving the problems of domestic violence and co-occurring child maltreatment ("When Violence Hits Home," *State Legislatures,* vol. 29, issue 6, June 2003). Walton added that child welfare workers and domestic violence agencies work against each other, with the former blaming the mother for exposing the child to her partner's violence and the latter protecting the mother from prosecution for failure to protect her child.

According to Thomas D. Morton, president and chief executive officer of Child Welfare Institute, child welfare agencies need to hold the batterers accountable for their actions (*Failure to Protect?* Child Welfare Institute, Duluth, GA, February 2002). Morton noted that some CPS caseworkers may equate a mother's victimization to her inability to protect her child, consequently removing the child from the home. CPS and/or state legislatures should clarify certain CPS practices, including what course of action to take when a nonrelated caregiver in a household is the child abuser. The author asked whether or not CPS should pursue family preservation (keeping the family together) if the abuser is not legally related to the child. He also raised such questions as to whether CPS may require the biological parent to end a relationship with the nonbiological caretaker as a requirement for keeping the child in the family.

Holding States Accountable

In 2004 the U.S. Department of Health and Human Services released the fourth in a series of annual reports on states' performances in meeting the needs of at-risk children who have entered the child welfare system. The *Child Welfare Outcomes 2001: Annual Report* (Administration for Children and Families, Administration on Children, Youth and Families, Children's Bureau, Washington, DC) was required by the 1997 Adoption and Safe Families Act (ASFA; Public Law 105-89).

TABLE 3.4

Children found at methamphetamine labs in the United States, 2000–02

		Number of children					
Year	Number of meth lab-related incidents	Present	Residing in seized meth labs [1]	Affected [2]	Exposed to toxic chemicals [3]	Taken into protective custody	Injured or killed
2002	15,353	2,077	2,023	3,167	1,373	1,026	26 injured, 2 killed
2001	13,270	2,191	976	2,191	788	778	14 injured
2000	8,971	1,803	216	1,803	345	353	12 injured, 3 killed

[1]Children included in this group were not necessarily present at the time of seizure.
[2]Includes children who were residing at the labs but not necessarily present at the time of seizure and children who were visiting the site; data for 2000 and 2001 may not show all children affected.
[3]Includes children who were residing at the labs but not necessarily present at the time of seizure.

SOURCE: "Children Found at Methamphetamine Labs in the United States," in *Children at Clandestine Methamphetamine Labs: Helping Meth's Youngest Victims,"* U.S. Department of Justice, Office of Justice Programs, Office for Victims of Crimes, June 2003 (accessed October 27, 2004)

ASFA gives states flexibility in interpreting the "reasonable efforts" required to reunify children with their birth families. When victims cannot safely return home, states can start proceedings to terminate parental rights for children who have been in foster care for fifteen of the previous twenty-two months. Children can then be placed in permanent homes. The *Child Welfare Outcomes 2001: Annual Report* showed that in fiscal year 2001 (October 1, 2000, to September 30, 2001) an estimated 290,000 children entered foster care. About 263,000 exited foster care. Fifty-seven percent were reunited with their parents or primary caretakers, 10% went to live with relatives, 18% were adopted, and 7% were emancipated (recognized by the court as an adult). Three percent were transferred to another CPS agency, and another 3% were put under guardianship. Two percent of foster children had run away. Another 528 children had died. (See Table 3.5.) As of September 30, 2002, an estimated 532,000 children remained in foster care.

Lives Saved

Although CPS agencies have had many problems and are often unable to perform as effectively as they should, many thousands of maltreated children have been identified, many lives have been saved, and many more have been taken out of dangerous environments. It is impossible to tally the number of child abuse cases that might have ended in death; these children have been saved by changes in the laws, by awareness and reporting, and by the efforts of the professionals who intervened on their behalf.

CPS'S PERCEPTION OF RACIAL DISPARITY IN THE CHILD WELFARE SYSTEM

In 2003 the Children's Bureau released the first study of its kind to explore the attitudes and perceptions of CPS personnel regarding the over-representation of minority children, particularly African-American children, in the child welfare system (Susan Chibnall, Nicole M. Dutch,

TABLE 3.5

Outcomes for children exiting foster care, fiscal year 2001

Reunification with parent(s) or primary caretaker(s)	57%	148,606
Living with other relative(s)	10%	26,084
Adoption	18%	46,668
Emancipation	7%	19,008
Guardianship	3%	8,969
Transfer to another agency	3%	7,918
Runaway	2%	5,219
Death of child	0%	528

Note: Deaths are attributable to a variety of causes including medical conditions, accidents, and homicide.

SOURCE: "What Were the Outcomes for the Children Exiting Foster Care during Fiscal Year 2001?" in *Child Welfare Outcomes 2001: Annual Report,* U.S. Department of Health and Human Services, Administration for Children and Families, Administration on Children, Youth, and Families, Children's Bureau, 2004, http://www.acf.hhs.gov/programs/cb/publications/cwo01/cwo01.pdf (accessed October 27, 2004)

Brenda Jones-Harden, Annie Brown, Ruby Gourdine, Jacqueline Smith, Anniglo Boone, and Shelita Snyder, *Children of Color in the Child Welfare System: Perspectives from the Child Welfare Community,* U.S. Department of Health and Human Services, Administration for Children and Families, Administration on Children, Youth and Families, Children's Bureau, Washington, DC). According to the authors, while African-American children make up 15% of all children in the United States, they represent 25% of substantiated maltreatment victims. In addition, these children account for 45% of all children in foster care.

Researchers conducted the study in nine child welfare agencies across the country. They interviewed agency administrators, supervisors, and caseworkers. The child welfare personnel gave a variety of reasons why minority children are over-represented in the child welfare system, including:

- Poverty and poverty-related issues—Child welfare personnel thought that African-American families are more likely to be poor than other ethnic/racial groups.

This makes them more vulnerable to social problems such as child maltreatment, domestic violence, and substance abuse. Moreover, these families typically live in areas lacking resources where they can go for assistance.

- Visibility—Poor families are more likely to use public services, such as public health care, making them more visible to mandated reporters when they are experiencing problems, including child abuse and neglect.

- Over-reporting—Many study participants proposed that, since poor families are more visible to mandated reporters such as doctors and nurses, they are more likely to be reported to CPS.

- Worker bias—When investigating particular families, some caseworkers may not understand the cultural norms and practices of minorities; this may influence their decisions at different stages of child welfare services, including child maltreatment reporting, investigation, substantiation, and the child's removal from home and placement in foster care.

- Media bias—According to child welfare personnel, the media frenzy that occurs after each high-profile child abuse case influences their decision to substantiate certain cases and remove children from their homes. Caseworkers in two sites (both located in areas that are mainly African-American) revealed that they felt "frightened and insecure" each time they came under media attention, which they thought has become quite frequent. One worker stated,

> [Workers] tend to feel safer placing children in care . . . because they've gotten pressure about leaving children in homes and something happens to them so they feel safer bringing a child into care. When in doubt, take them out. A lot of times, in African-American communities, they're going to take them out.

Perspectives on the Impact of Federal Policies on Children in the Child Welfare System

Some child welfare personnel who were interviewed for the study *Children of Color in the Child Welfare System: Perspectives from the Child Welfare Community* believed that the Multi-ethnic Placement Act (MEPA) of 1994 (Public Law 103-382), which allows the placement of African-American children in nonminority homes, does not serve children's best interests. They were concerned that transracial placements might be harmful to minority children's self-esteem and ethnic/racial identity.

On the other hand, child welfare personnel said MEPA has given them the alternative of placing some children with extended families. One supervisor quoted by the study commented, "The other thing that [MEPA] has done . . . is that it has broadened the role that family [are] able to play. For instance, we never used to recommend relative adoptions. It was seen as being very problematic and creating all kinds of difficult dynamics within the family system. And, now, that's a preferred plan, to have a relative that wants to adopt."

Study participants were also asked about their perspectives on the Adoption and Safe Families Act (ASFA) of 1997 (Public Law 105-89). Among its provisions, AFSA has accelerated the permanent placement of children waiting in foster care. ASFA allows the termination of parental rights in situations where family reunification is considered not possible. ASFA gives states incentive payments to find adoptive families for foster children within a certain time frame.

Participants reported concerns that families experiencing other issues, such as substance abuse and mental health problems, may take longer to resolve their problems. CPS workers admitted they feared that, under ASFA requirements, they might have to terminate parental rights before parents have had the time to sort out their problems. To aggravate the situation, these goals are hard to accomplish when they lack the financial resources to provide social services and treatments.

STATES SHOULD USE ASFA TO THEIR ADVANTAGE. Richard Wexler, executive director of the National Coalition for Child Protection Reform (Alexandria, VA), noted, "In passing ASFA, Congress failed to learn the lessons some states have begun to learn after experiencing foster care panics—huge, sudden increases in placements that follow intensive media coverage of the death of a child who was known to the [child welfare] system" ("Take the Child and Run: Tales from the Age of ASFA," *New England Law Review,* vol. 36, no. 1, Fall 2001). Wexler described how, in the aftermath of foster care panics, child abuse deaths tend to increase. Caseworkers, fearing the scrutiny of politicians and the media and overwhelmed with more cases, may remove children from homes that could have been made safe with the right services, while leaving others in dangerous homes.

Wexler observed that while ASFA encourages states to terminate parental rights within a restricted time period and provides monetary incentives for adoptions, nothing in the law prevents states from providing parents with housing or child care. States do not have to use the "take the child and run" approach. Instead, states can provide rent subsidies so that parents would not lose their children because of lack of decent housing. Moreover, states can provide daycare so that single working parents who leave children unsupervised in order to earn a living would not lose those children because they have been found neglectful.

CHAPTER 4

HOW MANY CHILDREN ARE MALTREATED?

Statistics on child abuse are difficult to interpret and compare because there is very little consistency in how information is collected. The definitions of abuse vary from study to study, as do the methods of counting incidents of abuse. Some methods count only reported cases of abuse. Some statistics are based on estimates projected from a small study, while others are based on interviews. In addition, it is virtually impossible to know the extent of child maltreatment that occurs in the privacy of the home.

INCIDENCE AND PREVALENCE OF CHILD MALTREATMENT

Researchers use two terms—incidence and prevalence—to describe the estimates of the number of victims of child abuse and neglect. Andrea J. Sedlak and Diane D. Broadhurst defined incidence as the number of new cases occurring in the population during a given period (*Third National Incidence Study of Child Abuse and Neglect* [NIS-3], U.S. Department of Health and Human Services, National Center on Child Abuse and Neglect, Washington, DC, 1996). The incidence of child maltreatment is measured in terms of incidence rate: the number of children per one thousand children in the U.S. population who are maltreated annually. Surveys based on official reports by child protective services (CPS) agencies and community professionals are a major source of incidence data.

Prevalence, as defined by NIS-3, refers to the total number of child maltreatment cases in the population at a given time. Some researchers use lifetime prevalence to denote the number of people who have had at least one experience of child maltreatment in their lives. To measure the prevalence of child maltreatment, researchers use self-reported surveys of parents and child victims. Examples of self-reported surveys are the landmark 1975 *National Family Violence Survey* and the 1985 *National Family Violence Resurvey* conducted by Murray A. Straus and Richard J. Gelles.

Official Reports

Studies based on official reports depend on a number of things happening before an incident of abuse can be recorded. The victim must be seen by people outside the home, and these people must recognize that the child has been abused. Once they have recognized this fact, they must then decide to report the abuse and find out where to report it. Once CPS receives and screens the report for appropriateness, it can then take action.

In some cases the initial call to CPS is prompted by a problem that needs to be handled by a different agency. It may be a case of neglect due to poverty rather than abuse, although the initial report is still recorded as abuse.

For the data to become publicly available, CPS must keep records of its cases and then pass them on to a national group that collects those statistics. Consequently, final reported statistics are understated estimates—valuable as indicators but not definitive findings. It is very unlikely that accurate statistics on child abuse will ever be available.

COLLECTING CHILD MALTREATMENT DATA

The 1974 Child Abuse Prevention and Treatment Act (CAPTA; Public Law 93-247) created the National Center on Child Abuse and Neglect (NCCAN) to coordinate nationwide efforts to protect children from maltreatment. As part of the former U.S. Department of Health, Education, and Welfare, NCCAN commissioned the American Humane Association (AHA) to collect data from the states. The first time the AHA collected data, in 1976, it recorded an estimated 416,000 reports, affecting 669,000 children. Between 1980 and 1985 the AHA reported a 12% annual increase in maltreatment reports to CPS agencies. By 1990 reports of child maltreatment had risen to 1.7 million, affecting about 2.7 million children.

In 1985 the federal government stopped funding data collection on child maltreatment. In 1986 the National

Committee to Prevent Child Abuse (NCPCA; now called Prevent Child Abuse America) picked up where the government left off. The NCPCA started collecting detailed information from the states on the number of children abused, the characteristics of child abuse, the number of child abuse deaths, and changes in the funding and extent of child welfare services.

In 1988 the Child Abuse Prevention, Adoption and Family Services Act (Public Law 100-294) replaced the 1974 CAPTA. The new law mandated that NCCAN, as part of the U.S. Department of Health and Human Services (HHS), establish a national data collection program on child maltreatment. In 1990 the National Child Abuse and Neglect Data System (NCANDS), designed to fulfill this mandate, began collecting and analyzing child maltreatment data from CPS agencies in the fifty states and the District of Columbia. The first three surveys were known as *Working Paper 1, Working Paper 2,* and *Child Maltreatment 1992.* NCANDS has since conducted the survey *Child Maltreatment.* The latest survey was *Child Maltreatment 2002,* released in April 2004.

As part of the 1974 CAPTA, Congress also mandated NCCAN to conduct a periodic *National Incidence Study of Child Abuse and Neglect* (NIS). Data on maltreated children are collected not only from CPS agencies but also from professionals in community agencies, such as law enforcement, public health, juvenile probation, mental health, and voluntary social services, as well as from hospitals, schools, and day care centers. The NIS is the single most comprehensive source of information about the incidence of child maltreatment in the United States, because it analyzes the characteristics of child abuse and neglect that are known to community-based professionals, including those characteristics not reported to CPS. The latest study, NIS-3, was released in 1996. In 2003 the Keeping Children and Families Safe Act (Public Law 108-36) directed the collection of data for NIS-4.

Pursuant to the CAPTA Amendments of 1996 (Public Law 104-235), NCCAN ceased operating as a separate agency. Since then all child maltreatment prevention functions have been consolidated within the Children's Bureau of the HHS.

CPS MALTREATMENT REPORTS

Collecting child maltreatment data from the states is difficult because each state has its own method of gathering and classifying the information. Most states collect data on an incident basis; that is, they count each time a child is reported for abuse or neglect. If the same child is reported several times in one year, each incident is counted. Consequently, the number of incidents of child maltreatment may be greater than the number of maltreated children.

In 2002 CPS agencies received an estimated 2,617,000 referrals, or reports, alleging the maltreatment of about 4.5 million children (*Child Maltreatment 2002,* U.S. Department of Health and Human Services, Administration for Children and Families, Administration on Children, Youth and Families, Children's Bureau, Washington, DC, 2004), which may include some children who were reported and counted more than once. States may vary in the rates of child maltreatment reported. States differ not only in definitions of maltreatment but also in the methods of counting reports of abuse. Some states count reports based on the number of incidents or the number of families involved, rather than on the number of children allegedly abused. Other states count all reports to CPS, while others count only investigated reports.

In 2002 forty-two states submitted child-level data for each report of alleged maltreatment. The data include, among other things, the demographics about the children and the perpetrators, types of maltreatment, and dispositions (findings after investigation or assessment of the case). The remaining eight states and the District of Columbia submitted only summary statistics, such as the number of child victims of maltreatment. CPS agencies screened in (accepted for further assessment or investigation) 1,141,820 referrals, or 67.1%, of referrals. Overall, the rate of maltreatment referrals ranged from 12.8 per one thousand children (Pennsylvania) to 78.1 per one thousand children (Montana) under age eighteen. (See Table 4.1.)

Dispositions of Investigated Reports

After a CPS agency screens in a report of child maltreatment, it initiates an investigation. Some states follow one time frame for responding to all reports, while others follow a priority system, investigating high-priority cases within one to twenty-four hours. According to the National Child Abuse and Neglect Data System (NCANDS), in 2002 twenty-three states that reported response time showed an average response time of fifty-two hours.

Following investigation of the report of child maltreatment, the CPS agency assigns a disposition, or finding, to the report. Prior to 2000, reports of alleged child maltreatment received one of three dispositions—indicated, substantiated, or unsubstantiated. In 2000 several states announced plans to establish an alternative response program to reports of alleged child maltreatment. If the child is at a serious and immediate risk of maltreatment, CPS responds with the traditional formal investigation, which may involve removing the child from the home. If it is determined, however, that the parent likely will not endanger the child, CPS workers use the alternative response to help the family. This involves a more informal approach. Instead of removing the child from the home environment, CPS steps in to assist the whole family by, for example, helping reduce stress that may lead to child abuse through provision of child care, adequate housing,

TABLE 4.1

Screened-in and screened-out referrals, 2002

State	Child population	Screened-out referrals		Screened-in referrals[1]		Total referrals	
		Number	%	Number	%	Number	Rate[2]
Alabama	1,107,108	339	1.7	19,281	98.3	19,620	17.7
Alaska	192,428	1,667	12.0	12,182	88.0	13,849	72.0
Arizona	1,476,856	5,381	14.0	33,151	86.0	38,532	26.1
Arkansas	677,522	11,417	37.9	18,697	62.1	30,114	44.4
California							
Colorado	1,151,118	12,265	30.5	27,889	69.5	40,154	34.9
Connecticut	872,853	11,114	24.4	34,513	75.6	45,627	52.3
Delaware	189,698	1,590	23.5	5,163	76.5	6,753	35.6
District of Columbia	112,128	189	3.6	5,049	96.4	5,238	46.7
Florida	3,882,271	83,331	36.9	142,547	63.1	225,878	58.2
Georgia	2,268,477	16,456	19.2	69,108	80.8	85,564	37.7
Hawaii							
Idaho	370,439	6,573	50.4	6,475	49.6	13,048	35.2
Illinois	3,254,523	0	0.0	58,704	100.0	58,704	18.0
Indiana	1,594,857	16,647	33.3	33,336	66.7	49,983	31.3
Iowa	698,045	12,397	34.8	23,215	65.2	35,612	51.0
Kansas	696,519	12,004	40.7	17,504	59.3	29,508	42.4
Kentucky	931,588	2,081	4.8	41,218	95.2	43,299	46.5
Louisiana							
Maine	279,058	11,653	72.3	4,474	27.7	16,127	57.8
Maryland							
Massachusetts	1,463,340	23,457	38.0	38,306	62.0	61,763	42.2
Michigan	2,570,264	50,018	40.7	72,999	59.3	123,017	47.9
Minnesota	1,252,125	15,289	46.2	17,770	53.8	33,059	26.4
Mississippi	760,747	4,878	29.5	11,670	70.5	16,548	21.8
Missouri	1,397,461	53,997	50.4	53,116	49.6	107,113	76.6
Montana	216,320	6,567	38.9	10,336	61.1	16,903	78.1
Nebraska	439,393	6,400	46.2	7,463	53.8	13,863	31.6
Nevada							
New Hampshire	308,371	9,806	56.6	7,509	43.4	17,315	56.1
New Jersey	2,127,391	0	0.0	39,148	100.0	39,148	18.4
New Mexico	500,506	9,886	41.4	13,995	58.6	23,881	47.7
New York							
North Carolina							
North Dakota	146,812	2,112	33.9	4,109	66.1	6,221	42.4
Ohio							
Oklahoma	873,560	19,370	32.9	39,592	67.1	58,962	67.5
Oregon	855,107	22,492	55.9	17,763	44.1	40,255	47.1
Pennsylvania	2,863,452	12,403	33.8	24,330	66.2	36,733	12.8
Rhode Island	239,248	6,051	45.6	7,211	54.4	13,262	55.4
South Carolina	979,163	7,225	28.0	18,579	72.0	25,804	26.4
South Dakota							
Tennessee							
Texas	6,102,316	22,527	14.8	129,956	85.2	152,483	25.0
Utah	713,012	9,676	33.8	18,965	66.2	28,641	40.2
Vermont							
Virginia	1,779,408	21,778	51.4	20,619	48.6	42,397	23.8
Washington	1,513,360	41,297	69.2	18,423	30.8	59,720	39.5
West Virginia	389,171	7,072	32.0	15,052	68.0	22,124	56.8
Wisconsin							
Wyoming	122,344	2,555	51.5	2,403	48.5	4,958	40.5
Total	**47,368,359**	**559,960**		**1,141,820**		**1,701,780**	
Weighted average/rate			32.9		67.1		35.9
Number reporting	39	39		39		39	

A national estimate of 2,600,000 referrals was calculated by multiplying the national referral rate (35.9) by the national population for all 51 states (72,894,483). The result was rounded to the nearest 100,000.

[1]For those states that submitted the Child File, the screened-in number is the sum of the reports by disposition. For SDC states, the number is taken directly from the state's report form.

[2]The national referral rate, 35.9 referrals per 1,000 children in the population, was calculated from the total number of referrals and the child populations in the 39 states reporting both screened in and screened-out referrals.

SOURCE: "Table 2-1. Screened-in and Screened-out Referrals, 2002," in *Child Maltreatment 2002*, U.S. Department of Health and Human Services, Administration for Children and Families, Administration on Children, Youth, and Families, Children's Bureau, 2004, http://www.acf.hhs.gov/programs/cb/publications/cm02/cm02.pdf (accessed October 27, 2004).

and education in parenting skills. In 2002 ten states implemented the alternative response program. NCANDS used the following dispositions for its 2002 report:

• A disposition of "substantiated" means that sufficient evidence existed to support the allegation of maltreatment or risk of maltreatment.

- A disposition of "indicated or reason to suspect" means that the abuse and/or neglect could not be confirmed, but there was reason to suspect that the child was maltreated or was at risk of maltreatment.

- A disposition of "unsubstantiated" means that no maltreatment occurred or sufficient evidence did not exist to conclude that the child was maltreated or was at risk of being maltreated.

- A disposition of "alternative response victim" means that, when a response other than investigation was provided, the child was identified as a victim of maltreatment.

- A disposition of "alternative response nonvictim" means that, when a response other than investigation was provided, the child was not identified as a victim of maltreatment.

Of the more than 1.1 million reports that were investigated, 60.4% were unsubstantiated. More than one-fourth (26.8%) were substantiated, and 3.5% were indicated. About 0.1% were determined alternative response victim, and 4.7% were alternative response nonvictim. Dispositions that were identified "closed with no finding" referred to cases in which the investigation could not be completed because the family moved out of the jurisdiction, the family could not be found, or the needed reports were not filed within the required time limit. Such dispositions accounted for 1.7%. (See Figure 4.1.)

VICTIMS OF MALTREATMENT

Rates of Victimization

In 2002 an estimated 896,000 children were victims of maltreatment in the United States, down from 903,000 in 2001. A total of 12.3 children for every one thousand children in the population were victims of abuse or neglect. While this rate of victimization was higher than that for 1999 (11.8 per one thousand children), it was lower than the rates for the previous years in the 1990s. The rate of maltreatment had peaked at 15.3 per one thousand children in 1993. (See Table 4.2.)

Types of Maltreatment

According to *Child Maltreatment 2002* more than three out of five maltreated children (60.5%) suffered neglect (including medical neglect). Nearly one-fifth (18.6%) were physically abused, and 9.9% were sexually abused. An additional 6.5% were subjected to emotional, or psychological, maltreatment. Another 18.9% experienced other types of maltreatment, including abandonment, congenital drug addiction, and threats to harm a child. Some children were victims of more than one type of maltreatment.

RATES OF MALTREATMENT BY TYPE. Between 1998 and 2002 the rates of the different types of maltreatment

FIGURE 4.1

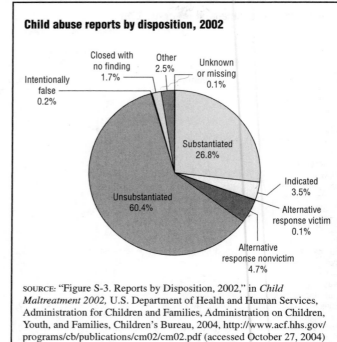

Child abuse reports by disposition, 2002

Closed with no finding 1.7%
Other 2.5%
Unknown or missing 0.1%
Intentionally false 0.2%
Substantiated 26.8%
Indicated 3.5%
Alternative response victim 0.1%
Alternative response nonvictim 4.7%
Unsubstantiated 60.4%

SOURCE: "Figure S-3. Reports by Disposition, 2002," in *Child Maltreatment 2002,* U.S. Department of Health and Human Services, Administration for Children and Families, Administration on Children, Youth, and Families, Children's Bureau, 2004, http://www.acf.hhs.gov/programs/cb/publications/cm02/cm02.pdf (accessed October 27, 2004)

fluctuated from year to year. The rate of neglect dropped from 6.9 per one thousand children in the population in 1998 to 6.5 per one thousand children in 1999, rising to 7.3 per one thousand children in 2000. The rate was about the same (7.2 per one thousand children) in 2002. The rates for medical neglect remained constant during the five-year period. The rates for physical abuse and sexual abuse declined, from 2.9 to 2.3 per one thousand children for the former, and from 1.5 to 1.2 per one thousand children for the latter. The rate for psychological abuse remained the same for 1998 and 2002 (0.8 per one thousand children). (See Figure 4.2.)

Gender and Age of Victims

In 2002 more female children (51.9%) were maltreated than their male counterparts (48.1%). Younger children represented most of the maltreated victims. Generally, the older the child gets, the more the likelihood of abuse decreases. The victimization rate for infants and toddlers up through age three was 16 per one thousand children of the same age group, compared to 13.7 per one thousand for children ages four to seven. The rate of victimization for children ages eight to eleven was 11.9 per one thousand; for ages twelve to fifteen, 10.6 per one thousand; and for ages sixteen and seventeen, six per one thousand. (See Figure 4.3.)

Race and Ethnicity of Victims

In 2002 more than half (54.2%) of maltreatment victims were white, and one-quarter (26.1%) were African-American. Hispanics, who may be of any race, accounted for 11% of the victims. Native Americans (1.8%) and

TABLE 4.2

Rates of children subjected to an investigation and rates of victimization, 1990–2002

Reporting year	Child population	Investigation rate	States reporting	Total children subjects of an investigation or assessment	Victim rate	States reporting	Total victims
1990	64,163,192	36.1	36	2,316,000	13.4	45	860,000
1991	65,069,507	38.2	39	2,486,000	14.0	46	911,000
1992	66,073,841	41.2	41	2,722,000	15.1	48	998,000
1993	66,961,573	42.1	42	2,819,000	15.3	47	1,025,000
1994	67,803,294	42.1	42	2,855,000	15.2	46	1,031,000
1995	68,437,378	42.2	43	2,888,000	14.7	47	1,006,000
1996	69,022,127	42.0	42	2,899,000	14.7	46	1,015,000
1997	69,527,944	41.9	44	2,913,000	13.7	45	953,000
1998	69,872,059	42.1	51	2,939,000	12.9	51	904,000
1999	70,199,435	41.0	50	2,878,000	11.8	50	828,000
2000	72,346,696	41.9	49	3,031,000	12.2	50	883,000
2001	72,616,308	43.2	48	3,137,000	12.4	51	903,000
2002	72,894,483	43.8	50	3,193,000	12.3	51	896,000

Data source: CAF (Combined Aggregate File, or combined numbers from child and agency files and other statistics).
Notes: Victimization and investigation rates were computed by dividing the respective counts of children by the population and multiplying by 1,000.
All totals are rounded to the nearest 100,000. If fewer than 51 states reported data, the total is an estimate based on multiplying the rate by the child population for that year.

SOURCE: "Table 3-3. Rates of Children Subjected to an Investigation and Rates of Victimization, 1990–2002," in *Child Maltreatment 2002*, U.S. Department of Health and Human Services, Administration for Children and Families, Administration on Children, Youth, and Families, Children's Bureau, 2004 (accessed October 27, 2004)

FIGURE 4.2

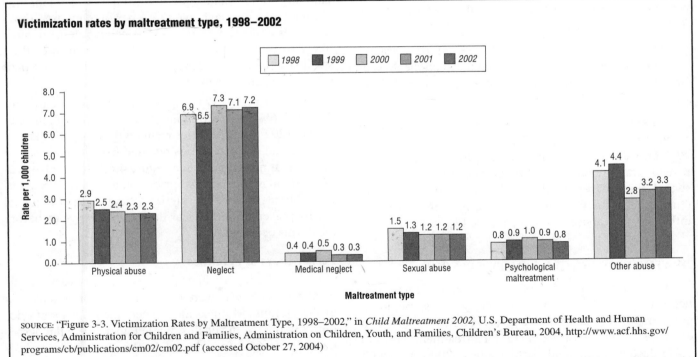

SOURCE: "Figure 3-3. Victimization Rates by Maltreatment Type, 1998–2002," in *Child Maltreatment 2002*, U.S. Department of Health and Human Services, Administration for Children and Families, Administration on Children, Youth, and Families, Children's Bureau, 2004, http://www.acf.hhs.gov/programs/cb/publications/cm02/cm02.pdf (accessed October 27, 2004)

Asians/Pacific Islanders (0.9%) made up the lowest proportions of victims. (See Figure 4.4.)

PERPETRATORS OF CHILD MALTREATMENT

The law considers perpetrators to be those persons who abuse or neglect children under their care. They may be parents, foster parents, other relatives, or other caretakers.

In 2002 more than two of five victims (40.3%) were maltreated by their mother acting alone. Another 19.1% experienced maltreatment from their father acting alone. Eighteen percent were maltreated by both parents. About 5.4% of the victims were maltreated by their mother and another person whose relationship with the mother was not known. One percent was maltreated by their father and another person

FIGURE 4.3

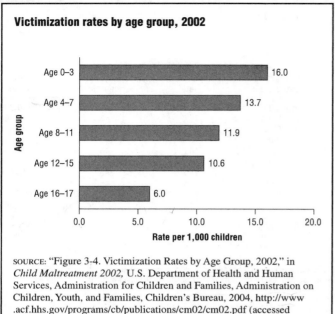

Victimization rates by age group, 2002

SOURCE: "Figure 3-4. Victimization Rates by Age Group, 2002," in *Child Maltreatment 2002*, U.S. Department of Health and Human Services, Administration for Children and Families, Administration on Children, Youth, and Families, Children's Bureau, 2004, http://www.acf.hhs.gov/programs/cb/publications/cm02/cm02.pdf (accessed October 27, 2004)

FIGURE 4.4

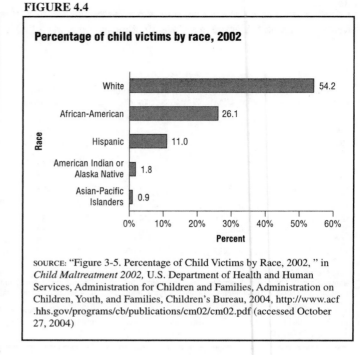

Percentage of child victims by race, 2002

SOURCE: "Figure 3-5. Percentage of Child Victims by Race, 2002, " in *Child Maltreatment 2002*, U.S. Department of Health and Human Services, Administration for Children and Families, Administration on Children, Youth, and Families, Children's Bureau, 2004, http://www.acf.hhs.gov/programs/cb/publications/cm02/cm02.pdf (accessed October 27, 2004)

whose relationship to the father was not known. Thirteen percent were maltreated by nonparental perpetrators, while 3.2% were maltreated by unknown individuals.

More than three-quarters (77.9%) of perpetrators were under age forty, with one-third between the ages of twenty and twenty-nine. Perpetrators were more likely to be female (58.3%) than male (41.7%).

Parents (including birth parents, adoptive parents, and stepparents) were responsible for the most cases of neglect, followed by child daycare providers and foster parents. Other relatives perpetrated more than a quarter of sexual abuse cases, while residential facility staff and unmarried partners of parents were the most likely to inflict physical abuse on children. (See Figure 4.5.)

DEATHS FROM CHILD MALTREATMENT

Child fatality is the most severe result of abuse and neglect. In 2002 CPS and other state agencies, including coroners' offices and fatality review boards, reported an estimated 1,390 deaths from child maltreatment, up from 1,373 deaths in 2001 and 1,306 deaths in 2000. The 2002 national fatality rate was nearly two deaths per one hundred thousand children in the general population. The District of Columbia reported the highest rate (11.6 per one hundred thousand), followed by West Virginia (7.5 per one hundred thousand) and Missouri (3.8 per one hundred thousand). (See Table 4.3.)

Children younger than four years of age accounted for a majority (76.1%) of deaths. Of these, infants younger than a year old comprised 41.2% of the fatalities.

More males under age one (18.8 per one hundred thousand boys of the same age) died from maltreatment than did females under age one (12.4 per one hundred thousand girls of the same age). Very young children are more likely to be victims of child fatalities because of their small size, their dependency on their caregivers, and their inability to defend themselves.

Neglect alone was responsible for more than one-third (37.6%) of maltreatment deaths. More than one-quarter (29.9%) of fatalities resulted from physical abuse. Another 28.9% of fatalities resulted from a combination of maltreatment types. (See Figure 4.6.) States also provided data on the victims' prior contact with CPS agencies. About 12% of the victims' families had received family preservation services during the five years before the deaths occurred.

Perpetrators of Fatalities

The 2002 report showed nearly four of five maltreatment deaths (78.9%) were inflicted by one or both parents of the victims. Mothers alone accounted for about one-third (32.6%) of the deaths, while fathers were the perpetrators in 16.6% of the deaths. In about one-fifth (19.2%) of cases, both parents were responsible for causing their children's death.

According to the National Clearinghouse on Child Abuse and Neglect Information (*Child Abuse and Neglect Fatalities: Statistics and Interventions,* Washington, DC, 2004), persons who commit fatal child abuse are often younger adults in their mid-twenties who did not finish high school and are living at or below the poverty level. They are likely to suffer from depression and are unable to cope with stress.

FIGURE 4.5

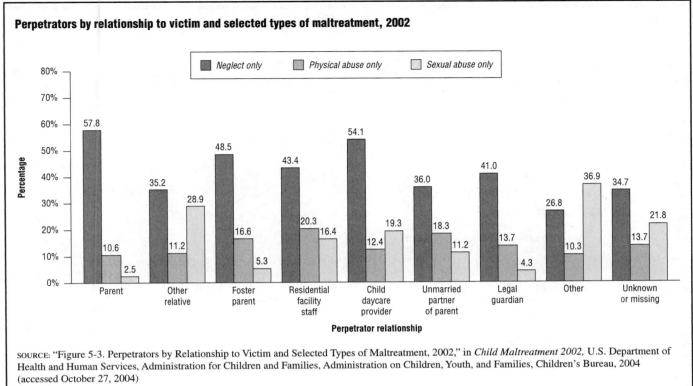

Perpetrators by relationship to victim and selected types of maltreatment, 2002

Legend: Neglect only | Physical abuse only | Sexual abuse only

Perpetrator relationship	Neglect only	Physical abuse only	Sexual abuse only
Parent	57.8	10.6	2.5
Other relative	35.2	11.2	28.9
Foster parent	48.5	16.6	5.3
Residential facility staff	43.4	20.3	16.4
Child daycare provider	54.1	12.4	19.3
Unmarried partner of parent	36.0	18.3	11.2
Legal guardian	41.0	13.7	4.3
Other	26.8	10.3	36.9
Unknown or missing	34.7	13.7	21.8

SOURCE: "Figure 5-3. Perpetrators by Relationship to Victim and Selected Types of Maltreatment, 2002," in *Child Maltreatment 2002*, U.S. Department of Health and Human Services, Administration for Children and Families, Administration on Children, Youth, and Families, Children's Bureau, 2004 (accessed October 27, 2004)

FIGURE 4.6

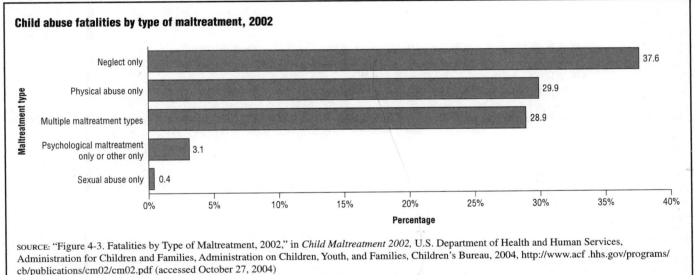

Child abuse fatalities by type of maltreatment, 2002

Maltreatment type	Percentage
Neglect only	37.6
Physical abuse only	29.9
Multiple maltreatment types	28.9
Psychological maltreatment only or other only	3.1
Sexual abuse only	0.4

SOURCE: "Figure 4-3. Fatalities by Type of Maltreatment, 2002," in *Child Maltreatment 2002*, U.S. Department of Health and Human Services, Administration for Children and Families, Administration on Children, Youth, and Families, Children's Bureau, 2004, http://www.acf .hhs.gov/programs/cb/publications/cm02/cm02.pdf (accessed October 27, 2004)

Child Fatality Review Teams

Historically, law enforcement, child protection agencies, and public health agencies worked separately in investigating child maltreatment deaths. In response to the increasing number of child deaths, all states have created multidisciplinary child fatality review teams to investigate the deaths and develop solutions to support families in crisis. These teams consist of prosecutors, medical examiners, law enforcement personnel, CPS personnel, health care providers, and other professionals.

State teams are formed to work with local teams, which are responsible for the management of individual cases. The number of child deaths reviewed by a local team depends on the county size. A local team in a large county may review just cases referred by the medical examiner, while a team in a smaller county may review child deaths from all causes.

TABLE 4.3

Child fatalities due to abuse, 2002

State	Child population	Child file and SDC fatalities	Agency file fatalities	Total child fatalities	Fatalities per 100,000 children
Alabama	1,107,108	29		29	2.62
Alaska	192,428	1		1	0.52
Arizona	1,476,856	21		21	1.42
Arkansas	677,522	13		13	1.92
California[1]	9,452,391		129	129	1.36
Colorado	1,151,118	25		25	2.17
Connecticut	872,853	9	2	11	1.26
Delaware	189,698	0	0	0	0.00
District of Columbia	112,128	7	6	13	11.59
Florida	3,882,271	97		97	2.50
Georgia	2,268,477	51		51	2.25
Hawaii	295,514	7		7	2.37
Idaho	370,439	2		2	0.54
Illinois	3,254,523	70		70	2.15
Indiana	1,594,857	58		58	3.64
Iowa	698,045	15		15	2.15
Kansas	696,519	1		1	0.14
Kentucky	931,588	23		23	2.47
Louisiana	1,185,674	37		37	3.12
Maine	279,058	0	3	3	1.08
Maryland	1,379,925		33	33	2.39
Massachusetts	1,463,340		17	17	1.16
Michigan					
Minnesota	1,252,125	16		16	1.28
Mississippi	760,747	7		7	0.92
Missouri	1,397,461	52	1	53	3.79
Montana	216,320	4		4	1.85
Nebraska	439,393	6	7	13	2.96
Nevada	572,590	3		3	0.52
New Hampshire	308,371		0	0	0.00
New Jersey	2,127,391	22	8	30	1.41
New Mexico	500,506		3	3	0.60
New York	4,613,251	68		68	1.47
North Carolina	2,068,840		26	26	1.26
North Dakota	146,812	2		2	1.36
Ohio	2,879,927	72		72	2.50
Oklahoma	873,560	23		23	2.63
Oregon	855,107	21		21	2.46
Pennsylvania	2,863,452	49	3	52	1.82
Rhode Island	239,248	1		1	0.42
South Carolina	979,163	13	3	16	1.63
South Dakota	195,625	5		5	2.56
Tennessee	1,404,661	18		18	1.28
Texas	6,102,316	206		206	3.38
Utah	713,012	12		12	1.68
Vermont	139,662	0	0	0	0.00
Virginia	1,779,408		22	22	1.24
Washington	1,513,360	1	14	15	0.99
West Virginia	389,171	13	16	29	7.45
Wisconsin	1,338,064	14		14	1.05
Wyoming	122,344	3		3	2.45
Total	**70,324,219**	**1,097**	**293**	**1,390**	
Rate					**1.98**
Number Reporting	**50**	**43**	**19**	**50**	**50**

Notes: SDC is Summary Data Component.
A national estimate of 1,400 fatalities was derived by multiplying the national rate of 1.98 by the total population—total population for all 51 states equals 72,894,483—and dividing by 100,000. The estimate was then rounded to the nearest 100.

SOURCE: "Table 4-1. Child Fatalities, 2002," in *Child Maltreatment 2002*, U.S. Department of Health and Human Services, Administration for Children and Families, Administration on Children, Youth, and Families, Children's Bureau, 2004, http://www.acf.hhs.gov/programs/cb/publications/cm02/cm02.pdf (accessed October 27, 2004)

Are Child Maltreatment Fatalities Properly Reflected in Death Certificates?

Although child fatality review teams have been formed in every state and the District of Columbia, NCANDS remains the sole national system that tracks child maltreatment deaths, typically just those cases that reach CPS.

Experts believe that there are likely more deaths each year due to child abuse and neglect than are reported to CPS and other agencies. According to researchers Tessa L. Crume, Carolyn DiGuiseppi, Tim Byers, Andrew P. Sirotnak, and Carol J. Garrett, although the federal government had concluded in 1993 that death certificates underreported child maltreatment fatalities, to date it has not done anything to remedy the problem. To determine whether child maltreatment is ascertained in death certificates, the researchers compared data collected by a child fatality review committee (CFRC) on child fatalities in Colorado between 1990 and 1998 with the death certificates issued for those fatalities ("Underascertainment of Child Maltreatment Fatalities by Death Certificates, 1990–1998," *Pediatrics,* vol. 110, no. 2, August 2002).

Crume and her colleagues found that only half of the maltreatment deaths were ascertained by death certificates. Of the 295 deaths confirmed by the CFRC to have resulted from maltreatment, just 147 were noted in the death certificates as such. Female children and non-Hispanic African-American children were more likely to be linked to higher ascertainment in the death certificates. Maltreatment was also more likely to be confirmed as the contributing factor when the death involved violence, such as bodily force, the use of firearms, or the use of sharp or blunt objects. A lower proportion of deaths (less than 20%) was attributed to less obvious child maltreatment, including neglect and abandonment.

NATIONAL INCIDENCE STUDY OF CHILD ABUSE AND NEGLECT

The *National Incidence Study of Child Abuse and Neglect* (NIS) was a congressionally mandated periodic survey of child maltreatment. The results of the first NIS were published in 1981, and those of the second NIS (NIS-2) in 1988. The most recent NIS, the *Third National Incidence Study of Child Abuse and Neglect,* (NIS-3) (U.S. Department of Health and Human Services, National Center on Child Abuse and Neglect, Washington, DC), was released in 1996. NIS-3 differed from the annual *Child Maltreatment* reports because NIS-3 findings were based on a nationally representative sample of more than 5,600 professionals in 842 agencies serving forty-two counties. NIS-3 included not only child victims investigated by CPS agencies, but also children seen by community institutions (such as daycare centers, schools, and hospitals) and other investigating agencies (such as public health departments, police, and courts). In addition, victim counts were unduplicated, which means that each child was counted only once.

Definition Standards

NIS-3 used two standardized definitions of abuse and neglect:

- Harm Standard—required that an act or omission must have resulted in demonstrable harm in order to be considered as abuse or neglect

- Endangerment Standard—allowed children who had not yet been harmed by maltreatment to be counted in

the estimates of maltreated children if a non-CPS professional considered them to be at risk of harm or if their maltreatment was substantiated or indicated in a CPS investigation

Incidence of Maltreatment

In 1993, under the Harm Standard, an estimated 1,553,800 children were victims of maltreatment, a 67% increase from the NIS-2 estimate (931,000 children) and a 149% increase from the first NIS estimate (625,100 children). Significant increases occurred for all types of abuse and neglect, as compared with the two earlier NIS surveys. The more than 1.5 million child victims of maltreatment in 1993 reflected a yearly incidence rate of 23.1 per one thousand children under age eighteen, or about one in forty-three children. (See Table 4.4.)

In 1993, under the Endangerment Standard, an estimated 2,815,600 children experienced some type of maltreatment. This figure nearly doubled the NIS-2 estimate of 1,424,400. As with the Harm Standard, marked increases occurred for all types of abuse and neglect. The incidence rate was 41.9 per one thousand children under age eighteen, or approximately one in twenty-four children. (See Table 4.5.)

COMPARISON OF MALTREATMENT ESTIMATES UNDER THE TWO STANDARDS. In 1993 the Endangerment Standard included an additional 1,261,800 children under age eighteen (an 81% difference) beyond those counted under the stricter Harm Standard. This means that children included under the Harm Standard represented 55% of those counted under the Endangerment Standard. Harm Standard children accounted for 61% of the Endangerment Standard total of all abused children, and 45% of the Endangerment Standard total of all neglected children.

Characteristics of Abused Children

GENDER. Under both the Harm and Endangerment Standards, more females were subjected to maltreatment than males. Females were sexually abused about three times more often than males. Males, however, were more likely to experience physical and emotional neglect under the Endangerment Standard. Under both standards, males suffered more physical and emotional neglect, while females suffered more educational neglect. Males were at a somewhat greater risk of serious injury and death than females. (See Table 4.6 and Table 4.7.)

AGE. NIS-3 found a lower incidence of maltreatment among younger children, particularly ages zero to five. This may be due to the fact that, prior to reaching school age, children are less observable to community professionals, especially educators—the group most likely to report suspected maltreatment. In addition, NIS-3 noted a disproportionate increase in the incidence of maltreatment among children between the ages of six and fourteen. (See

TABLE 4.4

National incidence of maltreatment under the Harm Standard in the NIS-3 (1993) and comparison with the NIS-2 (1986) and the NIS-1 (1980) Harm Standard estimates

Harm Standard Maltreatment Category	NIS-3 Estimates 1993 Total No. of Children	NIS-3 Estimates 1993 Rate per 1,000 Children	Comparisons With Earlier Studies NIS-2: 1986 Total No. of Children	NIS-2: 1986 Rate per 1,000 Children		NIS-1: 1980 Total No. of Children	NIS-1: 1980 Rate per 1,000 Children	
All Maltreatment	1,553,800	23.1	931,000	14.8	*	625,100	9.8	*
Abuse:								
All Abuse	743,200	11.1	507,700	8.1	m	336,600	5.3	*
Physical Abuse	381,700	5.7	269,700	4.3	m	199,100	3.1	*
Sexual Abuse	217,700	3.2	119,200	1.9	*	42,900	0.7	*
Emotional Abuse	204,500	3.0	155,200	2.5	ns	132,700	2.1	m
Neglect:								
All Neglect	879,000	13.1	474,800	7.5	*	315,400	4.9	*
Physical Neglect	338,900	5.0	167,800	2.7	*	103,600	1.6	*
Emotional Neglect	212,800	3.2	49,200	0.8	*	56,900	0.9	*
Educational Neglect	397,300	5.9	284,800	4.5	ns	174,000	2.7	*

* The difference between this and the NIS-3 estimate is significant at or below the p<.05 level.
m The difference between this and the NIS-3 estimate is statistically marginal (i.e., .I0>p>.05).
ns The difference between this and the NIS-3 estimate is neither significant nor marginal (p>.10).
Note: Estimated totals are rounded to the nearest 100.

SOURCE: Andrea J. Sedlak and Diane D. Broadhurst, "National Incidence of Maltreatment under the Harm Standard in the NIS-3 (1993), and Comparison with the NIS-2 (1986) and the NIS-1 (1980) Harm Standard Estimates," in *The Third National Incidence Study of Child Abuse and Neglect,* U.S. Department of Health and Human Services, National Center on Child Abuse and Neglect, 1996

TABLE 4.5

National incidence of maltreatment under the Endangerment Standard in the NIS-3 (1993), and comparison with the NIS-2 (1986) Endangerment Standard estimates

Endangerment Standard Maltreatment Category	NIS-3 Estimates 1993 Total No. of Children	NIS-3 Estimates 1993 Rate per 1,000 Children	Comparison With NIS-2 1986 Total No. of Children	Comparison With NIS-2 1986 Rate per 1,000 Children	
All Maltreatment	2,815,600	41.9	1,424,400	22.6	*
Abuse:					
All Abuse	1,221,800	18.2	590,800	9.4	*
Physical Abuse	614,100	9.1	311,500	4.9	*
Sexual Abuse	300,200	4.5	133,600	2.1	*
Emotional Abuse	532,200	7.9	188,100	3.0	*
Neglect:					
All Neglect	1,961,300	29.2	917,200	14.6	*
Physical Neglect	1,335,100	19.9	507,700	8.1	*
Emotional Neglect	584,100	8.7	203,000	3.2	*
Educational Neglect	397,300	5.9	284,800	4.5	ns

*The difference between this estimate and the NIS-3 estimate is significant at or below the p<.05 level.
Note: Estimated totals are rounded to the nearest 100.

SOURCE: Andrea J. Sedlak and Diane D. Broadhurst, "National Incidence of Maltreatment under the Endangerment Standard in the NIS-3 (1993), and Comparison with the NIS-2 (1986) Endangerment Standard Estimates," in *The Third National Incidence Study of Child Abuse and Neglect,* U.S. Department of Health and Human Services, National Center on Child Abuse and Neglect, 1996

TABLE 4.6

Sex differences in incidence rates per 1,000 children for maltreatment under the Harm Standard in the NIS-3 (1993)

Harm Standard Maltreatment Category	Males	Females	Significance of Difference
All Maltreatment	21.7	24.5	m
Abuse:			
All Abuse	9.5	12.6	*
Physical Abuse	5.8	5.6	ns
Sexual Abuse	1.6	4.9	*
Emotional Abuse	2.9	3.1	ns
Neglect:			
All Neglect	13.3	12.9	ns
Physical Neglect	5.5	4.5	ns
Emotional Neglect	3.5	2.8	ns
Educational Neglect	5.5	6.4	ns
Severity of Injury:			
Fatal	0.04	0.01	ns
Serious	9.3	7.5	m
Moderate	11.3	13.3	ns
Inferred	1.1	3.8	*

*The difference is significant at or below the p<.05 level.
m The difference is statistically marginal (i.e., .10>p>.05).
ns The difference is neither significant nor marginal (p>.10).

SOURCE: Andrea J. Sedlak and Diane D. Broadhurst, "Sex Differences in Incidence Rates per 1,000 Children for Maltreatment under the Harm Standard in the NIS-3 (1993)," in *The Third National Incidence Study of Child Abuse and Neglect,* U.S. Department of Health and Human Services, National Center on Child Abuse and Neglect, 1996

Figure 4.7 and Figure 4.8.) Sedlak and Broadhurst, the authors of NIS-3, noted a lower incidence of maltreatment among children older than fourteen years. Older children are more likely to escape if the abuse becomes more prevalent or severe. They are also more able to defend themselves and/or fight back.

TABLE 4.7

Sex differences in incidence rates per 1,000 children for maltreatment under the Endangerment Standard in the NIS-3 (1993)

Endangerment Standard Maltreatment Category	Males	Females	Significance of Difference
All Maltreatment	40.0	42.3	ns
Abuse:			
All Abuse	16.1	20.2	*
Physical Abuse	9.3	9.0	ns
Sexual Abuse	2.3	6.8	*
Emotional Abuse	8.0	7.7	ns
Neglect:			
All Neglect	29.2	27.6	ns
Physical Neglect	19.7	18.6	ns
Emotional Neglect	9.2	7.8	*
Educational Neglect	5.5	6.4	ns
Severity of Injury:			
Fatal	0.04	0.01	ns
Serious	9.4	7.6	m
Moderate	14.1	15.3	ns
Inferred	2.1	4.6	*
Endangered	14.5	14.8	ns

* The difference is significant at or below the p<.05 level.
m The difference is statistically marginal (i.e., .l0>p>.05).
ns The difference is neither significant nor marginal (p>.10).

SOURCE: Andrea J. Sedlak and Diane D. Broadhurst, "Sex Differences in Incidence Rates per 1,000 Children for Maltreatment under the Endangerment Standard in the NIS-3 (1993)," in *The Third National Incidence Study of Child Abuse and Neglect,* U.S. Department of Health and Human Services, National Center on Child Abuse and Neglect, 1996

FIGURE 4.7

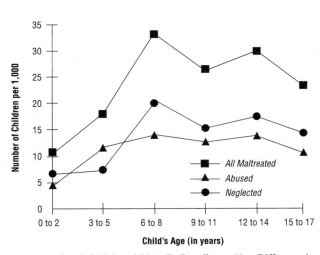

Age differences in all maltreatment, abuse, and neglect under the Harm Standard

SOURCE: Andrea J. Sedlak and Diane D. Broadhurst, "Age Difference in All Maltreatment, Abuse, and Neglect under the Harm Standard," in *The Third National Incidence Study of Child Abuse and Neglect,* U.S. Department of Health and Human Services, National Center on Child Abuse and Neglect, 1996

FIGURE 4.8

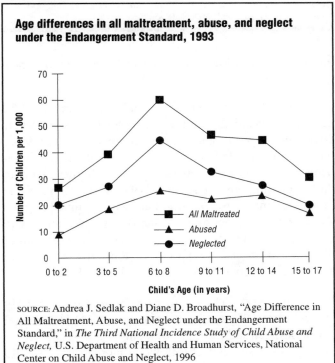

Age differences in all maltreatment, abuse, and neglect under the Endangerment Standard, 1993

SOURCE: Andrea J. Sedlak and Diane D. Broadhurst, "Age Difference in All Maltreatment, Abuse, and Neglect under the Endangerment Standard," in *The Third National Incidence Study of Child Abuse and Neglect,* U.S. Department of Health and Human Services, National Center on Child Abuse and Neglect, 1996

Under the Harm Standard, only ten per one thousand children in the zero to two age group experienced overall maltreatment. The numbers were significantly higher for children ages six to seventeen. Under the Endangerment Standard, twenty-six per one thousand children ages zero to two were subjected to overall maltreatment. A slightly higher number of children (29.7 per one thousand children) in the oldest age group (fifteen to seventeen years old) suffered maltreatment of some type. As with the Harm Standard, children between the ages of six and fourteen had a higher incidence of maltreatment. (See Figure 4.8.)

RACE. NIS-3 found no significant differences in race in the incidence of maltreatment. The authors noted that this finding may be somewhat surprising, considering the over-representation of African-American children in the child welfare population and in those served by public agencies. They attributed this lack of race-related difference in maltreatment incidence to the broader range of children identified by NIS-3, compared with the smaller number investigated by public agencies and the even smaller number receiving child protective and other welfare services. NIS-2 also had not found any disproportionate differences in race in relation to maltreatment incidence.

Family Characteristics

FAMILY STRUCTURE. Under the Harm Standard, among children living with single parents, an estimated 27.3 per one thousand under age eighteen suffered some type of maltreatment—almost twice the incidence rate for children living with both parents (15.5 per one thousand). The same rate held true for all types of abuse and neglect. Children living with single parents also had a greater risk of suffering serious injury (10.5 per one thousand) than

TABLE 4.8

Incidence rates per 1,000 children for maltreatment under the Harm Standard in the NIS-3 (1993) for different family structures

Harm Standard Maltreatment Category	Both Parents	Single Parent Either Mother or Father	Mother only	Father only	Neither Parent	Significance of Differences
All Maltreatment:	15.5	27.3	26.1	36.6	22.9	A, C, D
Abuse:						
All Abuse	8.4	11.4	10.5	17.7	13.7	D, e
Physical Abuse	3.9	6.9	6.4	10.5	7.0	a, D, e
Sexual Abuse	2.6	2.5	2.5	2.6	6.3	ns
Emotional Abuse	2.6	2.5	2.1	5.7	5.4	ns
Neglect:						
All Neglect	7.9	17.3	16.7	21.9	10.3	A, C, D
Physical Neglect	3.1	5.8	5.9	4.7	4.3	A, C
Emotional Neglect	2.3	4.0	3.4	8.8	3.1	a, G
Educational Neglect	3.0	9.6	9.5	10.8	3.1	A, B, f
Severity of Injury:						
Fatal	0.019	0.015	0.017	0.005	0.016	ns
Serious	5.8	10.5	10.0	14.0	8.0	A, C
Moderate	8.1	15.4	14.7	20.5	10.1	A
Inferred	1.6	1.4	1.3	2.1	4.8	ns

A Difference between "Both Parents" and "Either Mother or Father" is significant at or below the p<.05 level.
a Difference between "Both Parents" and "Either Mother or Father" is statistically marginal (i.e., .10>p>.05).
B Difference between "Either Mother or Father" and "Neither Parent" is significant at or below the p <.05 level.
C Difference between "Both Parents" and "Mother only" is significant at or below the p<.05 level.
D Difference between "Both Parents" and "Father only" is significant at or below the p<.05 level.
e Difference between "Mother only" and "Father only" is statistically marginal (i.e., .10>p>.05).
f Difference between "Mother only" and "Neither Parent" is statistically marginal (i.e., .10>p>.05).
G Difference between "Father only" and "Neither Parent" is significant at or below the p<.05 level.
ns No between-group difference is significant or marginal (all p's>.10)

SOURCE: Andrea J. Sedlak and Diane D. Broadhurst, "Incidence Rates per 1,000 Children for Maltreatment under the Harm Standard in the NIS-3 (1993) for Different Family Structures," in *The Third National Incidence Study of Child Abuse and Neglect,* U.S. Department of Health and Human Services, National Center on Child Abuse and Neglect, 1996

did those living with both parents (5.8 per one thousand). (See Table 4.8.)

Under the Endangerment Standard, an estimated 52 per one thousand children living with single parents suffered some type of maltreatment, compared with 26.9 per one thousand living with both parents. Children in single-parent households were abused at a 45% higher rate than those in two-parent households (19.6 versus 13.5 per one thousand) and suffered more than twice as much neglect (38.9 versus 17.6 per one thousand). Children living with single parents (10.5 per one thousand) were also more likely to suffer serious injuries than those living with both parents (5.9 per one thousand). (See Table 4.9.)

FAMILY SIZE. The number of children in the family was related to the incidence of maltreatment. Additional children meant additional tasks and responsibilities for the parents; therefore, it followed that the rates of child maltreatment were higher in these families. Among children in families with four or more children, an estimated 34.5 per one thousand under the Harm Standard and 68.1 per one thousand under the Endangerment Standard suffered some type of maltreatment.

Surprisingly, households with only one child had a higher maltreatment incidence rate than did households

with two to three children (22 versus 17.7 per one thousand children under the Harm Standard, and 34.2 versus 34.1 per one thousand children under the Endangerment Standard). The authors thought that an only child might have been in a situation where parental expectations were all focused on that one child. Another explanation was that "only" children might have been in households where the parents were just starting a family and were relatively young and inexperienced.

FAMILY INCOME. Family income was significantly related to the incidence rates of child maltreatment. Under the Harm Standard, children in families with annual incomes less than $15,000 had the highest rate of maltreatment (47 per one thousand). The figure is almost twice as high (95.9 per one thousand) using the Endangerment Standard. Children in families earning less than $15,000 annually also sustained more serious injuries. (See Table 4.10 and Table 4.11.)

Characteristics of Perpetrators

RELATIONSHIP TO THE CHILD. Most child victims (78%) were maltreated by their birth parents. Parents accounted for 72% of physical abuse and 81% of emotional abuse. Almost half (46%) of sexually abused children, however, were violated by someone other than a parent or

TABLE 4.9

Incidence rates per 1,000 children for maltreatment under the Endangerment Standard in the NIS-3 (1993), by family structure

Endangerment Standard Maltreatment Category	Both Parents	Single Parent			Neither Parent	Significance of Differences
		Either Mother or Father	Mother-only	Father-only		
All Maltreatment	26.9	52.0	50. 1	65.6	39.3	A, C, D, G
Abuse:						
All Abuse	13.5	19.6	18.1	31.0	17.3	a
Physical Abuse	6.5	10.6	9.8	16.5	9.2	d
Sexual Abuse	3.2	4.2	4.3	3.1	6.6	ns
Emotional Abuse	6.2	8.6	7.7	14.6	7.1	ns
Neglect:						
All Neglect	17.6	38.9	37.6	47.9	24.1	A, C, D, G
Physical Neglect	10.8	28.6	27.5	36.4	17.1	A, c, D
Emotional Neglect	6.4	10.5	9.7	16.2	8.3	a
Educational Neglect	3.0	9.6	9.5	10.8	3.1	A, B,C, f
Severity of Injury:						
Fatal	0.020	0.015	0.017	0.005	0.016	ns
Serious	5.9	10.5	10.0	14.0	8.0	A, C
Moderate	9.6	18.5	17.7	24.8	11.5	A, b
Inferred	2.1	2.5	2.0	6.0	4.7	ns
Endangered	9.3	20.5	20.4	20.7	15.1	A, C

A Difference between "Both Parents" and "Either Mother or Father" is significant at or below the p < .05 level.
a Difference between "Both Parents" and "Either Mother or Father" is statistically marginal (i.e., .10 > p >.05).
B Difference between "Either Mother or Father" and "Neither Parent" is significant at or below the p < .05 level.
b Difference between "Either Mother or Father" and "Neither Parent" is statistically marginal (i.e., .10 > p >.05).
C Difference between "Both Parents" and "Mother only" is significant at or below the p <.05 level.
c Difference between "Both Parents" and "Mother only" is statistically marginal (i.e., .10 > p >.05).
D Difference between "Both Parents" and "Father only" is significant at or below the p <.05 level.
d Difference between "Both Parents" and "Father only" is statistically marginal (i.e., .l0 > p >.05)
f Difference between "Mother only" and "Neither Parent" is statistically marginal (i.e., .10 > p >.05).
G Difference between "Father only" and "Neither Parent" is significant at or below the p <.05 level.
ns No between-group difference is significant or marginal (all p's >.10).

SOURCE: Andrea J. Sedlak and Diane D. Broadhurst, "Incidence Rates per 1,000 Children for Maltreatment under the Endangerment Standard in the NIS-3 (1993) for Different Family Structures," in *The Third National Incidence Study of Child Abuse and Neglect,* U.S. Department of Health and Human Services, National Center on Child Abuse and Neglect, 1996

parent-substitute. More than a quarter (29%) were sexually abused by a birth parent, and 25% were sexually abused by a parent-substitute, such as a stepparent or a mother's boyfriend. In addition, sexually abused children were more likely to sustain fatal or serious injuries or impairments when birth parents were the perpetrators. (See Table 4.12.)

PERPETRATORS' GENDERS. Overall, children were somewhat more likely to be maltreated by female perpetrators (65%) than by males (54%). Among children maltreated by their natural parents, most (75%) were maltreated by their mothers, and almost half (46%) were maltreated by their fathers. (Children who were maltreated by both parents were included in both "male" and "female" perpetrator counts.) Children who were maltreated by other parents and parent-substitutes were more likely to have been maltreated by a male (85%) than by a female (41%). Four of five children (80%) who were maltreated by other adults were maltreated by males, and only 14% were maltreated by other adults who were females. (See Table 4.13.) Note that the numbers will not add to 100% because many children were maltreated by both parents.)

Neglected children differed from abused children with regard to the gender of the perpetrators. Because mothers or other females tend to be the primary caretakers, children were more likely to suffer all forms of neglect by female perpetrators (87% versus 43% by male perpetrators). In contrast, children were more often abused by males (67%) than by females (40%). (See Table 4.13.)

SURVEY REVEALS YOUTH'S KNOWLEDGE OF PEER ABUSE

The most recent government survey revealed that, in 2002, an estimated 896,000 children under age eighteen were victims of maltreatment. Steve Crabtree reported that a 2003 nationwide survey of teenagers, ages thirteen to seventeen, found that more than one-third (36%) indicated they knew of a person their age who had been physically or sexually abused ("One-Third of Teens Know of Abuse Among Peers," *Gallup Youth Survey,* The Gallup Organization, Princeton, NJ, May 20, 2003). Nearly twice as many girls (47%) as boys (25%) said that they knew of a friend or a classmate who had been maltreated. (See Figure 4.9.)

According to Crabtree, the *Gallup Youth Survey* did not ask teens the direct question of whether or not they themselves had been victims of maltreatment, partly

TABLE 4.10

Incidence rates per 1,000 children for maltreatment under the Harm Standard in the NIS-3 (1993), by family income

Harm Standard Maltreatment Category	<$15K/yr	$15–29K/yr	$30K+/yr	Significance of Differences
All Maltreatment	47.0	20.0	2.1	a
Abuse:				
All Abuse	22.2	9.7	1.6	a
Physical Abuse	11.0	5.0	0.7	a
Sexual Abuse	7.0	2.8	0.4	b
Emotional Abuse	6.5	2.5	0.5	b
Neglect:				
All Neglect	27.2	11.3	0.6	a
Physical Neglect	12.0	2.9	0.3	a
Emotional Neglect	5.9	4.3	0.2	ns
Educational Neglect	11.1	4.8	0.2	a
Severity of Injury:				
Fatal	0.060	0.002	0.001	ns
Serious	17.9	7.8	0.8	a
Moderate	23.3	10.5	1.3	a
Inferred	5.7	1.6	0.1	b

a All between-group differences are significant at or below the p<.05 level.
b The highest income group ($30,000 or more) differs significantly from the others (p's < .05), but the difference between the <$15,000 group and the $15,000 to $29,999 group is statistically marginal (i.e., .10>p>.05).
ns No between-group difference is significant or marginal (all p's>.10)

SOURCE: Andrea J. Sedlak and Diane D. Broadhurst, "Incidence Rates per 1,000 Children for Maltreatment under the Harm Standard in the NIS-3 (1993) for Different Levels of Family Income," in *The Third National Incidence Study of Child Abuse and Neglect,* U.S. Department of Health and Human Services, National Center on Child Abuse and Neglect, 1996

TABLE 4.11

Incidence rates per 1,000 children for maltreatment under the Endangerment Standard in the NIS-3 (1993), by family income

Endangerment Standard Maltreatment Category	<$15K/yr	$15–29K/yr	$30K=/yr	Significance of Differences
All Maltreatment	95.9	33.1	3.8	*
Abuse:				
All Abuse	37.4	17.5	2.5	*
Physical Abuse	17.6	8.5	1.5	*
Sexual Abuse	9.2	4.2	0.5	*
Emotional Abuse	18.3	8.1	1.0	*
Neglect:				
All Neglect	72.3	21.6	1.6	*
Physical Neglect	54.3	12.5	1.1	*
Emotional Neglect	19.0	8.2	0.7	*
Educational Neglect	11.1	4.8	0.2	*
Severity of Injury:				
Fatal	0.060	0.002	0.003	ns
Serious	17.9	7.9	0.8	*
Moderate	29.6	12.1	1.5	*
Inferred	7.8	2.7	0.2	*
Endangered	40.5	10.3	1.3	*

*All between-group differences are significant at or below the p<.05 level.
ns No between-group difference is significant or marginal (all p's >.10).

SOURCE: Andrea J. Sedlak and Diane D. Broadhurst, "Incidence Rates per 1,000 Children for Maltreatment under the Endangerment Standard in the NIS-3 (1993) for Different Levels of Family Income," in *The Third National Incidence Study of Child Abuse and Neglect,* U.S. Department of Health and Human Services, National Center on Child Abuse and Neglect, 1996

because young people may be reluctant to reveal their own abuse. Some blame themselves for the abuse. Others feel ashamed of their experience, while still others are afraid of retaliation from the perpetrator. Interestingly, compared to adolescents who did not know of a friend or classmate who had been maltreated, those who revealed they were aware of a peer's experience with abuse were more likely to use alcohol (40% versus 30% of teens with no awareness of peer abuse), to have smoked in the past week (13% versus 6%), and to have tried marijuana (30% versus 15%). (See Table 4.14.)

FIGURE 4.9

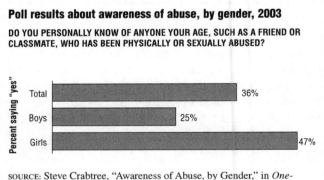

Poll results about awareness of abuse, by gender, 2003

DO YOU PERSONALLY KNOW OF ANYONE YOUR AGE, SUCH AS A FRIEND OR CLASSMATE, WHO HAS BEEN PHYSICALLY OR SEXUALLY ABUSED?

- Total: 36%
- Boys: 25%
- Girls: 47%

SOURCE: Steve Crabtree, "Awareness of Abuse, by Gender," in *One-Third of Teens Know of Abuse among Peers,* http://www.gallup.com/content/default.aspx?ci=8437 (accessed August 15, 2004). Copyright © 2004 by The Gallup Organization. Reproduced by permission of The Gallup Organization.

TABLE 4.12

Distribution of perpetrator's relationship to child and severity of harm, by the type of maltreatment, 1993

Category	Percent Children in Maltreatment Category	Total Maltreated Children	Percent of Children in Row with Injury/Impairment. . .		
			Fatal or Serious	Moderate	Inferred
Abuse:	100%	743,200	21%	63%	16%
Natural Parents	62%	461,800	22%	73%	4%
Other Parents and Parent/substitutes	19%	144,900	12%	62%	27%
Others	18%	136,600	24%	30%	46%
Physical Abuse	100%	381,700	13%	87%	+
Natural Parents	72%	273,200	13%	87%	+
Other Parents and Parent/substitutes	21%	78,700	13%	87%	+
Others	8%	29,700	*	82%	+
Sexual Abuse	100%	217,700	34%	12%	53%
Natural Parents	29%	63,300	61%	10%	28%
Other Parents and Parent/substitutes	25%	53,800	19%	18%	63%
Others	46%	100,500	26%	11%	63%
Emotional Abuse	100%	204,500	26%	68%	6%
Natural Parents	81%	166,500	27%	70%	2%
Other Parents and Parent/substitutes	13%	27,400	*	57%	24%
Others	5%	10,600	*	*	*
Neglect:	100%	879,000	50%	44%	6%
Natural Parents	91%	800,600	51%	43%	6%
Other Parents and Parent/substitutes	9%	78,400	35%	59%	*
Others	^	^	^	^	^
Physical Neglect	100%	338,900	64%	15%	21%
Natural Parents	95%	320,400	64%	16%	20%
Other Parents and Parent/substitutes	5%	18,400	*	*	*
Others	^	^	^	^	^
Emotional Neglect	100%	212,800	97%	3%	+
Natural Parents	91%	194,600	99%	*	+
Other Parents and Parent/substitutes	9%	*	*	*	+
Others	^	^	^	^	+
Educational Neglect	100%	397,300	7%	93%	+
Natural Parents	89%	354,300	8%	92%	+
Other Parents and Parent/substitutes	11%	43,000	*	99%	+
Others	^	^	^	^	+
All Maltreatment	100%	1,553,800	36%	53%	11%
Natural Parents	78%	1,208,100	41%	54%	5%
Other Parents and Parent/substitutes	14%	211,200	20%	61%	19%
Others	9%	134,500	24%	30%	46%

+This severity level not applicable for this form of maltreatment.
*Fewer than 20 cases with which to calculate estimate; estimate too unreliable to be given.
^These perpetrators were not allowed by countability requirements for cases of neglect.

SOURCE: Andrea J. Sedlak and Diane D. Broadhurst, "Distribution of Perpetrator's Relationship to Child and Severity of Harm by the Type of Maltreatment," in *The Third National Incidence Study of Child Abuse and Neglect,* U.S. Department of Health and Human Services, National Center on Child Abuse and Neglect, 1996

TABLE 4.13

Distribution of perpetrator's gender by type of maltreatment and perpetrator's relationship to child, 1993

Category	Percent Children in Maltreatment Category	Total Maltreated Children	Percent of Children in Row with Perpetrator Whose Gender was . . .		
			Male	Female	Unknown
Abuse:	100%	743,200	67%	40%	*
Natural Parents	62%	461,800	56%	55%	*
Other Parents and Parent/substitutes	19%	144,900	90%	15%	*
Others	18%	136,600	80%	14%	*
Physical Abuse	100%	381,700	58%	50%	*
Natural Parents	72%	273,200	48%	60%	*
Other Parents and Parent/substitutes	21%	78,700	90%	19%	*
Others	8%	29,700	57%	39%	*
Sexual Abuse	100%	217,700	89%	12%	*
Natural Parents	29%	63,300	87%	28%	*
Other Parents and Parent/substitutes	25%	53,800	97%	*	*
Others	46%	100,500	86%	8%	*
Emotional Abuse	100%	204,500	63%	50%	*
Natural Parents	81%	166,500	60%	55%	*
Other Parents and Parent/substitutes	13%	27,400	74%	*	*
Others	5%	10,600	*	*	*
All neglect:	100%	879,000	43%	87%	*
Natural Parents	91%	800,600	40%	87%	*
Other Parents and Parent/substitutes	9%	78,400	76%	88%	*
Others	^	^	^	^	^
Physical Neglect	100%	338,900	35%	93%	*
Natural Parents	95%	320,400	34%	93%	*
Other Parents and Parent/substitutes	5%	18,400	*	90%	*
Others	^	^	^	^	^
Emotional Neglect	100%	212,800	47%	77%	*
Natural Parents	91%	194,600	44%	78%	*
Other Parents and Parent/substitutes	9%	18,200	*	*	*
Others	^	^	^	^	^
Educational Neglect	100%	397,300	47%	88%	*
Natural Parents	89%	354,300	43%	86%	*
Other Parents and Parent/substitutes	11%	43,000	82%	100%	*
Others	^	^	^	^	^
All Maltreatment	100%	1,553,800	54%	65%	1%
Natural Parents	78%	1,208,100	46%	75%	*
Other Parents and Parent/substitutes	14%	211,200	85%	41%	*
Others	9%	134,500	80%	14%	7%

*Fewer than 20 cases with which to calculate, estimate too unreliable to be given
^These perpetrators were not allowed by countability requirements for cases of neglect.

SOURCE: Andrea J. Sedlak and Diane D. Broadhurst, "Distribution of Perpetrator's Gender by Type of Maltreatment and Perpetrator's Relationship to Child," in *The Third National Incidence Study of Child Abuse and Neglect,* U.S. Department of Health and Human Services, National Center on Child Abuse and Neglect, 1996

TABLE 4.14

Health behaviors of teens who know/do not know of someone their age who has been abused, 2003

	Know of someone their age who has been physically of sexually abused	Do not know of someone their age who has been physically or sexually abused
Use alcohol	40%	30%
Smoked in the past week	13%	6%
Tried marijuana	30%	15%

SOURCE: Steve Crabtree, "Health Behaviors," in *One-Third of Teens Know of Abuse among Peers,* http://www.gallup.com/content/default.aspx?ci=8437 (accessed August 15, 2004). Copyright © 2004 by The Gallup Organization. Reproduced by permission of The Gallup Organization.

CHAPTER 5
CAUSES AND EFFECTS OF CHILD ABUSE

Raising a child is not easy. Everyday stresses, strains, and sporadic upheavals in family life, coupled with the normal burdens of child care, cause most parents to feel angry at times. People who would not dream of hitting a colleague or an acquaintance when they are angry may think nothing of hitting their children. Some feel remorse after hitting a loved one; nevertheless, when they are angry, they still resort to violence. The deeper intimacy and greater commitment in a family make emotionally charged disagreements more frequent and more intense.

Murray A. Straus and Richard J. Gelles, experts in child abuse research, believe that cultural standards permit violence in the family. The family, which is the center of love and security in most children's lives, is also the place where the child is punished, sometimes physically.

The 1975 *National Family Violence Survey* and the 1985 *National Family Violence Resurvey,* conducted by Straus and Gelles, are the most complete studies of spousal and parent-child abuse yet prepared in the United States. The major difference between these two surveys and most other surveys discussed in Chapter 4 is that the data from these surveys came from detailed interviews with the general population, not from cases that came to the attention of official agencies and professionals. Straus and Gelles had a more intimate knowledge of the families and an awareness of incidences of child abuse that were not reported to the authorities. (Straus and Gelles incorporated research from the two surveys and additional chapters into the book *Physical Violence in American Families: Risk Factors and Adaptations to Violence in 8,145 Families,* New Brunswick, NJ: Transaction Publishers, 1990.)

SOME CONTRIBUTING FACTORS TO CHILD ABUSE

The factors contributing to child maltreatment are complex. The *Third National Incidence Study of Child Abuse and Neglect* (NIS-3; Andrea J. Sedlak and Diane D. Broadhurst, U.S. Department of Health and Human Services [HHS], National Center on Child Abuse and Neglect, Washington, DC, 1996), the most comprehensive federal source of information about the incidence of child maltreatment in the United States, found that family structure and size, poverty, alcohol and substance abuse, domestic violence, and community violence are contributing factors to child abuse and neglect.

For example, under the Harm Standard of NIS-3 (see Chapter 4 for a definition of the Harm and Endangerment Standards), children in single-parent households were at a higher risk of physical abuse and all types of neglect than were children in other family structures. Children living with only their fathers were more likely to suffer the highest incidence rates of physical abuse and emotional and educational neglect. (See Figure 5.1.) Under the Endangerment Standard, higher incidence rates of physical and emotional neglect occurred among children living with only their fathers than among those living in other family structures. (See Figure 5.2.)

Sedlak and Broadhurst noted that the increase in illicit drug use since the second *National Incidence Study of Child Abuse and Neglect* (NIS-2), in 1986, may have contributed to the increased child maltreatment incidence reported in NIS-3. Children whose parents are alcohol and substance abusers are at very high risk of abuse and neglect because of the physiological, psychological, and sociological nature of addiction.

While several factors increase the likelihood of child maltreatment, they do not necessarily lead to abuse. It is important to understand that the causes of child abuse and the characteristics of families in which child abuse occurs are only indicators. The vast majority of parents, even in the most stressful and demanding situations, and even with a personal history that might predispose them to be more violent than parents without such a history, do not abuse their children.

FIGURE 5.1

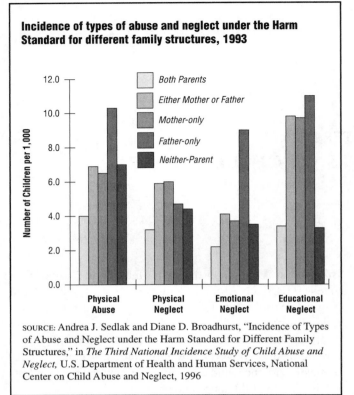

FIGURE 5.1

Incidence of types of abuse and neglect under the Harm Standard for different family structures, 1993

SOURCE: Andrea J. Sedlak and Diane D. Broadhurst, "Incidence of Types of Abuse and Neglect under the Harm Standard for Different Family Structures," in *The Third National Incidence Study of Child Abuse and Neglect,* U.S. Department of Health and Human Services, National Center on Child Abuse and Neglect, 1996

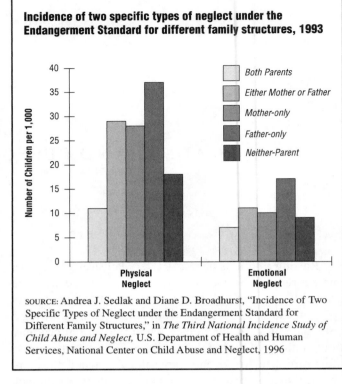

FIGURE 5.2

Incidence of two specific types of neglect under the Endangerment Standard for different family structures, 1993

SOURCE: Andrea J. Sedlak and Diane D. Broadhurst, "Incidence of Two Specific Types of Neglect under the Endangerment Standard for Different Family Structures," in *The Third National Incidence Study of Child Abuse and Neglect,* U.S. Department of Health and Human Services, National Center on Child Abuse and Neglect, 1996

Murray A. Straus and Christine Smith noted, in "Family Patterns and Child Abuse" (*Physical Violence in American Families: Risk Factors and Adaptations to Violence in 8,145 Families*), that one cannot simply single out an individual factor as the cause of abuse. The authors found that a combination of several factors is more likely to result in child abuse than is a single factor by itself. Also, the sum of the effects of individual factors taken together does not necessarily add up to what Straus and Smith called the "explosive combinations" of several factors interacting with one another. Nonetheless, even "explosive combinations" do not necessarily lead to child abuse.

Socioeconomic Status

POVERTY AND ABUSE: A COMPLEX RELATIONSHIP. Although the most comprehensive U.S. government report on the incidence of child maltreatment, NIS-3, found a correlation between family income and child abuse and neglect, most experts agree that the connection between poverty and maltreatment is not easily explained. According to Diana J. English, the stress that comes with poverty may predispose the parents to use corporal punishment that may lead to physical abuse ("The Extent and Consequences of Child Maltreatment," *The Future of Children: Protecting Children from Abuse and Neglect,* vol. 8, no. 1, Spring 1998).

English noted that most poor parents do not maltreat their children. Rather, the effects of poverty, such as

stress, may influence other risk factors, including depression, substance abuse, and domestic violence. These risk factors, in turn, may predispose the parents to violent behavior toward their children.

According to the National Center for Children in Poverty (NCCP), research has shown that the problems of depression, substance abuse, and domestic violence are interrelated and that these problems are more likely to be prevalent among low-income families (Sharmila Lawrence, Michelle Chau, and Mary Clare Lennon, *Depression, Substance Abuse, and Domestic Violence: Little Is Known about Co-Occurrence and Combined Effects on Low-Income Families,* June 2004). NCCP noted that federally funded and community-based programs, such as Early Head Start, designed to help low-income parents and their infants and toddlers, recognize the connection between poverty and parental and child well-being.

UNEMPLOYMENT. The 1975 *National Family Violence Survey* found rates of child abuse that were considerably higher among families suffering from unemployment than among those in which the husband was working full time. Families in which the husband was not working had a significantly higher rate of child abuse than other families (22.5 versus 13.9 per one hundred children). This finding did not recur, however, in the 1985 survey, although wives of unemployed husbands did have a higher rate of abuse than wives of husbands working full time (16.2 versus eleven per one hundred children). Straus and Smith ("Family Patterns and Child Abuse") thought that this higher rate for wives might have been caused by added family stress because the father was unemployed. Generally, workers in the lower economic class face greater stress because they often have less control over their employment situation, are more likely to find themselves unemployed, and have fewer resources to help ease their stress.

The rate of abuse in the 1985 *National Family Violence Resurvey* was considerably higher in families in which the husband was a blue-collar worker. Blue-collar fathers committed abuse at a rate of 11.9 per 100 children, compared with 8.9 per 100 children among white-collar workers. The abuse rate for the wives of blue-collar workers was even greater, 13.9 per 100 children versus 8.1 per 100 children among wives of white-collar workers.

Stress

There are no "vacations" from being a parent, and parenting stress has been associated with abusive behavior. When a parent who may be predisposed toward maltreating a child must deal with a particularly stressful situation, it is possible that little time, energy, or self-control is left for the children. In times of stress, the slightest action by the child can be "the last straw" that leads to violent abuse.

Often, when striking out at a child, the parent may be venting anger at his or her own situation rather than reacting to some misbehavior on the part of the child. Abused children have indicated that they never knew when their parents' anger would explode and that they were severely beaten for the most minor infractions. The child may also be hostile and aggressive, contributing to the stress.

Caring for Children with Disabilities

Children with disabilities are potentially at risk for maltreatment because society generally treats them as different and less valuable, thus possibly tolerating violence against them. These children require special care and attention, and parents may not have the social support to help ease stressful situations. A lack of financial resources further exacerbates the situation.

Some parents may feel disappointment at not having a "normal" child. Others may expect too much and feel frustrated if the child does not live up to their expectations. Children under the care of nonfamily members are at risk for maltreatment, not only from those caregivers who abuse their power or who feel no bond with them, but also from other children, especially in an institutional setting.

According to two committees of the American Academy of Pediatrics (AAP)—the Committee on Child Abuse and Neglect and the Committee on Children with Disabilities—children with disabilities may also be vulnerable to sexual abuse ("Assessment of Maltreatment of Children with Disabilities," *Pediatrics,* vol. 108, no. 2, August 2001).

Dependent on caregivers for their physical needs, these children may not be able to distinguish between appropriate and inappropriate touching of their bodies. The opportunities for sexual abuse may also be increased if the child depends on several caregivers for his or her needs.

The AAP also noted that children with disabilities may not be intellectually capable of understanding that they are being abused. They may not have the communication skills to disclose the abuse. In addition, children who experience some pain when undergoing therapy may not be able to distinguish between inflicted pain and therapy pain.

Patricia M. Sullivan called attention to the fact that the federal government does not collect specific data on children with disabilities in its crime statistics systems nor in national incidence studies mandated by law ("Violence against Children with Disabilities: Prevention, Public Policy, and Research Implications," *A Call to Action: Ending Crimes of Violence against Children and Adults with Disabilities: A Report to the Nation,* State University of New York Upstate Medical University, Department of Physical Medicine and Rehabilitation, Syracuse, NY, 2003). Although the Child Abuse and Prevention Treatment Act (CAPTA; Public Law 93-247) required that national incidence studies of child maltreatment include data on children with disabilities, the latest survey, the Third National Incidence Study of Child Abuse and Neglect (NIS-3), published in 1996, did not satisfy that mandate. The fourth mandated incidence study, NIS-4, still being conducted as of late 2004, would not include such data. Moreover, the National Child Abuse and Neglect Data System (NCANDS), which releases annual state data on maltreated children, does not gather information relating to children's disability status.

Sullivan and her colleagues undertook two epidemiological studies on maltreated children with disabilities. (Epidemiological studies take into consideration individuals' sex, age, race, social class, and other demographics.) The incidence of maltreatment (the number of new cases during a given period, such as per week, per month, or per year) and its prevalence (the total number of maltreated children with disabilities at a given time) are then measured. The hospital-based study of six thousand abused children found a 64% prevalence rate of maltreatment among disabled children, twice the prevalence rate (32%) among nondisabled children. The school-based study included 4,954 children, of which 31% of disabled children had been maltreated, 3.4 times that of the nondisabled comparison group.

Toilet Training

Toilet training can be one of the most frustrating events in the lives of parents and children. Researchers are now linking it to many of the more serious, even deadly, cases of abuse in children between the ages of one and four. Some parents have unrealistic expectations regarding bowel and bladder control for young children, and when their children are unable to live up to these standards, the parents explode in rage. Parental stress and inability to control emotions play a role in child abuse, but they require a trigger to set off the explosion. Soiled clothes and accidents frequently serve as this trigger.

When children are brought to the emergency room with deep, symmetrical scald burns on their bottoms, health care personnel conclude that they were deliberately immersed and held in hot water. This form of abuse is nearly always committed as the result of a toilet accident. Even a one-second contact with 147°F water can cause third-degree burns. Some parents think that immersing a child in hot water will make the child go to the bathroom.

Toileting accidents can be especially dangerous for children because the parent has to place his or her hands on the child to clean up the mess, making it easy for the parent's rage to be taken out on the child's body. This abuse is more common among less-educated, low-income mothers who mistakenly believe that children should be trained by twelve to sixteen months of age. Better-educated parents are more likely to be aware that successful training for girls happens at around two years of age and sometimes not until age three or later for boys.

THE VIOLENT FAMILY

Spousal Conflicts

Child abuse is sometimes a reflection of other forms of severe family conflict. Violence in one aspect of family life often flows into other aspects. Murray A. Straus and Christine Smith found that parents who were in constant conflict were also more likely to abuse their children ("Family Patterns and Child Abuse," *Physical Violence in American Families: Risk Factors and Adaptations to Violence in 8,145 Families*). The researchers measured the level of husband-wife conflict over such issues as money, sex, social activities, housekeeping, and children. The child abuse rate for fathers involved in high marital conflict was thirteen per one hundred children, compared with 7.4 per one hundred children for other men. Mothers in high-conflict relationships reported an even higher child abuse rate: 13.6 per one hundred children versus eight per one hundred children among mothers in lower-conflict homes.

Spousal Verbal Aggression and Child Abuse

Husbands and wives sometimes use verbal aggression to deal with their conflicts. The 1985 *National Family Violence Resurvey* found that spouses who verbally attacked each other were also more likely to abuse their children. Among verbally aggressive husbands, the child abuse rate was 11.2 per one hundred children, compared with 4.9 per one hundred children for other husbands. Verbally aggres-

sive wives had a child abuse rate of 12.3 per one hundred children, compared with 5.3 per one hundred children for other wives. Straus and Smith believed that verbal attacks between spouses, rather than clearing the air, tended to both mask the reason for the dispute and create further conflict. The resulting additional tension made it even harder to resolve the original source of conflict.

VERBAL ABUSE OF CHILDREN. Parents who verbally abuse their children are also more likely to physically abuse their children. Respondents to the 1975 *National Family Violence Survey* who verbally abuse their children reported a child abuse rate six times that of other parents (twenty-one versus 3.6 per one hundred children). The 1985 survey found that verbally abusive mothers physically abused their children about nine times more than other mothers (16.3 versus 1.8 per one hundred children). Fathers who were verbally aggressive toward their children physically abused the children more than three times as much as other fathers (14.3 versus 4.2 per one hundred children).

Spousal Physical Aggression and Child Abuse

In "Family Patterns and Child Abuse," Straus and Smith reported that one of the most distinct findings of the 1985 *National Family Violence Resurvey* was that violence in one family relationship is frequently associated with violence in other family relationships. In families in which the husband struck his wife, the child abuse rate was much higher (22.3 per one hundred children) than in other families (eight per one hundred children). Similarly, in families in which the wife hit the husband, the child abuse rate was also considerably higher (22.9 per one hundred children) than in families in which the wife did not hit the husband (9.2 per one hundred children).

In "Risk of Physical Abuse to Children of Spouse Abusing Parents" (*Child Abuse & Neglect*, vol. 20, no. 7, January 1996), Susan Ross, who did further research based on the 1985 *National Family Violence Resurvey*, reported that marital violence was a statistically significant predictor of physical child abuse. Ross noted that the probability of child abuse by a violent husband increased from 5% with one act of marital violence to near certainty with fifty or more acts of spousal abuse. The percentages were similar for violent wives.

Ross found that, of those husbands who had been violent with their wives, 22.8% had engaged in violence toward their children. Similarly, 23.9% of violent wives had engaged in at least one act of physical child abuse. These rates of child abuse were much higher than those of parents who were not violent toward each other (8.5% for fathers and 9.8% for mothers). In other words, the more frequent the spousal violence, the higher the probability of child abuse.

Psychological Abuse: Family Dynamics

Marie-Hélène Gagné and Camil Bouchard sought to determine the family characteristics that predispose parents to psychologically abuse their children ("Family Dynamics Associated with the Use of Psychologically Violent Parental Practices," *Journal of Family Violence*, vol. 19, no. 2, April 2004). Based on interviews with parents experiencing difficulties in their relationships with their children, parents with no apparent or acknowledged difficulties, and practitioners, the researchers gathered examples of psychological violence from parents who had experienced it and from practitioners who had come in contact with different family situations.

The researchers identified four family characteristics that are likely to result in parental psychological violence. The first involves a scapegoat child, who may be different from other family members by his or her unattractiveness, slow mental abilities, or disability. The scapegoat may be an unwanted child, the child of a former spouse, or an adopted child. This child is typically neglected by the parents, who favor his siblings. He is treated harshly and excluded from family intimacy. The second type of family has a domineering father, who intimidates the children and may even turn physically violent. The harsh treatment of the children is in reality a cover-up for his poor self-image and feelings of incompetence. The mother, assuming the role of peace-keeper, suffers stress and fatigue. In extreme cases, she herself may be a victim of spousal violence. The children may be psychologically abused by both parents.

The authoritarian mother typifies the third family characteristic leading to parental psychological abuse. She controls the household, and her spouse is powerless to defend the children. The children are expected to do as she bids. Despite the façade of control, this mother fears for her children. She overprotects them to the point of standing in the way of their independence. In turn, she demands full submission, so that the child who opposes her suffers psychological abuse. The fourth family characteristic involves the "broken parent," who has not attained maturity and a feeling of self-worth because of a difficult past. This type of parent takes care of the children when things are going smoothly, but falls apart when difficulties arise. They are not able to hold on to a job and/or maintain a relationship.

Woman Battering and Child Maltreatment

The National Clearinghouse on Child Abuse and Neglect Information reported that published studies have shown that there is a 30% to 60% overlap between violence against children and violence against women in the same families (*In Harm's Way: Domestic Violence and Child Maltreatment*, U.S. Department of Health and Human Services, Washington, DC, undated). (See Figure 5.3.) Although researchers and policy makers have studied

FIGURE 5.3

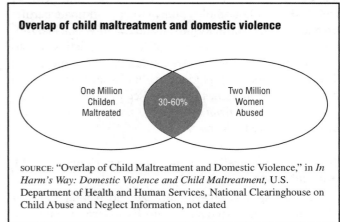

Overlap of child maltreatment and domestic violence

One Million Childen Maltreated | 30-60% | Two Million Women Abused

SOURCE: "Overlap of Child Maltreatment and Domestic Violence," in *In Harm's Way: Domestic Violence and Child Maltreatment,* U.S. Department of Health and Human Services, National Clearinghouse on Child Abuse and Neglect Information, not dated

TABLE 5.1

Violence by intimate partners, by type of crime and gender of victims, 2001

	Intimate partner violence					
	Total		Female		Male	
	Number	Rate per 1,000 persons	Number	Rate per 1,000 females	Number	Rate per 1,000 males
Overall violent crime	691,710	3.0	588,490	5.0	103,220	0.9
Rape/sexual assault	41,740	0.2	41,740	0.4	—	—
Robbery	60,630	0.3	44,060	0.4	16,570	0.1
Aggravated assault	117,480	0.5	81,140	0.7	36,350	0.3
Simple assault	471,860	2.1	421,550	3.6	50,310	0.5

—Based on 10 or fewer sample cases.

SOURCE: Callie Marie Rennison, "Table 1. Violence by Intimate Partners, by Type of Crime and Gender of Victims, 2001," in *Intimate Partner Violence, 1993–2001,* U.S. Department of Justice, Office of Justice Programs, Bureau of Justice Statistics, February 2003, http://www.ojp.usdoj.gov/bjs/pub/pdf/ipv01.pdf (accessed October 27, 2004)

the plight of battered women since the 1970s, no national data about children living in violent homes have ever been collected. A February 2003 report by Callie Marie Rennison (*Intimate Partner Violence, 1993–2001,* U.S. Department of Justice, Office of Justice Programs, Bureau of Justice Statistics, Washington, DC) showed that in 2001 588,490 women were victims of an intimate partner, accounting for 85% of total victimization by intimate partners as compared to male victims. (See Table 5.1.) *Child Maltreatment 2002* (U.S. Department of Health and Human Services, Administration for Children and Families, Administration on Children, Youth and Families, Children's Bureau, Washington, DC, 2004) reported that an estimated 896,000 children were victims of child maltreatment in 2002. Experts believe that many of these abused children and battered women come from the same homes.

Some government data illustrate that children indeed live in households where domestic violence occurs. The U.S. Department of Justice reported in July 2000 that between 1993 and 1998, children younger than twelve lived in 43% of households known to have intimate partner violence (Callie Marie Rennison and Sarah Welchans, *Intimate Partner Violence,* Bureau of Justice Statistics, Washington, DC). The Justice Department further reported in November 2000 that as many as half a million children may be present in homes where police make domestic violence arrests (*Safe from the Start: Taking Action on Children Exposed to Violence,* Washington, DC).

Exposure to Domestic Violence and Experiencing Child Maltreatment

According to John W. Fantuzzo and Wanda K. Mohr ("Prevalence and Effects of Child Exposure to Domestic Violence," *The Future of Children: Domestic Violence and Children,* vol. 9, no. 3, Winter 1999), various studies have found that child witnesses to domestic violence are more likely to exhibit aggression and behavior problems. These children experience internalizing behaviors, including depression, anxiety, suicidal tendencies, and low self-esteem. They have problems with schoolwork and attain lower scores in tests that gauge verbal, motor, and cognitive skills.

Linda Spears, in *Building Bridges between Domestic Violence Organizations and Child Protective Services* (Minnesota Center Against Violence and Abuse, University of Minnesota, St. Paul, MN, 2000), wrote that aside from seeing their mother being abused, children also witness the injuries resulting from the assault. Children may get hurt as a result of defending their mothers or of being battered themselves. Spears enumerated other effects of a child's exposure to domestic violence, including fearfulness, sleeplessness, withdrawal, anxiety, depression, and externalized problems such as delinquency and aggression.

Researchers compared a sample of one hundred New York City children from grades four to six who experienced physical abuse to a control group of one hundred nonabused children (Suzanne Salzinger, Richard S. Feldman, Daisy S. Ng-Mak, Elena Mojica, Tanya Stockhammer, and Margaret Rosario, "Effects of Partner Violence and Physical Child Abuse in Child Behavior: A Study of Abused and Comparison Children" *Journal of Family Violence,* vol. 17, no. 1, March 2002). Salzinger et al. sought to determine the relationship among family stress, partner violence, caretaker distress, and child abuse. They questioned each caretaker concerning stressful events that had occurred in their family during the lifetime of the child subject. These stress factors included, among other things, separation or divorce, drug abuse, alcohol abuse, deaths, serious illness in the past year, and job loss in the past year.

Salzinger and her associates found that, in households where partner violence and child maltreatment both occurred, the children suffered physical aggression from both the perpetrator and the victim. The perpetrator and victim could be either parent. In addition, in these households, the mothers who were typically the caretakers reported that they were more likely than the fathers to physically abuse the children. Interestingly, the researchers found that family stress, not partner violence, was responsible for caretaker distress, which in turn increased the risk for child abuse.

ABUSIVE MOTHERS

A national survey in the United Kingdom of the childhood experiences of young adults ages eighteen to twenty-four found that mothers were more likely than other household members to be violent toward their children. *Child Maltreatment in the United Kingdom—A Study of the Prevalence of Child Abuse and Neglect* (Pat Cawson, Corinne Wattam, Sue Brooker, and Graham Kelly, National Society for the Prevention of Cruelty to Children, London, England, November 20, 2000) was the most comprehensive report of childhood maltreatment ever conducted in that country, involving 2,869 interviews about young people's childhood experiences. Of the 11% of respondents who reported physical abuse, nearly half (49%) indicated that their mothers were the perpetrators of violence. Violence took the forms of knocking down the child, burning, threatening with a knife or a gun, kicking hard, shaking, or hitting with a fist or a hard implement. Another 40% of the respondents identified their attackers as their fathers.

Some Experts Say Social Factors Cause Abuse by Mothers

Straus and Smith, in "Family Patterns and Child Abuse," found that women are as likely, if not more likely, as men to abuse their children. The authors believed child abuse by women could be explained in terms of social factors rather than psychological factors. Women are more likely to abuse their children because they are more likely to have much greater responsibility for raising the children, which means that they are more exposed to the trials and frustrations of child rearing.

Women spend more "time at risk" while tending to their children. "Time at risk" refers to the time a potential abuser spends with the victim. This would apply to any form of domestic violence, such as spousal abuse and elder abuse. For example, elderly people are more likely to experience abuse from each other, not from a caregiver, if one is present. This is not because elderly couples are more violent than caregivers, but because they spend more time with each other.

Risk Factors and Chronic Child Maltreatment by Mothers

To determine the connection between psychological risk factors for child maltreatment and chronic maltreatment, researchers conducted interviews and tests of a group of abusive mothers in Quebec, Canada, on three separate occasions: during the initial recruitment for an intervention program, two years later at the end of the program, and four years after the initial recruitment as a follow-up (Louise S. Ethier, Germain Couture, and Carl Lacharité, "Risk Factors Associated with the Chronicity of High Potential for Child Abuse and Neglect," *Journal of Family Violence,* vol. 19, no. 1, February 2004). Fifty-six mothers were evaluated: twenty-one mothers whose files at the social agencies had been closed for at least four months (transitory problems group) and thirty-five mothers who were still abusive (chronic group). The risk factors were categorized into two general groups: the mother's history and her characteristics as an adult. The mother's history included placement in foster care, childhood sexual abuse, running away from home in her teens, break-ups with parental relationships, parental unavailability, neglect, and physical violence. The mother's adult characteristics included family unemployment, limited social support, past intimate partner violence, low level of intellectual functioning, low level of education, and high numbers of children and partners.

Ethier et al. found that mothers who reported a history of childhood sexual abuse, placement in foster care, and running away from home during adolescence were more likely to have chronic problems of child maltreatment. Overall, mothers exhibiting more than eight risk factors had about four times the risk for chronic child maltreatment. Those with a history of childhood sexual abuse had 3.75 times more risk of having chronic child maltreatment than those without this risk factor. The risk for chronic child maltreatment was 3.57 times for a childhood history of placement in foster care and 3.02 times for a history of running away from home in adolescence. The study also found that the following risk factors predispose mothers to chronic child maltreatment: childhood neglect (0.58 times more likely than those without this risk factor), physical violence (0.69 times), and unavailability of and break-up with parental figures (0.92 and 1.54 times, respectively). The authors concluded that traumatic experiences of childhood sexual abuse (77.8% of mothers in the study), placement in foster care (80%), and running away from home during adolescence (77.3%) had adverse effects on the mothers' ability to parent their children.

Results also showed that mothers with a low level of intelligence were 2.75 times more at risk for chronic child maltreatment. A total of 78.6% of the mothers showed such risk. However, the researchers cautioned that some studies have found that unless a parent's IQ (Intelligence Quotient) is below sixty, his or her low level of intelligence does not impair parenting abilities. Still other studies say IQ has nothing to do with parental competence. Mothers with a large family were found to have 3.13 times more risk for chronic maltreatment, with 80% of the sample displaying such risk.

ABUSIVE FATHERS

Katreena L. Scott and Claire V. Crooks noted that, despite the fact that some fathers are perpetrators of child maltreatment, very little research has been done on abusive fathers. According to the authors, for intervention services to be effective, it is important to know the characteristics of abusive fathers ("Effecting Change in Maltreating Fathers: Critical Principles for Intervention Planning," *Clinical Psychology: Science and Practice,* vol. 11, no. 1, Spring 2004). Abusive fathers tend to be very controlling of their children. Being self-centered, they demand respect and unconditional love. They are insecure and are constantly looking for signs of defiance or disrespect. An abusive father may feel that a child has more power than he does and may misinterpret a child's action as misbehavior. He therefore inflicts physical abuse to regain control. An abusive father has a sense of entitlement, expecting his children to do as he says. Scott and Crooks pointed out that sexual abuse may result from the father's sense of entitlement.

An abusive father's involvement with his children is usually based on his own needs, focusing on activities that he likes instead of what the children may want to do. However, his interest in his children may come and go, depending on his emotional state. Some fathers maltreat their children because they believe in the stereotypical role of fathers as disciplinarians. Some also feel that they have to show others that they are doing a good job as parents. Refusing to acknowledge that they may be having a tough time as parents, they take out their frustrations on the children.

ABUSIVE SIBLINGS

In *What Parents Need to Know about Sibling Abuse: Breaking the Cycle of Violence* (Springville, UT: Bonneville Books, 2002), Vernon R. Wiehe explored the reasons why siblings hurt each other. Sibling abuse may stem from a desire to control another person in order to take advantage of that person. The sibling in control typically does not know how to empathize (be aware and sensitive to the feelings of others). Wiehe noted that the reason most often given for sibling abuse is that an older sibling has been put in charge of younger siblings. Some parents may expect too much from older children, relegating parental responsibilities to them. Some children are too young to assume a parental role and may take out their frustration on younger siblings. Even if an older brother or sister is capable of babysitting their younger siblings, they lack the knowledge or skills to parent.

Wiehe pointed out that sibling abuse may be a learned behavior. Children who grow up in households where they see their parents abusing each other or are the recipients of such abuse may in turn use aggression toward one another. Children also learn abusive behavior from television programs, movies, videos, and computer games.

In "Sibling Abuse" (*Understanding Family Violence,* Thousand Oaks, CA: Sage Publications, Inc., 1998), Wiehe observed that abusive behavior between brothers and sisters is often considered sibling rivalry and is therefore not covered under mandatory reporting of abuse. The author conducted a nationwide survey of survivors of sibling abuse who had sought professional counseling for problems resulting from physical, emotional, and sexual abuse by a brother or sister.

The respondents were generally victims of more than one type of abuse: 71% reported being physically, emotionally, and sexually abused. An additional 7% indicated being just emotionally abused, pushing the total of emotionally abused victims to 78%. Emotional abuse took the forms of "name-calling, ridicule, degradation, exacerbating a fear, destroying personal possessions, and torturing or destroying a pet."

As far as the victims of sibling incest could remember, they were sexually abused at ages five to seven. The author, however, believed it was possible that the abuse started at an earlier age. The perpetrator was often a sibling older by three to ten years. The incest generally occurred over an extended period.

Effects of Sibling Abuse

In *What Parents Need to Know about Sibling Abuse,* Wiehe enumerated the effects of sibling abuse based on his interviews with survivors of such abuse:

• Poor self-esteem—Survivors indicated feelings of worthlessness and a lack of self-confidence. Those who experienced sexual abuse felt guilt and shame for their childhood victimization.

• Problems in relationships with the opposite sex— Women who had been sexually abused by their brothers reported problems with forming intimate relationships with men. They were suspicious and distrustful of men. Some had never married. Many continued to blame themselves for not having stopped the abuse.

• Difficulty with interpersonal relationships—Some survivors said they tried too hard to please others. Although they feared expressing anger and feared others' anger, they constantly lived with rage toward the sibling-perpetrators and their parents who responded inappropriately to the abuse.

• Revictimization—Because of their low self-esteem, survivors were likely to put themselves in a position of abuse as adults.

• Eating disorders, alcoholism, and drug abuse.

• Depression and posttraumatic stress disorder (PTSD)— Some survivors experienced severe depression to the point of contemplating and attempting suicide. Survivors reported PTSD symptoms, including anxiety attacks and reliving the experience of the abuse.

A LONGITUDINAL STUDY OF THE CONSEQUENCES OF CHILDHOOD MALTREATMENT

One of the most detailed longitudinal studies of the consequences of childhood maltreatment involved 908 children in a metropolitan area of the Midwest who were ages six to eleven when they were maltreated (between 1967 and 1971). A control group of 667 children with no history of childhood maltreatment was used for comparison. Each group had about two-thirds white and one-third African-American individuals, with about the same numbers of males and females. Cathy Spatz Widom examined the long-term consequences of childhood maltreatment on the subjects' intellectual, behavioral, social, and psychological development ("Childhood Victimization: Early Adversity, Later Psychopathology," *National Institute of Justice Journal,* January 2000). When the two groups were interviewed for the study, they had a median age (half were older, half were younger) of about twenty-nine years.

Widom found that, although both abused and control groups finished an average of 11.5 years of school, less than half of the abused group finished high school, compared with two-thirds of the control group. Thirteen percent of the abused group had stable marriages, compared with nearly 20% of the control group. The abused group was also more likely to experience frequent separation and divorce.

The Cycle of Violence

Widom is widely known for her work on the "cycle of violence." The cycle of violence theory suggests that childhood physical abuse increases the likelihood of arrest and of committing violent crime during the victim's later years. Widom found that, although a large proportion of maltreated children did not become juvenile delinquents or criminals, those who suffered childhood abuse or neglect were more likely than those with no reported maltreatment to be arrested as juveniles (31.2% versus 19%) and as adults (48.4% versus 36.2%). The maltreated victims (21%) were also more likely than those with no reported childhood maltreatment history (15.6%) to be arrested for a violent crime during their teen years or adulthood. (See Table 5.2.)

The author noted that the victims' later psychopathology (psychological disorders resulting from the childhood maltreatment) manifested itself in suicide attempts, antisocial personality, and alcohol abuse and/or dependence. Maltreatment victims were more likely than the control individuals to have attempted suicide (18.8% versus 7.7%) and to have manifested antisocial personality disorder (18.4% versus 11.2%). Both groups, however, did not

TABLE 5.2

Childhood victimization and later criminality

	Abuse/Neglect Group (676) %	Control Group (520) %
Arrest as juvenile	31.2[2]	19.0
Arrest as adult	48.4[2]	36.2
Arrest as juvenile or adult for any crime	56.5[2]	42.5
Arrest as juvenile or adult for any violent crime	21.0[1]	15.6

[1]$p \leq .05$ [2]$p \leq .001$
Note: Numbers in parentheses are numbers of cases.

SOURCE: Cathy Spatz Widom, "Table 1. Childhood Victimization and Later Criminality," in "Childhood Victimization, Early Adversity, Later Psychopathology," *National Institute of Justice Journal,* no. 242, January 2000

TABLE 5.3

Childhood victimization and later psychopathology

	Abuse/neglect group (676) %	Control group (520) %
Suicide attempt	18.8	7.7
Antisocial personality disorder	18.4	11.2
Alcohol abuse/dependence	54.5	51.0

Notes: Numbers in parentheses are numbers of cases.
Diagnoses of antisocial personality disorder and alcohol abuse/dependence were determined by using the National Institute of Mental Health DIS-III-R diagnostic interview.

SOURCE: Cathy Spatz Widom, "Table 2. Childhood Victimization and Later Psychopathology," in "Childhood Victimization, Early Adversity, Later Psychopathology," *National Institute of Justice Journal,* no. 242, January 2000, http://ncjrs.org/pdffiles1/jr000242b.pdf (accessed November 23, 2004)

TABLE 5.4

Childhood victimization and later psychopathology, by gender

	Abuse/Neglect Group %	Control Group %
Females	(338)	(224)
Suicide attempt	24.3[3]	8.6
Antisocial personality disorder	9.8[1]	4.9
Alcohol abuse/dependence	43.8[2]	32.8
Males	(338)	(276)
Suicide attempt	13.4[2]	6.9
Antisocial personality disorder	27.0[2]	16.7
Alcohol abuse/dependence	64.4	67.0

[1]$p \leq .05$
[2]$p \leq .01$
[3]$p \leq .001$
Note: Numbers in parentheses are numbers of cases.

SOURCE: Cathy Spatz Widom, "Table 3. Childhood Victimization and Later Psychopathology, by Gender," in "Childhood Victimization, Early Adversity, Later Psychopathology," *National Institute of Justice Journal,* no. 242, January 2000

differ much in the rates of alcohol abuse/dependence (54.5% for the abused or neglected group and 51% for the control group). (See Table 5.3.)

Gender played a role in the development of psychological disorders in adolescence and adulthood. Females (24.3%) with a history of childhood maltreatment were more likely to attempt suicide, compared with their male counterparts (13.4%). A significantly larger percentage of male victims (27%), however, than female victims (9.8%) were at a higher risk for future antisocial personality disorder. Although both male maltreated (64.4%) and control (67%) subjects had similar proportions of alcohol abuse or dependence, females who experienced abuse or neglect were more likely than the control group to have alcohol problems (43.8% versus 32.8%). (See Table 5.4.)

Cycle of Violence Updated

Another phase of the cycle of violence research was conducted when the maltreated and control groups had a median age of 32.5 years. Aside from collecting arrest records from federal, state, and local law enforcement, the researchers also conducted interviews with the subjects (Cathy S. Widom and Michael G. Maxfield, *An Update on the "Cycle of Violence,"* U.S. Department of Justice, National Institute of Justice, Washington, DC, February 2001). Overall, the study found that childhood abuse or neglect increased the likelihood of arrest in adolescence by 59% and in adulthood by 28%. Childhood maltreatment also increased the likelihood of committing a violent crime by 30%.

While earlier analysis of the maltreated group found that most of the victims did not become offenders, this study showed that nearly half (49%) of the victims had experienced a nontraffic offense as teenagers or adults. Comparison by race showed that, while both white and African-American maltreated children had more arrests than the control group, there was no significant difference among whites in the maltreated (21.8%) and control (15.2%) groups. Among African-American children, however, the maltreated group had higher rates of arrests. Maltreated African-Americans were nearly twice as likely as their counterparts in the control group to be arrested as juveniles (40.6% versus 20.9%). (See Table 5.5.)

Widom and Maxfield also examined the type of childhood maltreatment that might lead to violence later in life. They found that physically abused children (21.1%) were the most likely to commit a violent crime in their teen or adult years, closely followed by those who experienced neglect (20.2%). Although the study showed that just 8.8% of children who had been sexually abused were arrested for violence, the researchers noted that the victims were mostly females, and "females less often had a record of violent offenses." (See Table 5.6.)

MALTREATED GIRLS WHO BECOME OFFENDERS

Cathy Spatz Widom studied a group of girls who had experienced neglect and physical and sexual abuse from

TABLE 5.5

Involvement in criminality by race, in percent

Type of Arrest	Abused and Neglected Group (n = 900)	Comparison Group (n = 667)
Juvenile		
Black	40.6	20.9[3]
White	21.8	15.2[2]
Adult		
Black	59.8	43.6[3]
White	33.8	26.6[1]
Violent Crime		
Black	34.2	21.8[2]
White	11.0	9.7

[1]$p \leq .05$
[2]$p \leq .01$
[3]$p \leq .001$

SOURCE: Cathy S. Widom and Michael G. Maxfield, "Exhibit 4: Involvement in Criminality, by Race, in Percent" in *An Update on the "Cycle of Violence,"* U.S. Department of Justice, National Institute of Justice, February 2001

TABLE 5.6

Percentage of child abuse victims later arrested for violent offenses, by type of abuse

Abuse Group	Number of subjects	Percentage Arrested for Violent Offense
Physical Abuse Only	76	21.1
Neglect Only	609	20.2
Sexual Abuse Only	125	8.8
Mixed	98	14.3
Control	667	13.9

SOURCE: Cathy S. Widom and Michael G. Maxfield, "Exhibit 5: Does Only Violence Beget Violence?" in *An Update on the "Cycle of Violence"*, U.S. Department of Justice, National Institute of Justice, February 2001

ages zero to eleven through young adulthood ("Childhood Victimization and the Derailment of Girls and Women to the Criminal Justice System," *Research on Women and Girls in the Justice System,* U.S. Department of Justice, Washington, DC, September 2000). Widom found that abused and neglected girls were almost twice as likely to have been arrested as juveniles (20%), compared with 11.4% of a matched control group of nonabused girls, and almost twice as likely as the control group to be arrested as adults (28.5% versus 15.9%). Additionally, the maltreated girls were also more than twice as likely (8.2%) as the nonmaltreated girls (3.7%) to have been arrested for violent crimes. Widom, however, noted that although abused and neglected girls were at increased risk for criminal behavior, about 70% of the maltreated girls did not become criminals.

Abused and neglected girls who committed status offenses as minors tended to be arrested as adults (49% compared with 36% of the nonabused girls). Status offenses are acts that are illegal only when committed by minors: for example, drinking alcohol, skipping school, or violating curfews.

Widom, together with Peter Lambert and Daniel Nagin, found that 8% of the maltreated girls developed antisocial and criminal lifestyles that carried over to adulthood ("Does Childhood Victimization Alter Developmental Trajectories of Criminal Careers?," paper presented at the annual meeting of the American Society of Criminology, Washington, DC, November 1998). Among this group, nearly two of five (38%) had been arrested for status offenses as juveniles, but a larger percentage had been arrested for violence (46%) and property crimes (54%). Almost another third (32%) had been arrested for drug crimes. None of the girls in the control group exhibited these tendencies.

INMATES REPORT CHILDHOOD ABUSE

In midyear 2002 a total of 665,475 inmates were held in local jails (Doris J. James, *Profile of Jail Inmates, 2002,* U.S. Department of Justice, Office of Justice Programs, Bureau of Justice Statistics, Washington, DC, June 2004). Nearly 11% of inmates reported having experienced abuse before age eighteen. About twice as many females (20.3%) than males (9.7%) were abused during childhood. Overall, more than twice as many male inmates (59.7%) than female inmates (25.7%) reported that a parent or guardian abused them. About 16% of male inmates experienced abuse by other relatives, compared with 18.9% among female inmates. (See Table 5.7.)

CHILDHOOD MALTREATMENT, MENTAL HEALTH PROBLEMS, AND DATING VIOLENCE

Researchers in Ontario, Canada, investigated the relationship between childhood maltreatment and mental health problems and dating violence in adolescents with a history of childhood abuse and neglect (David A. Wolfe, Katreena Scott, Christine Wekerle, and Anna-Lee Pittman, "Child Maltreatment: Risk of Adjustment Problems and Dating Violence in Adolescence," *Journal of the American Academy of Child & Adolescent Psychiatry,* vol. 4, no. 3, March 2001). In a sample of 1,419 high school students ages fourteen to nineteen, nearly one-third (462 students) reported having experienced maltreatment as children. The researchers found that maltreated females were more than nine times as likely as nonmaltreated females to suffer from significant anxiety and posttraumatic stress, and more than seven times as likely to have problems with anger and depression. Maltreated females were nearly three times as likely to have committed nonviolent offenses, such as vandalism; four and a half times as likely to have committed violent acts, such as assault; and seven times as likely to have carried a concealed weapon during the past year. They reported being nearly three times as likely to use threatening behaviors with their partners. Maltreated females were also nearly twice as likely to have suffered sexual/physical abuse by a dating partner.

TABLE 5.7

Prior physical or sexual abuse of jail inmates, 2002 and 1996

	Percent of all jail inmates					
	All		Male		Female	
	2002	1996	2002	1996	2002	1996
Ever physically or						
sexually abused	18.2 %	16.4 %	13.4 %	12.9 %	55.3 %	47.5 %
Before age 18	10.9	11.6	9.7	10.6	20.3	20.8
After age 18	4.9	2.0	2.3	1.0	25.2	10.9
Both	2.3	2.7	1.4	1.3	9.7	15.8
Physically abused	15.1 %	13.3 %	11.2 %	10.7 %	44.9 %	37.2 %
Sexually abused	7.7	8.7	4.0	5.6	35.9	37.1
Relationship to abuser	Percent of abused inmates					
Knew abuser	92.4 %	86.6 %	92.5 %	87.9 %	92.1 %	90.3 %
Parent/guardian	47.9	53.2	59.7	60.1	25.7	36.3
Intimate*	30.0	16.6	10.5	3.5	66.7	47.7
Other relatives	17.3	24.4	16.4	21.6	18.9	31.3
Friend/acquaintance	20.7	23.1	13.9	21.7	33.5	26.4
Did not know abuser	7.6 %	13.4 %	7.5 %	12.1 %	7.9 %	17.9 %

Note: Details adds to more than total because more than 1 person may have abused inmates; or some inmates were both physically and sexually abused.
*Includes (ex) spouse, (ex) boyfriend, and (ex) girlfriend.

SOURCE: Doris J. James, "Table 17. Prior Physical or Sexual Abuse of Jail Inmates, 2002 and 1996," in *Profile of Jail Inmates, 2002,* U.S. Department of Justice, Office of Justice Programs, Bureau of Justice Statistics, July 2004, http://www.ojp.usdoj.gov/bjs/pub/pdf/ipv01.pdf (accessed October 27, 2004)

In comparison, maltreated males reported lesser degrees of mental problems. They were more than three times as likely as nonmaltreated males to experience anger and posttraumatic stress and more than twice as likely to report depression. Although maltreated boys did not report significant delinquency, they were more than three times as likely as maltreated males to physically abuse their partners and almost twice as likely to be sexually abusive. They were also nearly three times as likely to threaten their partners. Maltreated males were twice as likely to have been sexually abused, two and a half times as likely to have experienced physical abuse, and three times as likely to have been threatened by their partners.

CHILDHOOD MALTREATMENT AND THE RISK OF ILLICIT DRUG USE

It is recognized that illicit drug use is associated with behaviors leading to violence, sexually transmitted diseases, other health problems, and crime. A study population of 8,613 adult members of a health plan filled out a questionnaire relating to their adverse childhood experiences (ACEs) during the first eighteen years of life. The aim of the study was to determine the effects of related ACEs on various health outcomes and behaviors (Shanta R. Dube, Vincent J. Felitti, Maxia Dong, Daniel P. Chapman, Wayne H. Giles, and Robert F. Anda, "Childhood Abuse, Neglect, and Household Dysfunction and the Risk of Illicit Drug Use: The Adverse Childhood Experiences Study," *Pediatrics,* vol. 3, no. 3, March 2003).

The participants included more females (54%) than males (46%). About three-fourths (73% of females and 75% of males) were white. The mean age was fifty-five years for females and fifty-seven years for males. A total of 32% of females and 42% of males were college graduates. Another 42% of females and 39% of males had some college education. Just a small proportion (8% females and 7% males) did not finish high school.

The researchers used the following ten categories of ACEs:

Abuse

• Physical
• Emotional
• Sexual

Neglect

• Physical
• Emotional

Household Dysfunction

• Battered mother
• Parental separation/divorce
• Mental illness at home
• Substance abuse in home
• Incarcerated household member

The researchers found that each ACE increased two to four times the likelihood of initiation to illicit drug use by age fourteen and increased the risk of drug use into adulthood. They noted that several ACEs usually occur together. Their cumulative effect on illicit drug use is strongest during early adolescence because the young teen has just been through those painful experiences and is at the same time undergoing the turmoil characteristic of that age group.

ACEs were also found to increase the likelihood of initiation to illicit drug use among adolescents ages fifteen to eighteen and persons age nineteen and over. This shows that ACEs have long-term effects past early adolescence. Moreover, persons who had experienced more than five ACEs were seven to ten times more likely to have illicit drug use problems, addiction to illicit drugs, and injected-drug use. Finally, the authors determined the connection between ACEs and lifetime illicit drug use by analyzing four birth cohorts, or persons of approximately the same age, starting in 1900. They found the greatest impact of ACEs on illicit drug use among the oldest group, showing that adverse childhood experiences, such as child abuse and neglect, can have persistent effects throughout a person's lifetime.

CHILDHOOD MALTREATMENT AND EARLY BRAIN DEVELOPMENT

Increasing research has shown that child abuse or neglect during infancy and early childhood affects early brain development. The National Clearinghouse on Child Abuse and Neglect Information, in *Understanding the Effects of Maltreatment on Early Brain Development* (U.S. Department of Health and Human Services, Washington, DC, October 2001), defined "brain development, or learning," as "the process of creating, strengthening, and discarding connections among the neurons; these connections are called synapses." Neurons, or nerve cells, send signals to one another through synapses, which in turn form the neuronal pathways that enable the brain to respond to specific environments.

An infant is born with very few synapses formed. These include those responsible for breathing, eating, and sleeping. During the early years of life the brain develops synapses at a fast rate. Scientists have found that repeated experiences strengthen the neuronal pathways, making them sensitive to similar experiences that may occur later on in life. Unfortunately, if these early life experiences are of a negative nature, the development of the brain may be impaired. For example, if an infant who cries for attention constantly gets ignored, his brain creates the neuronal pathway that enables him to cope with being ignored. If the infant continually fails to get the attention he or she craves, the brain strengthens that same neuronal pathway.

Childhood abuse or neglect has long-term consequences on brain development. When children suffer abuse or neglect, their brains are preoccupied with reacting to the chronic stress. As the brain builds and strength-ens neuronal pathways involved with survival, it fails to develop social and cognitive skills. Later on in life, maltreatment victims may not know how to react to kindness and nurturing because the brain has no memory of how to respond to those new experiences. They may also have learning difficulties because the brain has focused solely on the body's survival so that the thinking processes may not have been developed or may have been impaired.

Hyperarousal is another consequence of maltreatment on brain development. During the state of hyperarousal, the brain is always attuned to what it perceives as a threatening situation. The brain has "learned" that the world is a dangerous place, and it has to be constantly on the alert. The victim experiences extreme anxiety at any perceived threat, or he or she may use aggression to control the situation. For example, children who have been physically abused may start a fight just so they can control the conflict and be able to choose their adversary. Males and older children are more likely to exhibit hyperarousal.

Researchers have found that, while males and older children tend to suffer from hyperarousal, younger children and females are more likely to show dissociation. In the dissociative state victims disconnect themselves from the negative experience. Their bodies and minds do not react to the abusive experience, "pretending" not to be there.

Childhood maltreatment can result in the disruption of the attachment process, which refers to the development of healthy emotional relationships with others. Under normal circumstances the first relationship that infants develop is with their caregivers. Such relationships form the basis for future emotional connections. In maltreated children, the attachment process may not be fully developed, resulting in the inability to know oneself as well as to put oneself in another's position.

CHILD NEGLECT

When most people think of child maltreatment, they think of abuse and not neglect. Furthermore, research literature and conferences dealing with child maltreatment have generally overlooked child neglect. The congressional hearings that took place before the passage of the landmark Child Abuse Prevention and Treatment Act of 1974 (CAPTA; Public Law 93-247) focused almost entirely on examples of physical abuse. Barely three pages of the hundreds recorded pertained to child neglect.

Nonetheless, every year the federal government reports a very high incidence of child neglect. According to the U.S. Department of Health and Human Services (*Child Maltreatment 2002*, Administration for Children and Families, Administration on Children, Youth and Families, Children's Bureau, Washington, DC, 2004), in 2002 more than three times as many children were victims of neglect as of physical abuse (7.5 versus 2.3 children per one thousand child population). In addition, 37.6% of the children who died of child maltreatment died of neglect alone. (See Figure 4.2 and Figure 4.6 in Chapter 4.) It is important to note that these numbers pertain only to children reported to child protective services (CPS) whose cases had been substantiated. Experts believe these numbers are underreported.

Child Neglect—A Major Social Problem

Neglect is an act of omission, or the absence of action. While the consequences of child neglect can be devastating, it leaves no visible marks. Moreover, it usually involves infants and very young children who cannot speak for themselves.

James M. Gaudin Jr., in "Child Neglect: Short-Term and Long-Term Outcomes" (*Neglected Children: Research, Practice, and Policy,* Thousand Oaks, CA: Sage Publications, Inc., 1999), reported that, compared with nonmaltreated and abused children, neglected children have the worst delays in language comprehension and expression. Psychologically neglected children also score lowest in IQ (Intelligence Quotient) tests.

Emotional neglect, in its most serious form, can result in the "non-organic failure to thrive syndrome," a condition in which a child fails to develop physically or even to survive. According to Gaudin, studies have found that, even with aggressive intervention, the neglected child continues to deteriorate. The cooperation of the neglectful parents, which is crucial to the intervention, usually declines as the child's condition worsens. This shows that it is sometimes not that easy to change the parental attributes that have contributed to the neglect in the first place.

Child Neglect around the World

In a paper presented at the Ninth ISPCAN (International Society for Prevention of Child Abuse and Neglect) European Conference on Child Abuse and Neglect, Warsaw, Poland, August 31, 2003, Murray A. Straus and Sarah A. Savage reported on experiences of child neglect among university students in seventeen countries (*Neglectful Behavior by Parents in the Life History of University Students in Seventeen Countries and its Relation to Violence against Dating Partners*). A total of 6,900 students from thirty-three universities were recruited to answer questions pertaining to their experience of childhood neglect. The participants, attending classes in psychology and sociology, were mostly female (69%). The study population ranged in age from eighteen to forty years. The students were also questioned regarding violence in their relationship with a dating partner to test the theory that childhood neglect is a risk factor for violence against a dating partner as an adult.

The parental neglectful behaviors included not keeping the child clean, not providing enough clothes for keeping warm, not making sure the child attended school, not caring if the child got into trouble in school, not helping with homework, not helping the child do his best, not providing comfort when the child was upset, and not helping when the child had problems. The authors pointed out, "One of the most ambiguous aspects of defining and measuring neglect concerns how pervasive the neglectful behavior must be for a parent to be classified as neglectful." For purposes of the study, three or more neglectful behaviors constituted having experienced childhood neglect.

The prevalence of childhood neglect ranged from 3.2% in New Hampshire, United States, to 10% in Montreal, Quebec, Canada, 19.4% in Singapore, and 36.4% in Pusan, Korea. Straus and Savage pointed out that, although the neglectful behaviors represented in their study may seem "relatively minor," they are associated with physical violence toward a dating partner in adulthood. The proportion of childhood neglect victims who reported assaulting their dating partners ranged from 15% to 45%. Those reporting severe assault of dating partners ranged from 4% to 22%, with up to 13% indicating they inflicted severe injuries. The authors added that neglected children, whose parents do not respond to their emotional needs and fail to provide consistent discipline, will not learn to use nonaggressive means to attain their goals.

Child Neglect and Fathers' Involvement in the Child's Life

One area of interest in the subject of child maltreatment involves the link between father involvement and child neglect. Researchers examined this link in the first study of its kind (Howard Dubowitz, Maureen M. Black, Mia A. Kerr, Raymond H. Starr, and Donna Harrington, "Fathers and Child Neglect," *Archives of Pediatrics & Adolescent Medicine,* vol. 154, no. 2, February 2000). The participants included 244 low-income, inner-city families who were involved in a long-term study of child health and development in families at risk for child maltreatment. The children were under two years old when the study began, and this particular portion of the study was conducted when the children were five years old. A total of 176 children (72%) had a father or father figure.

The study found an overall range of 11% to 30% of child neglect in the households. The nature of father involvement, however, not the absence of the father, was associated with neglect. The researchers found that less child neglect was associated with the following: a longer duration of father involvement in the child's life, the positive feelings the father had about his parenting skills, the father's greater involvement with household chores, and the father's less involvement with child care. Interestingly, the father's greater involvement with child care resulted in more child neglect. Dubowitz et al. explained that other studies have shown that fathers tended to be more involved in child care when the mothers were unavailable.

HOUSEHOLD COMPOSITION AND RISK OF MALTREATMENT DEATH

In 2002 an estimated 1,390 children died of abuse or neglect in the United States. About 76% of these children were younger than four, making maltreatment the main cause of injury death in this age group. Another 12% of victims were ages four to seven. To determine the role of family composition as a risk factor for fatal child maltreatment, researchers examined all information related to Missouri resident children under five years old who died in that state within a three-year period (Michael N. Stiffman, Patricia G. Schnitzer, Patricia Adam, Robin L. Kruse, and Bernard G. Ewigman, "Household Composition and Risk of Fatal Child Maltreatment," *Pediatrics*, vol. 109, no. 4, April 2002).

Stiffman et al. used the comprehensive data of child deaths (birth through age seventeen) collected by the Missouri Child Fatality Review Panel (CFRP) system between 1992 and 1994. The CFRP data contained information on all household members and their relationship to the deceased child. For comparison, the researchers used a control group consisting of children under age five who had died of natural causes. Of the 291 injury deaths that were examined, 60% (175 children) were determined to have died of maltreatment. Nearly one-third (31%, or fifty-five children) of the deaths resulted from injury caused by a parent or other caregiver. Of this group, thirty-nine of the children died from being shaken, hit, or dropped. Eleven children died from the use of physical objects, including guns. The cause of death for the remaining five children was unknown.

The study found that children living in households with one or more biologically unrelated adult males and boyfriends of the child's mother had the highest risk of death from maltreatment. These children were eight times more likely to die of maltreatment than children living with two biological parents with no other adults. Children residing with foster and adoptive parents, as well as with stepparents, were nearly five times as likely to suffer maltreatment deaths. Those living in households with other adult relatives present were twice as likely to die from maltreatment. Children living with just one biological parent, however, with no other adult present, were not at increased risk for fatal maltreatment.

CORPORAL PUNISHMENT

Corporal Punishment by Parents

All fifty states allow parents to use corporal punishment for purposes of disciplining their children. This means that the parent may use objects such as belts as long as the child does not suffer injury, as well as the more typical spanking with the hand. When states passed child abuse laws in the 1960s, provisions allowing parents to use corporal punishment helped facilitate passage of the legislation.

According to the Center for Effective Discipline, as of September 2004, thirteen countries prohibited corporal punishment by parents, caretakers, and teachers. In 1979 Sweden became the first country to ban all corporal punishment of children. The other twelve countries were: Finland (1983), Norway (1987), Austria (1989), Cyprus (1994), Denmark (1997), Latvia (1998), Croatia (1999), Germany (2000), Israel (2000), Iceland (2003), Ukraine (2004), and Romania (2004). Since January 2003, Canada bans corporal punishment for children under two and over twelve years of age, as well as the use of any object, such as a paddle.

Corporal Punishment in Schools

As of 2004, among industrialized countries, only Australia (just Outback areas) and the United States allowed spanking in schools. A total of twenty-two U.S. states allowed corporal punishment in public schools, although in some schools parents can request that their children not be spanked. Most are southern states. (See Figure 5.4.) The most recent school year (1999–2000) for which U.S. Department of Education figures are available showed that 342,038 students were paddled in public schools (Center for Effective Discipline, "U.S. Statistics on Corporal Punishment by State and Race," http://www.stophitting.com/disatschool/statesbanning.php [accessed November 20, 2004]).

American Attitudes about Corporal Punishment

The latest Gallup poll (1997) that surveyed Americans' attitudes about corporal punishment showed that 65% of Americans favored spanking children, a slightly lower percentage than the 74% who approved of spanking about fifty years ago in 1946. The 1997 poll also showed that, among parents, 66% favored spanking. An October 2002 ABC News poll found almost the same proportion (65%) of American parents in favor of spanking. Half of the respondents (50%) who had minor children at home indicated they sometimes spanked their children. Respondents in the southern states were more likely to favor corporal punishment, compared with the rest of the country (73% versus 60%). More parents in the South (62%) reported spanking their children, compared to parents in the rest of the states (41%). On the subject of physical punishment administered by teachers, just a quarter (26%) of parents with children thought spanking should be allowed in school. Among parents in the South, about one-third (35%) felt spanking should be allowed in schools.

The Trend of Corporal Punishment by Parents

The 1985 *National Family Violence Resurvey* found that more than 90% of parents of children ages three and

FIGURE 5.4

States banning corporal punishment in school, 2003

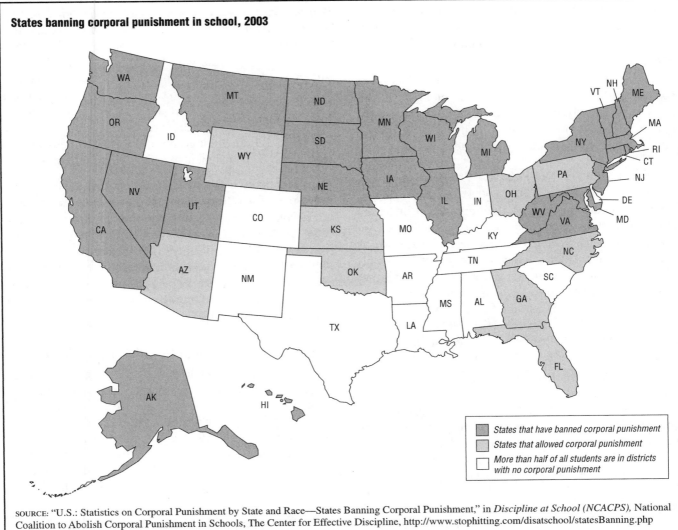

SOURCE: "U.S.: Statistics on Corporal Punishment by State and Race—States Banning Corporal Punishment," in *Discipline at School (NCACPS)*, National Coalition to Abolish Corporal Punishment in Schools, The Center for Effective Discipline, http://www.stophitting.com/disatschool/statesBanning.php (accessed November 23, 2004)

four used some form of corporal punishment, ranging from a slap on the hand to severe spanking. While spanking generally decreased as the child got older, about 49% of thirteen-year-olds were still being physically punished.

The National Center for Health Statistics of the U.S. Department of Health and Human Services conducted the first nationwide survey to examine the health and development of children under three years of age. Using data from the 2000 survey, researchers examined, among other things, the parental use of corporal punishment for discipline (Michael Regalado, Harvinder Sareen, Moira Inkelas, Lawrence S. Wissow, and Neal Halfon, "Parents' Discipline of Young Children: Results from the National Survey of Early Childhood Health," *Pediatrics,* vol. 113, no. 6, June 2004). Six percent of parents surveyed indicated they ever spanked their children ages four to nine months old. Twenty-nine percent spanked their children ten to eighteen months old, and 64% spanked their children who were nineteen to thirty-five months old. Fre-

quent spankings were also administered by some parents (11%) of children ten to eighteen months old and nineteen to thirty-five months old (26%).

Prevalence and Chronicity of Corporal Punishment

Murray A. Straus and Julie H. Stewart, in "Corporal Punishment by American Parents: National Data on Prevalence, Chronicity, Severity, and Duration, in Relation to Child and Family Characteristics" (*Clinical Child and Family Psychology Review,* vol. 2, no. 2, 1999), reported on a national survey of American parents regarding their use of corporal punishment.

Overall, based on the chronological age of the children, more than a third (35%) of parents surveyed used corporal punishment on their infants, reaching a peak of 94% for parents of children who were three to four years old. The prevalence rate of parents using corporal punishment decreased after age five, with just over 50% of parents using it on children at age twelve, one-third (33%) at age fourteen, and 13% at age seventeen. The survey also found that corporal punishment was more prevalent among African-Americans and parents in the low socioeconomic level. It was also more commonly inflicted on boys, by mothers, and in the South.

Chronicity refers to the frequency of the infliction of corporal punishment during the year. Corporal punishment was most frequently used by parents of two-year-olds, averaging eighteen times a year. After age two, chronicity declined, averaging six times a year for teenagers.

Corporal Punishment and Behavior Problems in Children Starting Elementary School

Studies on the spanking of children have mostly used sample populations of children age two and older. Eric P. Slade and Lawrence S. Wissow conducted the first study of its kind in the United States, following a group of 1,966 children younger than two years old to test the hypothesis that "spanking frequency before age two is positively associated with the probability of having significant behavior problems four years later" ("Spanking in Early Childhood and Later Behavior Problems: A Prospective Study of Infants and Young Toddlers," *Pediatrics,* vol. 113, no. 5, May 2004).

The researchers collected data about 1,966 children and their mothers who participated in the National Longitudinal Survey of Mother-Child Sample, a large-scale national study of youth ages fourteen to twenty-one. Some of these young people were mothers with children. Data were collected on the mother-children groups when the children were under two years of age. Four years later, after the children had entered elementary school, the researchers interviewed the mothers to explore their hypothesis. Mothers were asked if they spanked their child the previous week and how frequently they spanked their children. They were also questioned about the child's temperament, mother-child interactions, and whether they had ever met with the child's teacher due to behavioral problems.

Slade and Wissow found that, compared with children who were never spanked, white non-Hispanic children who were frequently spanked (five times a week) before age two were four times more likely to have behavioral problems by the time they started school. No connection was found between spanking and later behavioral problems among African-American and Hispanic children. According to the authors, the same results were found in studies involving children older than two. The authors explained that the way white families and other ethnic groups view the spanking of children may influence the impact of spanking. For example, African-American families typically do not consider spanking as "harsh or unfair."

Corporal Punishment Increases the Risk of Physical Abuse

Murray A. Straus presented a model called "path analysis" to illustrate how physical punishment could escalate to physical abuse ("Physical Abuse," Chapter 6 in *Beating the Devil out of Them: Corporal Punishment in American Families and Its Effects on Children,* 2nd ed., New Brunswick, NJ: Transaction Publishers, 2001). Straus theorized that parents who have been physically disciplined as adolescents are more likely to believe that it is acceptable to use violence to remedy a misbehavior. These parents tend to be depressed and to be involved in spousal violence. When a parent resorts to physical punishment and the child does not comply, the parent increases the severity of the punishment, eventually harming the child.

Corporal punishment experienced in adolescence produces the same effect on males and females. Parents who were physically punished thirty or more times as adolescents (24%) were three times as likely as those who never received physical punishment (7%) to abuse their children physically. Straus noted, however, that his model also shows that three-quarters (76%) of parents who were hit many times (thirty or more) as adolescents did not, in turn, abuse their children.

Corporal Punishment and Cognitive Development

In "Corporal Punishment by Mothers and Child's Cognitive Development: A Longitudinal Study" (Family Research Laboratory, University of New Hampshire, Durham, NH; a paper presented at the 14th World Congress of Sociology, Montreal, Quebec, Canada, 1998), Murray A. Straus and Mallie J. Paschall found that corporal punishment was associated with a child's failure to keep up with the average rate of cognitive development.

Straus and Paschall followed the cognitive development of 960 children born to mothers who participated in the *National Longitudinal Study of Youth.* The women were fourteen to twenty-one years old in 1979, at the start of the study. In 1986, when the women were between the ages of twenty-one and twenty-eight, those with children were interviewed regarding the way they were raising their children. The children underwent cognitive, psychosocial, and behavioral assessments. Children ages one to four were selected, among other reasons, because "the development of neural connections is greatest at the youngest ages." The children were tested again in 1990.

About seven in ten (71%) mothers reported spanking their toddlers in the past week, with 6.2% spanking the child during the course of their interview for the study. Those who used corporal punishment reported using it an average of 3.6 times per week. This amounted to an estimated 187 spankings a year.

COGNITIVE DEVELOPMENT. Straus and Paschall found that the more prevalent the corporal punishment, the greater the decrease in cognitive ability. Considering other studies, which showed that talking to children, including infants, is associated with increased neural connections in the brain and cognitive functioning, the researchers hypothesized that if parents are not using corporal punishment to discipline their child, they are very likely verbally interacting with that child, thus positively affecting cognitive development.

Moreover, corporal punishment has been found to affect cognitive development in other ways. It is believed that experiencing corporal punishment can be very stressful to children. Stress hampers children's ability to process events, which is important for their cognitive development. And since corporal punishment generally occurs over a long period, children's bonding with their parents may be minimized to the point that the children will not be motivated to learn from their parents.

OTHER FINDINGS. Straus and Paschall also found that, contrary to some beliefs that corporal punishment is acceptable if the parent provides emotional support to the child, the adverse effects of physical punishment on cognitive development remained the same whether or not there was maternal support. The results of the study also debunked the general belief among African-Americans that corporal punishment benefits children. The adverse consequences on cognitive development held true for all racial and ethnic groups.

Consequences of Reducing the Use of Corporal Punishment

Ron L. Pitzer, a University of Minnesota Extension Service sociologist, conducted a six-year study of changes in parental disciplinary practices, specifically the use of corporal punishment, and their effects on aggressive child behaviors ("Changes in Goodhue County Parenting Practices 1993–1998," *Family Forum*, Minnesota Council of Family Relations, St. Paul, MN, 2002). The *Positive Parenting* study randomly selected 1003 parents with children under age thirteen. The participants were residents of Goodhue County (501) and Rice County (502) in Minnesota. In this report, Pitzer discussed data concerning the Goodhue County participants.

Researchers interviewed the parents regarding their parenting practices in 1993, 1995, and 1998. During the six-year period, many parents attended positive-parenting classes. At the same time, a multiagency citizen group ran a public awareness and educational campaign to bring the message of "Kids: Handle with Care" to the county residents. Overall, parents' use of corporal punishment declined from 36% (1993) to 21% (1995) to 12% (1998) during the six months prior to the interviews. Those parents who attended public-awareness activities reported lesser use of corporal punishment. In 1993, 11% reported spanking their children eleven or more times in the past six months before the interview. By 1998 no parent reported spanking that often during the past six months. In 1993, 20% indicated spanking six or more times the previous six

months. Just 2% said they used physical punishment in 1998. Parents who took parenting classes reported, among other things, that they learned to set limits by explaining to the child what was expected of him or her. Fathers who actively participated in the parenting classes and public-awareness programs did just as well as or better than the mothers in changing their parenting practices.

The researchers also found changes in some children's aggression. Nonaggressive children at the start of the study who were spanked were twice as aggressive by the end of the study. Those who were aggressive in 1993 but were not spanked throughout the study were half as aggressive in 1998. Overall, the percentage of parents who reported their children hitting siblings dropped from 80% in 1993 to 56% in 1998. Hitting other children declined from 45% to 27%, damaging things, from 47% to 31%, and hitting adults, including parents, from 28% to 9%. The study did not take into account, however, that much of this change would be expected because of the difference in the children's age from the beginning to the end of the study.

Not All Experts Oppose Physical Punishment

Some experts believe nonabusive spanking can play a role in effective parental discipline of young children. According to Robert E. Larzelere, spanking can have beneficial results when it is "nonabusive (e.g., two swats to the buttocks with an open hand) and used primarily to back up milder disciplinary tactics with 2- to 6-year-olds by loving parents" ("Child Outcomes of Nonabusive and Customary Physical Punishment by Parents: An Updated Literature Review," *Clinical Child and Family Psychology Review*, vol. 3, no. 4, 2000). Larzelere reviewed thirty-eight studies on corporal punishment to determine the effects of nonabusive and customary spanking. The author described researches on customary spanking as "studies that measure physical punishment without emphasizing the severity of its use."

Generally, the thirty-eight studies were nearly equally divided in their reports of beneficial child outcomes, detrimental child outcomes, and neutral or mixed outcomes: 32%, 34%, and 34%, respectively. The author examined seventeen studies he considered to be causally conclusive, that is, the research showed that nonabusive spanking was associated with the child outcomes. Nine studies in which children two to six years of age received nonabusive spankings after noncompliance with room time-out found beneficial child outcomes, such as subsequent compliance with parental orders. Of these nine studies, two studies in which parents used reasoning with the child followed by nonabusive spanking revealed a longer delay in between misbehaviors. A study involving extended disciplining by mothers showed that child compliance occurred at higher rates when the mothers used spanking as a final resort after other disciplinary measures had been tried.

Of the eight controlled longitudinal studies that examined spanking frequency, five reported negative child outcomes, such as low self-esteem. Controlled studies refer to studies that excluded initial child misbehavior. The author noted that three of these studies showed that the detrimental effects were a result of frequent spankings.

Larzelere found that the child's age was associated with the outcome of nonabusive spanking. Of twelve studies involving children with mean ages under six, eleven reported beneficial outcomes. Among children ages seven-and-a-half to ten years, just one study reported beneficial outcomes, while six studies found detrimental outcomes.

Larzelere noted that confounding factors in some studies were responsible for a conclusion of detrimental child outcomes. In other words, studies that used opposing or unclear factors found negative outcomes. According to Larzelere, studies that did not show detrimental child outcomes shared three common factors: very serious corporal punishment was not included in those studies; spanking was measured as a back-up for other disciplinary practices and not in terms of frequency; and a large number of children exhibited behavior problems at the start of the study.

CHAPTER 6
CHILD SEXUAL ABUSE

A BETRAYAL OF TRUST

Many experts believe that sexual abuse is the most underreported type of child maltreatment. A victim, especially a very young child, may not know what he or she is experiencing. In many cases the child is sworn to secrecy. Adults who may be aware of the abuse sometimes get involved in a conspiracy of silence.

Child sexual abuse is the ultimate misuse of an adult's trust and power over a child. When the abuser is particularly close to the victim, the child feels betrayed, trapped in a situation where an adult who claims to care for the child is assaulting him or her.

FREUD

The first person to present childhood sexual abuse as a source of psychological problems was Austrian psychoanalyst Sigmund Freud (1856–1939). Early in his career Freud proposed that the hysteria he saw in some of his patients was the result of childhood sexual abuse. He thought his patients' symptoms represented symbolic manifestations of their repressed sexual memories. Freud later changed his mind, denying that he thought sexual abuse had taken place. Instead, he proposed that young children have an unconscious sexual attachment to the parent of the opposite sex and a sense of rivalry with the parent of the same sex. This is called the Oedipus complex in males and the Electra complex in females. In other words, the adult's memories of incestuous experiences were remnants of his or her childhood desires to be seduced by an adult. Freud theorized that, under the normal psychological development process, the child starts to identify with the parent of the same sex. He claimed that if this does not occur, the individual will develop personality disorders in adulthood.

Some scholars have proposed that Freud revised his theory because he was pressured by colleagues to recant. Psychoanalyst Alice Miller claimed that Freud suppressed the truth so that he, his colleagues, and men in Viennese society would be spared having to examine their own histories. Some experts believe that the testimonies Freud originally elicited from his patients were cases of incestuous abuse. Others believe that he changed his theory to preserve his concept of repression, on which he based the whole structure of psychoanalysis.

WHAT IS CHILD SEXUAL ABUSE?

Federal Definition

The Child Abuse Prevention and Treatment Act of 1974 (CAPTA; Public Law 93-247) specifically identified parents and caretakers as the perpetrators of sexual abuse. Sexual molestation by other individuals was considered sexual assault. The 1996 amendments to this law, however, included a more comprehensive definition, one that also included sexually abusive behavior by individuals other than parents and caregivers.

The CAPTA Amendments of 1996 (Public Law 104-235; Sec. 111 [42 U.S.C. 5106g]) defines child sexual abuse as:

- The employment, use, persuasion, inducement, enticement, or coercion of any child to engage in, or assist any other person to engage in, any sexually explicit conduct or simulation of such conduct for the purpose of producing a visual depiction of such conduct; or

- the rape, and in cases of caretaker or interfamilial relationships, statutory rape, molestation, prostitution, or other form of sexual exploitation of children, or incest with children.

Specific Definition Varies by State

Whereas the federal government has established a broad definition of child sexual abuse, it leaves it up to state child abuse laws to specify detailed provisions. All states have laws prohibiting child sexual molestation and generally consider incest illegal. States also specify the age of consent, or the age at which a person can consent to sexual activity with an adult—generally between the ages of fourteen and eighteen. Sexual activity between an adult and a person below the age of consent is against the law.

Types of Child Sexual Abuse

Familial abuse, or incest, involves the use of a child for sexual satisfaction by family members—blood relatives who are too close to marry legally. Extrafamilial abuse involves a person outside the family. Extrafamilial predators may be strangers, but they may also be persons in a position of trust, such as family friends, teachers, and spiritual advisers.

HOW FREQUENT IS ABUSE?

Each year the National Child Abuse and Neglect Data System (NCANDS) of the U.S. Department of Health and Human Services (DHHS) collects child maltreatment data from child protective services (CPS) agencies in the fifty states and the District of Columbia, releasing the compiled information as *Child Maltreatment*. The federally mandated *National Incidence Study of Child Abuse and Neglect* (NIS) is another source that shows the extent of child sexual abuse. As of 2004 three national incidence studies had been conducted—NIS-1 (1980), NIS-2 (1986), and NIS-3 (1993). In 2003 the Keeping Children and Families Safe Act (Public Law 108-36) directed the collection of data for NIS-4. A third source of sexual abuse data is retrospective studies, which are surveys of adults about their childhood experience of sexual abuse. Within this source type are periodic federal government surveys of jail inmates and prisoners regarding their experience of child sexual abuse.

According to the DHHS, in 1976 an estimated six thousand substantiated child sexual abuse cases were reported by CPS agencies in the United States, representing a rate of 0.86 per 10,000 children. By 1986, the number of reported cases had risen to 132,000, with a rate of 20.9 per 10,000 children. The number of substantiated child sexual abuse cases peaked at an estimated 149,800 in 1992, a rate of 23 per 10,000 children. (The current rate used by the DHHS is 2.3 per one thousand children.) Since then the numbers declined to approximately 129,000 cases in 1995, about 89,000 in 2000, and an estimated 89,700 in 2002.

Determining the Extent of Child Sexual Abuse through Retrospective Studies

David Finkelhor, director of the Crimes against Children Research Center at the University of New Hampshire in Durham, is a national authority on child sexual abuse. In "Current Information on the Scope and Nature of Child Sexual Abuse" (*The Future of Children: Sexual Abuse of Children,* vol. 4, no. 2, Summer/Fall 1994), Finkelhor noted that surveys of adults regarding their childhood experiences (called retrospective studies) probably give the most complete estimates of the actual extent of child sexual abuse. He reviewed nineteen adult retrospective surveys and found that the proportion of adults who indicated sexual abuse during childhood ranged widely, from 2% to 62% for females and from 3% to 16% for males.

Finkelhor observed that the surveys that reported higher levels of abuse were those that asked multiple questions about the possibility of abuse. Multiple questions are more effective because they provide respondents various "cues" about the different kinds of experiences the researchers are asking about. Multiple questions also give the respondents ample time to overcome their embarrassment. Many experts accept the estimate that one of five (20%) American women and one of ten (10%) American men have experienced some form of childhood sexual abuse.

Some Victims May Not Be Counted

Estimates of the number of sexual abuse cases generally do not include victims of pornographic exploitation and child prostitution. These types of child abuse have only recently become subjects of research, and while they are known to involve multimillion-dollar businesses, little is known about the numbers of child victims involved.

The estimates also do not include stranger abductions, often for sexual purposes, that result in the death of the child. The Second National Incidence Studies of Missing, Abducted, Runaway, and Thrownaway Children (NISMART-2) found that, during the study year 1999, an estimated 58,200 children were victims of nonfamily abductions (David Finkelhor, Heather Hammer, and Andrea J. Sedlak, *Nonfamily Abducted Children: National Estimates and Characteristics,* U.S. Department of Justice, Office of Justice Programs, Office of Juvenile Justice and Delinquency Prevention, October 2002). The study also reported an estimated 115 cases of stereotypical kidnapping, the kind that make it to the news because of their seriousness or duration. The authors noted that the larger number of 58,200 resulted from using a broad definition of nonfamily abduction.

Abduction is typically associated with very serious life-and-death situations involving strangers. Abduction, however, according to legal definition, may involve less serious cases. For its incidence study, NISMART-2 used two definitions: stereotypical kidnapping and nonfamily abduction. Stereotypical kidnapping refers to kidnapping committed by a stranger or a slight acquaintance who keeps the child overnight, transports the child fifty or more miles, takes the child for ransom, or takes the child to keep him permanently or to kill him. (A slight acquaintance may be a person the child has known for less than six

TABLE 6.1

Characteristics of nonfamily abducted children, 1999

Characteristic of Child	All Nonfamily Abduction Victims (n=58,200) Percent	All Nonfamily Abduction Victims (n=58,200) Estimate	Stereotypical Kidnapping Victims (n=115) Percent	Stereotypical Kidnapping Victims (n=115) Estimate	Percent of U.S. Child Population* (N=70,172,700)
Age (years)					
0–5	7[1]	4,300[1]	19	20	33
6–11	12[1]	6,800[1]	24	25	34
12–14	22[1]	13,000[1]	38	45	17
15–17	59	34,100	20	20	17
Gender					
Male	35[1]	20,300[1]	31	35	51
Female	65	37,900	69	80	49
Race/ethnicity					
White, non-Hispanic	35	20,500	72	80	65
Black, non-Hispanic	42[1]	24,500[1]	19	20	15
Hispanic	23[1]	13,200[1]	8[1]	10[1]	16
Other	<1[1]	<100[1]	2[1]	<5[1]	5
Region					
Northeast	<1[2]	<100[1]	n/a[2]	n/a	18
Midwest	33	19,300	n/a	n/a	23
South	38[2]	21,900[1]	n/a	n/a	35
West	29[1]	16,900[1]	n/a	n/a	24
No information	<1[2]	100[2]	100	115	—

Note: All estimates are rounded to the nearest 100. Percents may not sum to 100 because of rounding.

* Age, gender, and race for the U.S. population were based on the average monthly estimates of the population ages 0–17 years for 1999 (U.S. Census Bureau, 2000a). The regional distribution of the population was computed from State-by-State estimates of the population ages 0–17 as of July 1, 1999 (U.S. Census Bureau, 2000b).
[1]Estimate is based on too few sample cases to be reliable.
[2]n/a = not available.

SOURCE: David Finkelhor, Heather Hammer, and Andrea J. Sedlak, "Table 2: Characteristics of Nonfamily Abducted Children," in *Nonfamily Abducted Children: National Estimates and Characteristics,* U.S. Department of Justice, Office of Justice Programs, Office of Juvenile Justice and Delinquency Prevention, October 2002

TABLE 6.2

Characteristics of nonfamily abduction perpetrators, by relationship, gender, and age, 1999

Characteristic of perpetrator	Percent of all nonfamily abduction victims (n=58,200)	Percent of stereotypical kidnapping victims (n=115)
Identity of main perpetrator		
Friend	17*	—
Long-term acquaintance	21*	—
Neighbor	5*	—
Authority person	6*	—
Caretaker or babysitter	4*	—
Stranger	37*	71[†]
Slight acquaintance	8*	29[†]
Someone else	3*	—
More than one perpetrator		
Yes	21*	48
No	79	41
No information	<1*	11*
Main perpetrator's gender		
Male	75	86
Female	25*	7*
No information	<1*	7*
Main perpetrator's age (years)		
13–19	25*	21
20–29	42*	36
30–39	12*	21
40–49	16*	7*
50–89	5*	4*
No information	<1*	10*

*Estimate based on too few sample cases to be reliable.

Notes: n =sample size. By definition, stereotypical kidnappings are limited to cases involving strangers and slight acquaintances.

SOURCE: David Finkelhor, Heather Hammer, and Andrea J. Sedlak, "Table 3: Characteristics of Nonfamily Abduction Perpetrators," in *Nonfamily Abducted Children: National Estimates and Characteristics,* U.S. Department of Justice, Office of Justice Programs, Office of Juvenile Justice and Delinquency Prevention, October 2002, http://www.ncjrs.org/html/ojjdp/nismart/03/ns4.html (accessed November 23, 2004)

months. The person may be someone the child has known for more than six months but has seen less than once a month. A slight acquaintance may also be a person the child does not know well enough to have spoken to.) Nonfamily abduction includes stereotypical kidnapping as well as less serious kidnappings. It may involve luring a child for purposes of collecting ransom or keeping the child permanently. It may also involve the forceful transporting of a child or the detention of a child for at least an hour.

Children ages twelve to seventeen accounted for an estimated 81% of nonfamily abductions and for about 58% of stereotypical kidnappings. About two-thirds of the victims of both nonfamily (65%) and stereotypical (69%) abductions were girls. The authors noted that, in most cases, abductions were carried out for sexual purposes. Although the sample cases showed that more non-Hispanic African-American children (42%) than non-Hispanic white children (35%) were involved in nonfamily abductions, the larger proportion for African-Americans may just be due to the sample studied. Among child victims of stereotypical kidnapping, there were nearly four times as many white victims (72%) as African-Americans (19%). (See Table 6.1.)

More than half (53%) of perpetrators of nonfamily abductions were people known to the child, including neighbors, authority figures, friends, long-term acquaintances, and caregivers. Strangers made up more than one-third (37%) of nonfamily abductors. Most perpetrators of nonfamily (75%) and stereotypical (86%) kidnapping were males. (See Table 6.2.) Almost half of the victims of nonfamily abductions (46%) and stereotypical kidnappings (49%) were sexually assaulted.

WHAT MAKES A VICTIM DISCLOSE CHILDHOOD SEXUAL ABUSE?

A review of studies of child sexual abuse shows that more females than males seem to disclose childhood sexual abuse. This is because females are more likely to participate in research studies. Researchers at the Medical University of South Carolina and of the College of Charleston, South Carolina, sought to discover the factors that contribute to the likelihood that an adolescent will disclose sexual abuse. The authors also sought to examine whether, among the different ethnic/racial groups, adolescents differ in rates of disclosure and in the factors contributing to that disclosure (Rochelle F. Hanson, Lisha W. Kievit, Benjamin E. Saunders, Daniel W. Smith, Dean G. Kilpatrick, Heidi S. Resnick, and Kenneth J. Ruggiero, "Correlates of Adolescent Reports of Sexual Assault: Findings from the National Survey of Adolescents," *Child Maltreatment,* vol. 8, no. 4, November 2003).

Participants in the National Survey of Adolescents were a national, random sample of 4,023 U.S. adolescents ages twelve to seventeen. The sample was made up of 51.3% males and 48.7% females. A majority (70.2%) were white non-Hispanic. The children were grouped into several age cohorts (groups with like characteristics). Interviews were conducted by telephone, with the consent of the parent or guardian.

A total of 326 adolescents (8.1%) indicated that they had experienced child sexual abuse. Approximately four of five (78.1%) participants were female, and one of five (21.9%) was male. Most (58.2%) were white, 23.6% were African-American, and 9.4% were Hispanic. Other ethnic groups made up 8.2%.

Of the 326 victims almost one-third (30.7%) had been raped, more than one-quarter (26.8%) reported fearing for their life during the assault, and about 10% had suffered physical injuries. Alcohol or drugs were involved in 6.7% of the incidents. Single incidents were reported by about two-thirds (64.1%) of the victims. Three-quarters (76.4%) knew the perpetrator (4.3% identified their father or stepfather as the abuser), 17.5% named another relative, and 52.8% reported an unrelated acquaintance. Nearly one-quarter (23%) said the perpetrator was a stranger, 1.8% (six adolescents) knew the perpetrator but did not identify the person, and two victims did not name the perpetrator.

About two-thirds (68.1%, or 222 adolescents) of the victims told interviewers they disclosed their sexual abuse to a person. Just 4.5% (ten victims) first disclosed the abuse to a police officer or social worker. One-third (34.3%) told their mother or stepmother, and more than a third (39.3%) told a close friend. The other victims told another relative (6.1%), a teacher (1.8%), a father or stepfather (1.7%), or a doctor or other health professional (1.3%). About 3.4% indicated they disclosed the abuse to someone but did not say who it was. Another 3.9% would not say who they told of the abuse, or could not remember who they first told. Overall, just one-third·(33.6%) indicated they reported the abuse to police or other authorities.

More females (74%) than males (46.5%) disclosed having been sexually abused. White victims (75.1%) were more likely than Hispanics (67.7%) and African-Americans (55.8%) to tell someone of their abuse. Having feared for their lives during the assault (80.7% of victims) increased the likelihood of disclosing the abuse, compared with having suffered physical injury (70.6%), hav-

ing used substances (68.2%), having been assaulted once (67.9%), or having experienced a penetration assault (72%). The likelihood of telling someone of the abuse was also influenced by the relationship between the victim and the perpetrator. Nearly nine of ten victims (87.7%) who were sexually abused by a relative disclosed the incident, compared to those abused by a stranger (70.7%), an unrelated acquaintance (62.2%), or a father (57.1%).

The study showed that the gender of the adolescent is related to disclosure of sexual abuse, with girls more likely to do so. The authors reiterated previous findings that males might fear being thought of as gay if the abuser were male. Also, society tells males that they are powerful creatures and that it is all right for them to engage in any sexual relationship with females. The authors also noted that other studies have shown that African-American females are reluctant to disclose sexual abuse because of fear of not being believed. Although no similar studies have been done of their male counterparts, the authors thought the same reason might keep African-American male adolescents from reporting child sexual abuse. In this study African-American females were seven times more likely than their male counterparts to tell someone they had experienced sexual abuse. White adolescents did not differ in disclosure of abuse based on gender.

ARE CHILD SEXUAL ABUSE CASES DECLINING?

According to CPS agencies across the United States, reported and substantiated cases of child sexual abuse have declined since 1992. Lisa Jones and David Finkelhor examined the possible factors responsible for the decline (*The Decline in Child Sexual Abuse Cases,* U.S. Department of Justice, Office of Justice Programs, Office of Juvenile Justice and Delinquency Prevention, Washington, DC, January 2001).

Reported child sexual abuse cases declined 26% from an estimated 429,000 in 1991 to 315,400 in 1998. Substantiated, or confirmed, cases dropped from a peak of 149,800 in 1992 to 103,600 in 1998, a 31% decrease. (See Figure 6.1.) Between 1990 and 1992 just three states experienced a decrease in cases of substantiated child sexual abuse, compared to fourteen states reporting increases of 20% or more. The decreasing trend started between 1992 and 1994, with twenty-two states reporting a decline of 20% or more, followed by eighteen states reporting declines between 1994 and 1996. From 1996 to 1998 thirteen states showed decreases of 20% or more substantiated child sexual abuse cases. (See Figure 6.2.)

According to the authors, several factors may have influenced the decline in substantiated cases of child sexual abuse. (See Figure 6.3.) Since the 1990s the incidence of child sexual abuse may have been reduced by such factors as child victimization prevention programs, incarcer-

FIGURE 6.1

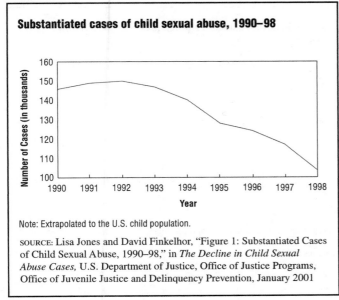

Substantiated cases of child sexual abuse, 1990–98

Note: Extrapolated to the U.S. child population.

SOURCE: Lisa Jones and David Finkelhor, "Figure 1: Substantiated Cases of Child Sexual Abuse, 1990–98," in *The Decline in Child Sexual Abuse Cases,* U.S. Department of Justice, Office of Justice Programs, Office of Juvenile Justice and Delinquency Prevention, January 2001

FIGURE 6.2

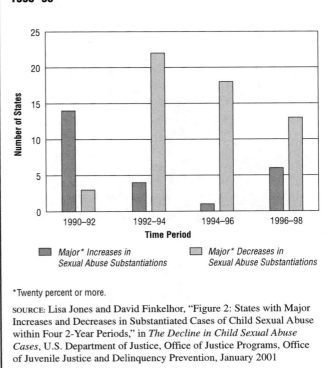

States with major increases and decreases in substantiated cases of child sexual abuse within four 2-year periods, 1990–98

*Twenty percent or more.

SOURCE: Lisa Jones and David Finkelhor, "Figure 2: States with Major Increases and Decreases in Substantiated Cases of Child Sexual Abuse within Four 2-Year Periods," in *The Decline in Child Sexual Abuse Cases,* U.S. Department of Justice, Office of Justice Programs, Office of Juvenile Justice and Delinquency Prevention, January 2001

ation of sexual offenders, treatment programs for sex offenders, as well as other variables that may cause child sexual abuse. These variables include female victimization by intimate partners and poverty. In other words, declining trends in these causal variables may play a role in the decreasing cases of child sexual abuse. Experts have shown a 30% to 60% overlap in the victimization of children and the victimization of their mothers. (See Figure 5.3 in Chapter 5.) Since 1993 a 21% decrease in female victimization by intimate partners has been reported. Poverty, down 18% between 1993 and 1998, while more often linked to cases of neglect and physical abuse, has also been found to contribute to child sexual abuse.

Jones and Finkelhor suggested that the drop in reports of child sexual abuse from 1991 to 1998 may be due to people's reluctance to report their suspicions because of widely publicized cases of false accusations. The public and mandated reporters, such as health care professionals, may also have learned accurate identification of the signs of abuse. In addition, the large numbers of sexual abuse cases that had surfaced as a result of increased vigilance starting in the 1980s may have been exhausted.

The investigation of child sexual abuse may have changed in scope. The authors noted that some CPS agencies may not be screening certain cases, such as sexual abuse by nonfamily members. Agencies with large caseloads may be investigating only cases they deem serious enough to warrant their time. These factors also affect the sexual abuse count. Changes in agency criteria of which investigated cases are substantiated may also affect the final count of substantiated cases.

Jones and Finkelhor pointed out that, if declining numbers of child sexual abuse resulted from intimidation

of child abuse reporters or changes in CPS investigative and substantiating policies, more research is needed. They suggested better training of professionals in identifying abuse. They also suggested exploring the cases that had not been investigated or substantiated and the changes in CPS procedures that caused the decline.

Researchers Revisit the Decline in Child Sexual Abuse Cases

In January 2004 David Finkelhor and Lisa M. Jones revisited the factors they discussed in 2001, which they believed might have influenced the decline in substantiated cases of child sexual abuse since 1992 (*Explanations for the Decline in Child Sexual Abuse Cases,* U.S. Department of Justice, Office of Justice Programs, Office of Juvenile Justice and Delinquency Prevention, Washington, DC, January 2004). They examined, among other things, four states with large decreases in substantiated child sexual abuse, as well as extensive information for the 1990s. The four states were Illinois, Minnesota, Oregon, and Pennsylvania. The researchers found little or no evidence that the decline resulted from CPS agencies not investigating certain cases or the diminishing number of older cases. They could not determine whether or not fear of repercussions, such as lawsuits, had contributed to the decline in mandated reporting by physicians because the states had mixed results in physician reports.

FIGURE 6.3

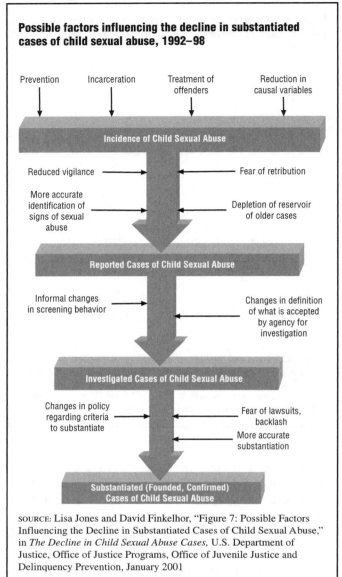

Possible factors influencing the decline in substantiated cases of child sexual abuse, 1992–98

SOURCE: Lisa Jones and David Finkelhor, "Figure 7: Possible Factors Influencing the Decline in Substantiated Cases of Child Sexual Abuse," in *The Decline in Child Sexual Abuse Cases,* U.S. Department of Justice, Office of Justice Programs, Office of Juvenile Justice and Delinquency Prevention, January 2001

FIGURE 6.4

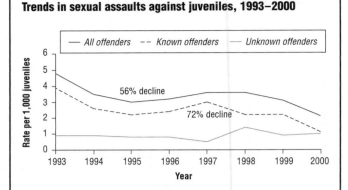

Trends in sexual assaults against juveniles, 1993–2000

Note: Juvenile victims are ages 12–17. Known offenders are family members or acquaintances, and unknown offenders are strangers or unidentified.

SOURCE: David Finkelhor and Lisa M. Jones, "Figure 12. Trends in Sexual Assaults against Juveniles, 1993–2000," in *Explanations for the Decline in Child Sexual Abuse Cases,* U.S. Department of Justice, Office of Justice Programs, Office of Juvenile Justice and Delinquency Prevention, January 2004, http://www.ncjrs.org/pdffiles1/ojjdp/199298 .pdf (accessed October 27, 2004)

FIGURE 6.5

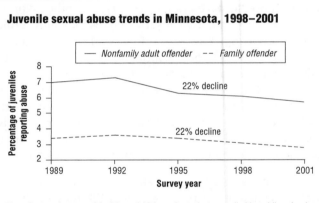

Juvenile sexual abuse trends in Minnesota, 1998–2001

Note: Respondents are 6th, 9th, and 12th grade students enrolled in public schools in selected Minnesota school districts.

SOURCE: David Finkelhor and Lisa M. Jones, "Figure 13. Juvenile Sexual Abuse Trends in Minnesota, 1998–2001," in *Explanations for the Decline in Child Sexual Abuse Cases,* U.S. Department of Justice, Office of Justice Programs, Office of Juvenile Justice and Delinquency Prevention, January 2004, http://www.ncjrs.org/pdffiles1/ojjdp/199298 .pdf (accessed October 27, 2004)

Although Finkelhor and Jones found "no solid and convincing explanation" for the decline of child sexual abuse in the 1990s, they offered two pieces of evidence for some true decline in sexual abuse cases. One piece of evidence was the results of two self-reports of sexual assault (by nonfamily members) and sexual abuse (by family members). The National Crime Victimization Survey (NCVS), an annual survey of one hundred thousand persons ages twelve to seventeen, found an overall 56% decline in self-reported sexual assault against juveniles between 1993 and 2000, with a 72% decline for sexual abuse. (See Figure 6.4). The Minnesota Student Survey, administered five times between 1989 and 2001, to students in grades six, nine, and twelve (more than 100,000 individuals), found a slight increase in the sexual abuse trend from 1989 to 1992, then a 22% decline for sexual abuse by family and nonfamily members. (See Figure 6.5.)

A SURVEY CONSIDERED A LANDMARK STUDY OF CHILD SEXUAL ABUSE

One of the early landmark studies of child sexual abuse was conducted by sociologist Diana E. H. Russell in 1978. Russell surveyed 930 adult women in San Francisco about their early sexual experiences (*The Secret Trauma: Incest in the Lives of Girls and Women,* New York, NY: Basic Books, 1986). Russell reported that 38% of the women had suffered incestuous and extrafamilial sexual abuse before their eighteenth birthday. About 16% had been abused by a family member.

Russell's study is still frequently cited by experts who believe that much more abuse occurs than is officially reported by government studies. They suggest the high results recorded in her study reflect the thoroughness of her preparation. While other studies have asked one question concerning childhood sexual abuse, she asked fourteen different questions, any one of which might have set off a memory of sexual abuse.

In 2000 Diana E. H. Russell and Rebecca M. Bolen revisited the prevalence rates reported in Russell's 1978 survey (*The Epidemic of Rape and Child Sexual Abuse in the United States,* Thousand Oaks, CA: Sage Publications, Inc.). The authors believed those rates to be underestimates. The 1978 survey subjects did not include two groups regarded to be highly probable victims of child sexual abuse: females in institutions and those not living at home. The authors also found that some women were reluctant to reveal experiences of abuse to survey interviewers, while others did not recall these experiences.

An Expert Disagrees

Richard Wexler, executive director of the National Coalition for Child Protection Reform and an expert on the child welfare system, disagreed with Russell's finding that 38% of the women in her study had experienced childhood sexual abuse (*Wounded Innocents: The Real Victims of the War against Child Abuse,* Buffalo, NY: Prometheus Books, 1990). Wexler contended that if this were correct then sexual abuse would be an enormous problem. He pointed out that the 38% included other nonfamily offenders, which did not fall under CPS jurisdiction. When only parents, stepparents, and siblings were counted, the number came out to be seven of one hundred women, instead of the one in three women Russell reported.

MULTIPLE ABUSE AND POLYINCEST

M. Sue Crowley and Brenda L. Seery sought to address what they believed to be a gap in studies on childhood sexual abuse—the study of multiple abuse and polyincest. In "Exploring the Multiplicity of Childhood Sexual Abuse with a Focus on Polyincestuous Contexts of Abuse" (*Journal of Child Sexual Abuse,* vol. 10, no. 4, 2001), the authors found that, in a sample of eighty-eight adult women undergoing treatment for childhood sexual abuse, 43% reported having been sexually molested by multiple (three or more) abusers and 23% reported having experienced polyincest. The authors described a polyincestuous situation as one in which more than one family member related by blood, adoption, or marriage is involved in the sexual abuse of other family members.

Of the eighty-eight women, thirty agreed to extensive interviews. Among this group, fourteen women reported polyincestuous abuse, including six who were molested by female relatives in addition to experiencing sexual abuse by male perpetrators. Upon disclosure of abuse, all single-abuse, multiple-abuse, and polyincest victims suffered different forms of silencing, including minimizing and denial of the abuse. Compared to single-abuse and multiple-abuse victims, victims of polyincest received very little or no support from friends and authorities. They also suffered threats from family members for revealing their abuse, therefore allowing the perpetrator to victimize the child again over time.

THE VICTIMS

Virtually all studies indicate that girls are far more likely than boys to suffer sexual abuse. Under the Harm and Endangerment Standards of NIS-3 (See Chapter 4), girls were sexually abused about three times more often than boys (Andrea J. Sedlak and Diane D. Broadhurst, *Third National Incidence Study of Child Abuse and Neglect* [NIS-3], U.S. Department of Health and Human Services, National Center on Child Abuse and Neglect, Washington, DC, 1996).

Adolescents Experience Abuse by Dating Partners

In the most comprehensive study of dating abuse among adolescents, researchers found that one of five adolescent females ages fourteen to eighteen had been a victim of physical or sexual abuse, or both, by dating partners (Jay G. Silverman, Anita Raj, Lorelei A. Mucci, and Jeanne E. Hathaway, "Dating Violence against Adolescent Girls and Associated Substance Use, Unhealthy Weight Control, Sexual Risk Behavior, Pregnancy, and Suicidality," *Journal of the American Medical Association,* vol. 286, no. 5, August 1, 2001).

The researchers analyzed the responses of Massachusetts public high school students grades nine to twelve to the 1997 and 1999 *Youth Risk Behavior Survey,* a national assessment survey conducted by states. Massachusetts was the first state to include a question about sexual and physical abuse from dating partners. Female respondents to the two surveys consisted of more than 4,100 students. The survey found that about one of five female high school students (20.2% in 1997 and 18% in 1999) in Massachusetts had been sexually and/or physically abused by a date. Silverman et al. suggested that the same proportions may be applied to the students' counterparts in the rest of the states.

Is Sexual Abuse of Boys Underreported?

Dr. William C. Holmes of the University of Pennsylvania School of Medicine claims that sexual abuse of boys is not only common but also underreported and undertreated. In "Sexual Abuse of Boys: Definition, Prevalence, Correlates, Sequelae, and Management" (*Journal of the American Medical Association,* vol. 280, no. 21, December 2, 1998), Dr. Holmes reviewed 149 studies of male sexual abuse. These studies, conducted between 1985 and 1997, included face-to-face interviews, telephone surveys, medical chart reviews, and computerized and paper questionnaires. The respondents included adolescents (ninth- through twelfth-graders, runaways, non-sex-offending delinquents, and detainees), college students, psychiatric patients, Native Americans, sex offenders (including serial rapists), substance-abusing patients, and homeless men. Dr. Holmes found that, overall, one of five boys had been sexually abused.

Dr. Holmes found that boys younger than thirteen years of age, nonwhite, of low socioeconomic status, and not living with their fathers were at a higher risk for sexual abuse. Boys whose parents had abused alcohol, had criminal records, and were divorced, separated, or remarried were more likely to experience sexual abuse. Sexually abused boys were fifteen times more likely than boys who had never been sexually abused to live in families in which some members had also been sexually abused.

Start and Duration of Abuse

Kathleen Kendall-Tackett and Roberta Marshall, in "Sexual Victimization of Children: Incest and Child Sexual Abuse" (*Issues in Intimate Violence,* Raquel Kennedy Bergen, ed., Thousand Oaks, CA: Sage Publications, Inc., 1998), reported that studies have found that the age of victims at the start of the abuse could be anywhere between seven and thirteen, although there had been cases of sexual abuse among children six years of age or younger. The sexual abuse may be a one-time occurrence or it may last for several years. The authors found durations of abuse ranging from two and a half to eight years.

In *Sexual Assault of Young Children as Reported to Law Enforcement: Victim, Incident, and Offender Characteristics* (U.S. Department of Justice, Bureau of Justice Statistics, Washington, DC, 2000), Howard N. Snyder found that 34.1% of all victims of sexual assault reported to law enforcement from 1991 to 1996 were under age twelve, with 14% (one of seven victims) under six years of age. (See Table 6.3.) (Some researchers distinguish between child sexual abuse as perpetrated by parents or caregivers and sexual assault as committed by other individuals. In this report, the term "sexual assault" included child sexual abuse.)

START AND DURATION OF ABUSE AMONG MALE VICTIMS. In his research on male child victims, Dr. Holmes found that sexual abuse generally began before puberty. About 17% to 53% of the respondents reported repeated abuse, with some victimization continuing over periods of less than six months and some victimization enduring for eighteen to forty-eight months.

THE PERPETRATORS

Howard N. Snyder (in *Sexual Assault of Young Children as Reported to Law Enforcement*) found that the

TABLE 6.3

Age profile of the victims of sexual assault, 1991–96

Victim age	All sexual assault	Forcible rape	Forcible sodomy	Sexual assault with object	Forcible fondling
Total	**100.0%**	**100.0%**	**100.0%**	**100.0%**	**100.0%**
0 to 5	14.0%	4.3%	24.0%	26.5%	20.2%
6 to 11	20.1	8.0	30.8	23.2	29.3
12 to 17	32.8	33.5	24.0	25.5	34.3
18 to 24	14.2	22.6	8.7	9.7	7.7
25 to 34	11.5	19.6	7.5	8.3	5.0
Above 34	7.4	12.0	5.1	6.8	3.5

SOURCE: Howard N. Snyder, "Table 1: Age Profile of the Victims of Sexual Assault, 1991–96," in *Sexual Assault of Young Children as Reported to Law Enforcement: Victim, Incident, and Offender Characteristics,* U.S. Department of Justice, Bureau of Justice Statistics, July 2000

abusers of young victims were more likely than the abusers of older victims to be family members. Sexual abusers whose victims were children five years old and younger were family members nearly half the time (48.6%), a number that decreased for those ages six to eleven (42.4%), and further decreased for victims ages twelve to seventeen (24.3%). (See Table 6.4.) More female victims (51.1% of those five years old and younger and 43.8% of those ages six to eleven) were abused by family members, compared with their male counterparts (42.4% of those five years old and younger and 37.7% of those ages six to eleven). (See Table 6.5.)

Fathers

David Finkelhor and Linda Meyer Williams, in *The Characteristics of Incestuous Fathers* (Family Research Laboratory, University of New Hampshire, Durham, NH, 1992), found that, generally, incestuous fathers had lonely childhoods (82%). Almost half (47%) had not lived with their own fathers and had changed living arrangements (43%), perhaps as a result of parental divorce or remarriage. Their own parents' alcohol problem, however, was no different from that of the nonabused comparison group. Incestuous fathers were far more likely to have been juvenile delinquents and to have been rejected by their parents. The researchers also found that the sex education of incestuous fathers while growing up did not come from friends or peers, but from being victims of sexual abuse. About 70% had a history of sexual abuse, with 45% having multiple abusers. Nearly three of five were sexually abused by nonfamily adults.

INCESTUOUS FATHERS' MOTIVES TO OFFEND. Carolyn Copps Hartley observed that, while incestuous fathers may share some common characteristics, there does not seem to be a single profile of these offenders. Hartley sought to explore "incest offenders' perceptions of their own motives for sexually offending" ("Incest Offenders' Perceptions of Their Motives to Sexually

TABLE 6.4

Victim-offender relationship in sexual assault, 1991–96

Victim age	Total	Family member	Acquaintance	Stranger
		Offenders		
All victims	**100.0%**	**26.7%**	**59.6%**	**13.8%**
Juveniles	**100.0%**	**34.2%**	**58.7%**	**7.0%**
0 to 5	100.0	48.6	48.3	3.1
6 to 11	100.0	42.4	52.9	4.7
12 to 17	100.0	24.3	66.0	9.8
Adults	**100.0%**	**11.5%**	**61.1%**	**27.3%**
18 to 24	100.0	9.8	66.5	23.7
Above 24	100.0	12.8	57.1	30.1

SOURCE: Howard N. Snyder, "Table 6: Victim–Offender Relationship in Sexual Assault," in *Sexual Assault of Young Children as Reported to Law Enforcement: Victim, Incident, and Offender Characteristics*, U.S. Department of Justice, Bureau of Justice Statistics, July 2000

TABLE 6.5

Victim-offender relationship in sexual assault, by victim gender, 1991–96

Victim age	Total	Family member	Acquaintance	Stranger
		Offenders		
Female victims	**100.0%**	**25.7%**	**59.5%**	**14.7%**
Juveniles	100.0%	33.9	58.7	7.5
0 to 5	100.0	51.1	45.9	3.0
6 to 11	100.0	43.8	51.4	4.8
12 to 17	100.0	24.3	65.7	10.0
Adults	100.0%	11.5	61.0	27.5
18 to 24	100.0	9.8	66.4	23.8
Above 24	100.0	12.9	56.9	30.2
Male victims	**100.0%**	**32.8%**	**59.8%**	**7.3%**
Juveniles	100.0%	35.8	59.2	5.0
0 to 5	100.0	42.4	54.1	3.5
6 to 11	100.0	37.7	57.7	4.6
12 to 17	100.0	23.7	68.7	7.6
Adults	100.0%	11.3	63.9	24.8
18 to 24	100.0	10.7	68.4	20.9
Above 24	100.0	11.8	60.3	27.9

SOURCE: Howard N. Snyder, "Table 6: Victim–Offender Relationship in Sexual Assault, by Victim Gender, 1991–96" in *Sexual Assault of Young Children as Reported to Law Enforcement: Victim, Incident, and Offender Characteristics*, U.S. Department of Justice, Bureau of Justice Statistics, July 2000

Offend within Their Past and Current Life Context," *Journal of Interpersonal Violence,* vol. 16, no. 5, May 2001). Study participants were eight incestuous fathers or father figures. Three were biological fathers, four were stepfathers, and one was an adoptive father. All victims were females who were between the ages of six and fifteen when the sexual abuse was revealed. The offenders were undergoing treatment when they participated in the study. Seven were white and one was Hispanic. The duration of the sexual abuse ranged from several incidents within six months to ongoing contacts spanning five years.

All participants reported that sexual gratification was part of their motive for sexually abusing their daughters. Half of the men gave sexual gratification as their primary motive, saying that sex was very important in their lives. All fathers reported being dissatisfied with their lives when the abuse began; however, just three men said their abuse of their daughters was an outlet for that dissatisfaction. Three fathers thought they sexually abused their daughters because they were angry with their wives or to get back at someone because they themselves had suffered sexual abuse during childhood. Half of the fathers felt they had sex with their daughters out of affection, perceiving the girls as adults.

Hartley also explored how the incestuous fathers perceived their motives to sexually offend within the context of their childhood and current life circumstances. While the men felt their life circumstances at the time of the abuse might have influenced their decision to abuse their daughters, they could not make a connection between their unstable childhood environments and the sexual offense against their daughters. The men reported that, at the time of the abuse, they were experiencing marital/partner problems. As children, the participants had little or no relationship with their fathers. Although they reported having more of a relationship with their mothers, their mothers were physically present but not nurturing. Half

reported childhood physical abuse, and six men reported emotional abuse. The author noted that research has shown that these childhood experiences may result in poor attachment (failure to form meaningful relationships in early age) and low self-esteem that may be factors in the sexual offending of children.

Women Who Abuse

Until recently, experts thought female sex abusers were uncommon. When women were involved in abuse, it was thought to be a situation in which a man had forced the woman to commit the abuse. Some experts postulate that women are more maternal and, therefore, less likely to abuse a child. Women are also thought to have different attitudes toward sex. While a man ties his feelings of self-worth to his sexual experiences, a woman is supposedly less concerned with sexual prowess and tends to be more empathetic toward others.

Some researchers have proposed that the abusive behavior of women is influenced by severe psychiatric disturbance, mental retardation, brain damage, or male coercion. C. Allen studied female offenders in *A Comparative Analysis of Women Who Sexually Abuse Children* (Final Report to the National Center on Child Abuse and Neglect, Iowa State University, 1990) and found that their lives involved particularly harsh childhoods marked by instability and abuse.

Comparing male and female offenders, Allen found that the women reported more severe incidents of physical and emotional abuse in their pasts, had run away from home more often, were more sexually promiscuous than male offenders, and had more frequent incidents of being paid for sex. Both male and female offenders reported that their victims were most often members of their own families.

Because they perceived child sexual abuse as a great social deviance, female offenders were less likely to admit guilt. They were less cooperative than men during the investigations and were angrier with informants and investigators. Following disclosure, they also appeared to experience less guilt and sorrow than male offenders.

MOTHERS. Sexual abuse by mothers may remain undetected because it occurs at home and is either denied or never reported. Mothers generally have more intimate contact with their children, and the lines between maternal love and care and sexual abuse are not as clear-cut as they are for fathers. Furthermore, society is reluctant to see a woman as a perpetrator of incest, portraying the woman as someone likely to turn her pain inward into depression, compared with the man who acts out his anger in sexually criminal behavior.

Siblings

Sibling incest is another form of abuse that has not been well studied. Some experts, however, believe that sibling sexual abuse is more common than father–daughter incest. Vernon R. Wiehe believed that the problem of sibling incest had not received much attention because of the families' reluctance to report to authorities that such abuse is happening at home, the parents' playing down the fact that "it" is indeed a problem, and the perception that it is normal for brothers and sisters to explore their sexuality ("Sibling Abuse," *Understanding Family Violence: Treating and Preventing Partner, Child, Sibling, and Elder Abuse,* Thousand Oaks, CA: Sage Publications, Inc., 1998).

Wiehe also felt that a very serious factor is that the victim may be living with threats of real harm from the abusive sibling. Indeed, in the author's nationwide survey of survivors of sibling abuse, the incest victims reported an interaction of physical abuse and incest, such as threats of physical harm, or even death, if the parents were told. An interaction of emotional abuse and incest might involve constant humiliation of the victim from the sibling perpetrator, such as comments that the victim was no longer a virgin.

Wiehe believed that sexual abuse by a sibling should be considered a crime of rape because the perpetrator uses aggression, force, or threats. Moreover, the consequences to the victim are the same whether the sexual abuse takes the form of fondling or intercourse.

Educators

Sex between educators and students is nothing new. However, except for sensational cases, such as that of Washington teacher Mary Kay Letourneau who was charged with child rape of her twelve-year-old student and served a seven-and-a-half-year term, other cases have not received much attention. Some experts have observed that there seems to be a double standard in cases involving a female teacher and a male student. They point to an example in New Jersey. In 2002 Superior Court Judge Bruce A. Gaeta refused to sentence Pamela Diehl-Moore to prison for pleading guilty to sexual assault and instead ordered probation. The teacher admitted having sex for six months with a thirteen-year-old student. The judge claimed he saw no harm done to the student and that the relationship might have been a way for the boy to satisfy his sexual needs. Gaeta received public reprimand for his comments. Diehl-Moore was sentenced to three years in prison upon appeal.

In 2004 Charol Shakeshaft, a professor of educational policies at Hofstra University in Huntington, New York, reported that no national study of public school educators who have abused students had even been done. In compliance with the No Child Left Behind Act of 2001 (Public Law 107-110), the U.S. Department of Education commissioned Shakeshaft to conduct a national study of sexual abuse in schools. After identifying about nine hundred literature citations that discussed educator sexual misconduct and contacting over one thousand researchers, educators, and policymakers on the issue, Shakeshaft found just fourteen U.S. and five Canadian/British empirical studies on educator sexual misconduct. (Empirical studies are based on practical observations and not theory.) With scant empirical studies on hand, she based her conclusion on two American Association of University Women (AAUW) *Hostile Hallways* surveys conducted in 1993 and 2000 involving about 2,065 public school students in grades eight to eleven. Both were the author's own work. In addition, Shakeshaft used her 2003 reanalysis of the surveys for additional data on educator sexual misconduct.

In *Educator Sexual Misconduct: A Synthesis of Existing Literature* (U.S. Department of Education, Office of the Under Secretary, Washington, DC, 2004), Shakeshaft projected the numbers in her surveys to the whole public school system. She concluded that 9.6% of public school children, accounting for 4.5 million students, experienced sexual misconduct by educators. Educators included teachers and other school officials, such as principals, coaches, counselors, substitute teachers, teacher's aides, security guards, bus drivers, and other employees.

The studies Shakeshaft analyzed did not reveal the number or proportion of educators who were perpetrators of sexual misconduct. However, Shakeshaft's surveys showed that students reported sexual misconduct by 18% teachers, 15% coaches, and 13% substitute teachers. Principals accounted for 6%, and school counselors made up 5%. The author observed that teachers whose jobs involve dealing with individual students, such as coaches and music teachers, are more likely than other educators to sexually abuse students. With regard to the gender of the perpetrators, the different studies showed a range of 4% to 43% for female educators and a range of 57% to 96% for male educators.

Deputy Secretary of Education Eugene W. Hickok wrote in the preface of the report that Shakeshaft's use of the terms "sexual abuse" and "sexual misconduct" interchangeably might be confusing to the reader. The law that mandated the study used "sexual abuse," a term that has a specific definition under the law and carries a penalty of a fine or imprisonment, or both. Moreover, he noted that Shakeshaft included several types of inappropriate behaviors under "sexual misconduct," ranging from telling sexual jokes, to showing pictures of a sexual nature, to sexual intercourse. Some critics claimed the report is based not on a synthesis of several studies but only on studies by the author. Some teachers' unions believe the report is misleading and will harm their profession. Shakeshaft believed that the AAUW studies provided the most reliable data on educator sexual conduct across the nation. She recommended that the Education Department should revisit the issue and that educators should play an active role in examining the problem.

Babysitters

As more and more working parents depend on outside help to care for their children, law enforcement has recognized the importance of collecting information about these caregivers. Although the Federal Bureau of Investigation National Incident-Based Reporting System will eventually replace its Uniform Crime Report program as the national statistical database of crimes reported to law enforcement, it has not yet evolved into a complete national system. Nonetheless, its four-year (1995 through 1998) compiled data about the offenses against children committed by babysitters showed more than 1,435 victimizations.

In *Crimes against Children by Babysitters* (U.S. Department of Justice, Office of Justice Programs, Office of Juvenile Justice and Delinquency Prevention, Washington, DC, September 2001), David Finkelhor and Richard Ormrod reported that about two-thirds (65%) of babysitter offenses reported to police were sex offenses. Forcible fondling comprised 41% of the sex offenses, followed by 11% of sodomy, and 9% of rape. Another 3% represented sexual assault with an object. (See Figure 6.6.) In comparison, simple assault accounted for approximately 25% of babysitter offenses, and aggravated assault accounted for another 9%.

Overall, 63% of babysitters reported for offenses against children were male and 37% were female. Males were more likely to be involved in sexual offenses, accounting for 77% of these cases. A majority (71%) of

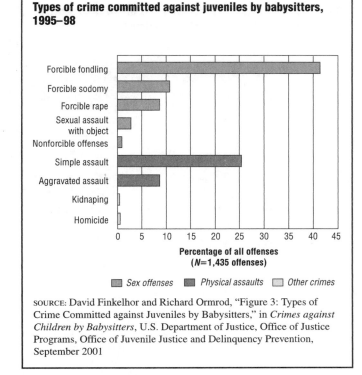

FIGURE 6.6

Types of crime committed against juveniles by babysitters, 1995–98

Percentage of all offenses
(*N*=1,435 offenses)

■ Sex offenses   ■ Physical assaults   □ Other crimes

SOURCE: David Finkelhor and Richard Ormrod, "Figure 3: Types of Crime Committed against Juveniles by Babysitters," in *Crimes against Children by Babysitters*, U.S. Department of Justice, Office of Justice Programs, Office of Juvenile Justice and Delinquency Prevention, September 2001

male sex offenders victimized females and more than half (54%) victimized children under six years of age. Female sex offenders, however, nearly equally victimized female (46%) and male (54%) children, and more than two-thirds (68%) of their victims were younger children ages zero to six. (See Figure 6.7.) Babysitter sex offenders were generally teens (48%). Nevertheless, while female sex offenders were more likely to be adolescents ages thirteen to fifteen (67%), male sex offenders tended to be adults (58%).

Sexual Abusers of Boys

Dr. William C. Holmes's review of 149 studies of boys and young male adolescents who experienced sexual abuse revealed that more than 90% of their abusers were male ("Sexual Abuse of Boys: Definition, Prevalence, Correlates, Sequelae, and Management"). Male abusers of older male teenagers and young male adults, however, made up 22% to 73% of perpetrators. This older age group also experienced abuse by females, ranging from 27% to 78%. Adolescent babysitters accounted for up to half of female sexual abusers of younger boys.

More than half of those who sexually abused male children were not family members, but were known to the victims. Boys younger than six years old were more likely to be sexually abused by family and acquaintances, while those older than twelve were more likely to be victims of strangers. While male perpetrators used physical force, with threats of physical harm increasing with victim age, female perpetrators used persuasion and promises of spe-

FIGURE 6.7

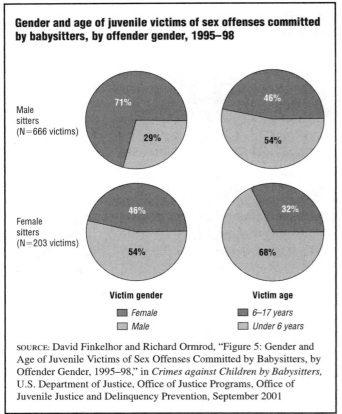

Gender and age of juvenile victims of sex offenses committed by babysitters, by offender gender, 1995–98

Male sitters (N=666 victims)

71% 29%

46% 54%

Female sitters (N=203 victims)

46% 54%

32% 68%

Victim gender

- ■ Female
- □ Male

Victim age

- ■ 6–17 years
- □ Under 6 years

SOURCE: David Finkelhor and Richard Ormrod, "Figure 5: Gender and Age of Juvenile Victims of Sex Offenses Committed by Babysitters, by Offender Gender, 1995–98," in *Crimes against Children by Babysitters,* U.S. Department of Justice, Office of Justice Programs, Office of Juvenile Justice and Delinquency Prevention, September 2001

cial favors. One study reviewed by Dr. Holmes found that up to one-third of boys participated in the abuse out of curiosity.

Pedophiles

At one time, a pedophile was stereotyped as a lonely, isolated man who generally sought employment that permitted contact with children. Experts now know that men or women, heterosexual or gay, married or single, may be pedophiles. Examples include the pediatric dentist who anesthetized his patients and photographed them in lewd positions. Another molester was a high school teacher who had sex with her students during tutoring sessions at her home. Still another was a police officer who made more than one thousand videotapes of young boys performing sex acts.

PEDOPHILES ON THE INTERNET. Many pedophiles have found that the Internet gives them easy access to children. According to the Office for Victims of Crime of the U.S. Department of Justice, child predators who look for victims in places where children typically congregate, such as schoolyards, playgrounds, and shopping malls, now have cyberspace to commit their criminal acts (*Internet Crimes against Children,* February 2001). The Internet presents an even more attractive venue because predators can commit their crimes anonymously and are able to contact the same child on a regular basis. They may groom

children online for the production of child pornography. They have been known to prey on vulnerable children, gaining their confidence online, and then traveling for the purpose of engaging their victims in sex acts.

Increasingly large numbers of children use the Internet (*A Nation Online: How Americans Are Expanding Their Use of the Internet,* U.S. Department of Commerce, Economics and Statistics Administration, National Telecommunications and Information Administration, February 2002). In 2001 more than thirty-two million children ages three to seventeen used the Internet, up from about eighteen million in 1998. More than three-fourths (75.6%) of those ages fourteen to seventeen used the Internet at some location, up from 51.2% in 1998. Among children ages ten to thirteen, the proportion of those using the Internet rose from 39.2% (1998) to 65.4% (2001). Even children ages five to nine more than doubled their Internet use, from 16.8% (1998) to 38.9% (2001). (See Figure 6.8.)

Julian Fantino, chief of police of the Toronto Police Service of Ontario, Canada, noted that more and more younger children were being used in child pornography, with a large proportion being infants and preschool children ("Child Pornography on the Internet: New Challenges Require New Ideas," *The Police Chief,* International Association of Chiefs of Police, Alexandria, VA, December 2003). Offenders form secret clubs, sharing modes of operation and protecting one another's identities. According to Fantino, in 2003 more than 100,000 Web sites contained child pornography.

FIRST NATIONAL SURVEY ON THE ONLINE VICTIMIZATION OF CHILDREN. In the first national survey on the risks children face on the Internet, researchers found that nearly one of five youths (19%) using the Internet in the last year had received an unwanted sexual solicitation or approach. Sexual solicitations involved requests to do sexual things the children did not want to do, while sexual approaches involved incidents in which persons tried to get children to talk about sex when they did not want to or asked them intimate questions (*Online Victimization: A Report on the Nation's Youth,* David Finkelhor, Kimberly J. Mitchell, and Janis Wolak, Crimes against Children Research Center, University of New Hampshire, Durham, NH, and the National Center for Missing and Exploited Children, Alexandria, VA, June 2000). In addition, one of four children (25%) reported at least one unwanted exposure to sexual material (pictures of naked people or people having sex) while surfing the Web the past year.

TEENS COMMUNICATE WITH STRANGERS ONLINE. A study released by the Pew Internet & American Life Project found that adolescents who have Internet access do communicate with strangers they meet online (Amanda Lenhart, Lee Rainie, and Oliver Lewis, *Teenage Life Online: The Rise of the Instant-Message Generation and*

FIGURE 6.8

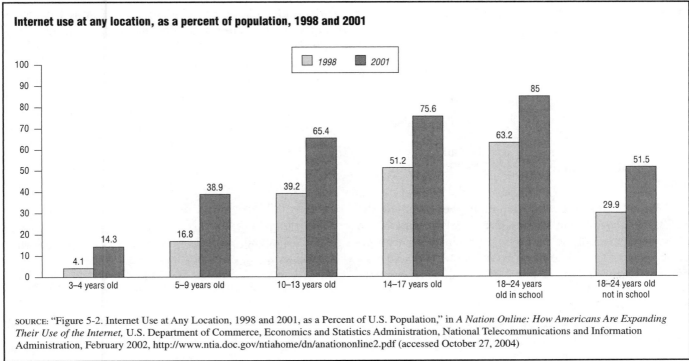

Internet use at any location, as a percent of population, 1998 and 2001

SOURCE: "Figure 5-2. Internet Use at Any Location, 1998 and 2001, as a Percent of U.S. Population," in *A Nation Online: How Americans Are Expanding Their Use of the Internet,* U.S. Department of Commerce, Economics and Statistics Administration, National Telecommunications and Information Administration, February 2002, http://www.ntia.doc.gov/ntiahome/dn/anationonline2.pdf (accessed October 27, 2004)

the Internet's Impact on Friendships and Family Relationships, Washington, DC, June 20, 2001). About three of five (60%) of online teens (ages twelve to seventeen) surveyed by Pew reported that they had received e-mails or instant messages from strangers. About 63% of those who had received e-mails or instant messages from strangers had answered such messages. Teens also said that they had lied about their age to get on a Web site with pornography. Boys (19%) were more likely than girls (11%) to have done so.

Pedophile Priests

On July 23, 2003, Massachusetts Attorney General Thomas F. Reilly released a report, *The Sexual Abuse of Children in the Roman Catholic Archdiocese of Boston: A Report by the Attorney General,* describing the culture of secrecy involving the sexual abuse of an estimated one thousand minors in the Archdiocese of Boston since 1940. Reilly's eighteen-month investigation found, "There is overwhelming evidence that for many years Cardinal [Bernard] Law and his senior managers had direct, actual knowledge that substantial numbers of children in the Archdiocese had been sexually abused by substantial numbers of priests."

Attorney General Reilly started the investigation in March 2002 soon after John Geoghan, a former priest in the Archdiocese of Boston, was sentenced to nine to ten years in prison for sexually abusing a ten-year-old boy. Reilly's investigators found that starting in 1979 the archdiocese had received complaints of child sexual abuse against Geoghan. Some 130 more people had brought accusations

against the priest. Church documents, which had previously been sealed, revealed that the church not only moved him from parish to parish but had also paid settlements amounting to $15 million to the victims' families. Reilly reported that the archdiocese's own files showed that 789 persons had brought sexual complaints against the Boston clergy. The attorney general believed the actual number of victims is higher. About 240 priests and church workers had been accused of rape and sexual assault.

EXTENT OF CHILD SEXUAL ABUSE BY PRIESTS. In June 2002 the United States Conference of Catholic Bishops commissioned a study of the nature and scope of the problem of child sexual abuse in the Catholic Church. The John Jay College of Criminal Justice of the City University of New York (New York, NY) conducted the study based on information provided by 195 dioceses, representing 98% of all diocesan priests in the United States. The researchers also collected data from 140 religious communities, accounting for about 60% of religious communities and 80% of all priests in the religious communities.

A report of the study was released on February 27, 2004. *The Nature and Scope of the Problem of Sexual Abuse of Minors by Catholic Priests and Deacons in the United States* (United States Conference of Catholic Bishops, Washington, DC) covered the period 1950–2002. Of the 109,694 priests and deacons (collectively referred to as priests) who served during this time period, 4,392 (4%) allegedly abused children under age eighteen. Most of the priests (55.7%) had a single allegation of abuse. Nearly

27% had two to three allegations, 13.9% had four to nine allegations, and 3.5% had ten or more allegations.

The survey showed that 10,667 individuals made allegations of child sexual abuse by priests between 1950 and 2002. About 81% of the victims were male and 19% were female. About half (50.9%) were between the ages of eleven and fourteen. More than a quarter (27.3%) were fifteen to seventeen years old, 16% were ages eight to ten, and 6% were younger than seven. One survey question asked whether or not a sibling was also allegedly abused. Of the 6,350 individuals that provided this information, 1,842 answered "yes."

The largest number of allegations were made in the 1970s (35.3%) and the 1960s (26.1%). At the time of the allegations, most of the priests were serving in the capacity of pastors (25.1%), associate pastors (42.3%), and resident priests (10.4%). About 7.2% of the priests were teachers, 2.7% were chaplains, and 1.8% were seminary administrators or faculty members. The remaining 10.5% were bishops, vicars, cardinals, chancellors, deacons, seminarians, priests performing other functions, and priests who were relatives of the victims.

Most of the abuse occurred in the priest's home or parish residence (40.9%), in church (16.3%), and in the victim's home (12.4%). Nearly half (49.6%) of the priests socialized with the alleged victim's family, mostly (79.6%) in the family's home.

THE EFFECTS OF CHILD SEXUAL ABUSE

Effects on Children and Adults

According to the American Psychological Association (APA), children who have been sexually abused exhibit a range of symptoms (*Understanding Child Sexual Abuse: Education, Prevention, and Recovery,* Washington, DC, October 1999). The immediate effects may include thumb sucking and/or bed wetting; sleep disturbances; eating problems; and school problems, including misconduct, problems with performing schoolwork, and failure to participate in activities.

The APA also detailed long-term effects of childhood sexual abuse. Adult victims of childhood sexual abuse may suffer from depression, sexual dysfunction, and anxiety. Anxiety may manifest itself in such behaviors as anxiety attacks, insomnia, and alcohol and drug abuse. Adult survivors of childhood sexual abuse also report revictimization, as rape victims or as victims of intimate physical abuse.

A Longitudinal Study of the Effects of Child Sexual Abuse

In the first study of its kind, researchers sought to determine the impact of child sexual abuse on adult mental health, parenting relationships, and the adjustment of the children of mothers who had been victims of childhood sexual abuse (Ron Roberts, Tom O'Connor, Judy Dunn, Jean Golding, and the ALSPAC Study Team, "The Effects of Child Sexual Abuse in Later Family Life: Mental Health, Parenting and Adjustment of Offspring," *Child Abuse & Neglect,* vol. 28, issue 5, May 2004). Roberts et al. investigated 8,292 families, a subsample of the Avon Longitudinal Study of Parents and Children (ALSPAC), a continuing study of women and their families in Avon, England. The participating women had self-reported experiences of sexual assault before adolescence. Four family groups were included:

- Single mother families (9% of the study sample)—Consist of a nonmarried woman with no partner and her children

- Biological families (79.5%)—Consist of two parents and their biological children with no other children from previous relationships

- Stepmother/Complex stepfamilies (4.6%)—Consist of fathers with at least one biological child (living in the household or visiting regularly) who is not the biological offspring of the mother

- Stepfather families (6.9%)—Consist of a mother and at least one biological child (living in the household or visiting regularly) who is not the biological offspring of the father

The study revealed that more than a quarter (26%) of survivors of child sexual abuse had teen pregnancies. These women were disproportionately likely to be currently living in a nontradional family—single mother families (3%) and stepfather families (2.9%)—than to be living in biological families (1.3%). The researchers did not have a similar finding when it came to stepmother/complex stepfamilies. In this group just 0.8% reported child sexual abuse. They surmised that a woman who has experienced child sexual abuse tends to choose a partner without children because she might feel inadequate to take care of more children.

Child sexual abuse also has consequences on the adult survivors' mental health. Mothers who reported child sexual abuse were likely to report more depression and anxiety and lower self-esteem. These mental problems in turn affect the mothers' relationship with their children and the children's adjustment. Mothers with a history of child sexual abuse reported less confidence in themselves and less positive relationships with their children. The children were hyperactive and had emotional, peer, and conduct problems.

High-Risk Sexual Behaviors in Adolescent Girls

A sample of 125 adolescents ages twelve to seventeen comprised the subjects of a study designed to examine the sexual at-risk behaviors of female adolescents who had experienced sexual abuse (Caroline Cinq-Mars, John Wright, Mireille Cyr, and Pierre McDuff, "Sexual At-Risk

Behaviors of Sexually Abused Adolescent Girls," *Journal of Child Sexual Abuse,* vol. 12, no. 2, 2003). The researchers administered a self-report questionnaire that asked about the subjects' sexual activities, which did not involve sexual abuse experiences. Then the subjects were interviewed regarding their sexual abuse experiences, including information about the perpetrator (both family and nonfamily members), frequency and duration of abuse, severity of the abuse, and whether or not they told someone of the abuse.

Among offending family members, fathers were the perpetrators in 30.4% of incidents. Stepfathers and extended family members each were responsible for 28.8% of the sexual abuse, and brothers accounted for another 9.6% of abuse. The victims experienced more than one incident of sexual abuse, with the mean number of perpetrators per victim being 1.8. The mean age for the start of abuse was 9.3 years. More than one-third (36.8%) of the victims experienced sexual abuse before age eleven.

More than half (55.3%) of the participants reported being sexually active. More than half (54.5%) had their first consensual intercourse before the age of fifteen. The rate of pregnancy was 15%. The researchers found three sexual abuse characteristics that were associated with the adolescents' sexual at-risk behavior. Adolescents who experienced childhood sexual abuse involving penetration were more than thirteen times as likely to have been pregnant and twice as likely to have more than one consensual partner in the past year. Having been abused by more than one perpetrator (in one or more incidents) was also closely associated with at-risk behaviors—pregnancy (eight times as likely), more than one consensual sexual partner (four times as likely), and irregular condom use (three times as likely). Finally, physical coercion during abuse increased the odds of pregnancy (four times as likely), more than one consensual sexual partner (five times as likely), and irregular condom use (three times as likely).

Relationship between Male Child Sexual Abuse and Teen Pregnancy

More than 4,100 men in a primary care setting were interviewed regarding whether or not they had ever impregnated an adolescent girl (Robert F. Anda, Vincent J. Felitti, Daniel P. Chapman, Janet B. Croft, David F. Williamson, John Santelli, Patricia M. Dietz, and James S. Marks, "Abused Boys, Battered Mothers, and Male Involvement in Teen Pregnancy," *Pediatrics,* vol. 107, no. 2, February 2001). The study found that men with a history of childhood sexual or physical abuse or of witnessing physical abuse of their mother were more likely to have been involved in teenage pregnancy. About 19% of the men reported ever getting a girl pregnant during adolescence and adulthood. The girls were between twelve and nineteen years old. About 59% of the men were age twenty or older at the time they impregnated the girls.

One-fourth (25.5%) of men who experienced childhood sexual abuse indicated having impregnated teen girls, compared to 17.8% of those who had not been sexually abused as children. Those whose sexual abuse was characterized by physical force or threat of harm were about twice as likely to have impregnated a teenage girl. Those who were abused at age ten and under showed an 80% increased risk of getting a teenage girl pregnant.

Effects of Abuse by Females

Myriam S. Denov of the University of Ottawa, Ontario, Canada, conducted a qualitative study of the long-term effects of childhood sexual abuse by women. Unlike quantitative research, which involves collecting samples of quantitative data and performing some form of statistical analysis, qualitative research is based on a smaller sample of individuals and does not represent the general population. However, according to Denov, the qualitative approach "is particularly appropriate for a study of this nature as it can give depth and detail of phenomena that are difficult to convey with quantitative methods" ("The Long-Term Effects of Child Sexual Abuse by Female Perpetrators: A Qualitative Study of Male and Female Victims," *Journal of Interpersonal Violence,* vol. 19, no. 10, October 2004).

The study sample consisted of seven males and seven females, who ranged in age from twenty-three to fifty-nine years. The sexual abuse occurred when they were fourteen years old or younger. All participants reported at least one incident of sexual abuse by a lone female perpetrator. Five participants reported having been sexually abused by more than one lone perpetrator. Nine participants were abused by a female relative—six by their mother, two by their mother and grandmother, and one by his mother and sister. Four participants were abused by an unrelated person—three by a babysitter and one by a nun at a local church. While the study concerns abuse perpetrated by women, half (or seven) of the participants reported having also been sexually abused by a man (in a separate incident from the abuse by women)—four by their father, two by an unrelated male babysitter, and one by his older half-brother.

The sexual abuse started, on average, at age five and ended, on average, at age twelve. It lasted about six years. Five participants were abused more than once a week, three were abused once a week, and four were abused once a month. Two participants reported a single episode of abuse. All participants reported mild abuse (for example, kissing in a sexual way and sexual invitations). In addition, ten reported moderate abuse (genital contact or fondling [without penetration] and simulated intercourse). Nine participants experienced severe abuse (such as intercourse and penetration with fingers or objects).

Denov observed that, while many effects of sexual abuse by females seem similar to that by males, female sexual abuse has long-term effects that are unique. Of the fourteen study participants, just one (a male) indicated he did not feel damaged by the sexual abuse by a woman. The other thirteen said they felt damaged by the abuse. All seven participants who were also abused by males reported that the sexual abuse by women was more damaging. The effects of child sexual abuse included substance abuse (used to "silence their rage and numb the pain"), self-injury, thoughts of suicide, depression, and rage. All victims reported a great mistrust of women and a discomfort with sexual intimacy. Most of the female victims were confused about their sense of identity and self-concept. Five of seven said that, as young girls, they did not want to grow up to be women. Four women confessed that they continued to deny their femininity, one victim admitting that she dressed in an unwomanly fashion because she would be safest to herself and to others. Twelve participants feared they might sexually abuse their own children. In fact, two men and two women reported having sexually abused children. One man and three women decided not to have children.

Male Victims' Perception of Childhood Sexual Abuse and Clinical Findings

Dr. Holmes's review of studies of male child sexual abuse ("Sexual Abuse of Boys: Definition, Prevalence, Correlates, Sequelae, and Management," *Journal of the American Medical Association,* vol. 280, no. 21, December 2, 1998) found that only 15% to 39% of victims who responded to the studies thought that they were adversely affected by the sexual abuse. The victims stressed that the adverse effects were linked to the use of force, a great difference in victim–perpetrator age, or cases in which the perpetrator was much older, or the victim was very young. Dr. Holmes noted, however, that negative clinical results (in contrast to what the studies' subjects reported) included posttraumatic stress disorder, major depression, paranoia, aggressive behavior, poor self-image, poor school performance, and running away from home.

Dr. Holmes also found a connection between sexual abuse and subsequent substance abuse among male victims. Sexually abused males were also more likely to have sex-related problems, including sexual dysfunction, hypersexuality, and the tendency to force sex on others. He surmised that the discrepancy between the respondents' perceptions of the negative consequences of their sexual victimization and those discovered in clinical outcomes may be due to several factors. Dr. Holmes observed that perhaps abused males believe they have failed to protect themselves as society expects them to do. Instead of owning up to their failure, they resort to not giving much gravity to their experiences. Moreover, if the victims had experienced pleasure while being abused, they may be confused by their feelings about it.

A Risk for Substance Abuse

Studies have shown that childhood abuse increases the risk for substance abuse later in life. A five-year study by McLean Hospital researchers in Belmont, Massachusetts, uncovered how this occurs (Carl M. Anderson, Martin H. Teicher, Ann Polcari, and Perry F. Renshaw, "Abnormal T2 Relaxation Time in the Cerebellar Vermis of Adults Sexually Abused in Childhood: Potential Role of the Vermis in Stress-Enhanced Risk for Drug Abuse," *Psychoneuroendocrinology,* vol. 27, no. 1–2, January 2002). Anderson et al. found that the vermis, the region flanked by the cerebellar hemispheres of the brain, may play a key role in the risk for substance abuse among adults who have experienced child abuse. The vermis develops gradually and continues to produce neurons, or nerve cells, after birth. It is known to be sensitive to stress, so that stress can influence its development.

The researchers compared young adults ages eighteen to twenty-two, including eight with a history of repeated childhood sexual abuse (CSA) and sixteen others as the control group. Using functional magnetic resonance imaging (fMRI) technology, the researchers measured the resting blood flow in the vermis. They found that the subjects who had been victims of CSA had diminished blood flow. Anderson and his colleagues suggested that the stress experienced with repeated CSA may have caused damage to the vermis, which in turn could not perform its job of controlling irritability in the limbic system. The limbic system in the center of the brain, a collection of connected clusters of nerve cells, is responsible for, among other things, regulating emotions and memory. The damaged vermis, therefore, induces a person to use drugs or alcohol to suppress the irritability.

Since the CSA subjects had no history of alcohol or substance abuse, Anderson and his colleagues wanted to confirm their findings, which linked an impaired cerebellar vermis and the potential for substance abuse in CSA victims. The researchers analyzed test data collected from the 537 college students recruited for the study. They found that students who reported frequent substance abuse showed higher irritability in the limbic system. They also exhibited symptoms usually associated with drug use, including depression and anger.

A Risk for Illicit Drug Use

A total of 1,478 noninjecting female sexual partners of male injection-drug users were the subjects of a study by Robert C. Freeman, Karyn Collier, and Kathleen M. Parillo ("Early Life Sexual Abuse as a Risk Factor for Crack Cocaine Use in a Sample of Community-Recruited Women at High Risk for Illicit Drug Use," *American Journal of Drug and Alcohol Abuse,* vol. 28, no. 1, February 2002). Nearly two-thirds (63.7%) of the women reported having used crack cocaine. The researchers found that an equal proportion of all women had suffered sexual abuse before age twelve (39.5%) and during adolescence (38.8%). Overall, nearly 22% were sexually abused during both childhood and adolescence.

While Freeman et al. found a relationship between childhood sexual abuse and lifetime crack use, they found no direct link between sexual abuse during adolescence and lifetime crack use. They did find, however, some indirect connections between the two. Female teens who were victims of sexual abuse were more likely to run away, and these runaways were more likely to use crack because of the type of people with whom they associated.

Sexual Revictimization

Abused females were the subjects in a longitudinal study that examined the impact of child sexual abuse on female development. This was the first prospective study that followed children from the time sexual abuse was reported through adolescence and into early adulthood (Jennie G. Noll, Lisa A. Horowitz, George A. Bonanno, Penelope K. Trickett, and Frank W. Putnam, "Revictimization and Self-Harm in Females Who Experienced Childhood Sexual Abuse: Results from a Prospective Study," *Journal of Interpersonal Violence,* vol. 18, no. 12, December 2003). Referred by child protective services agencies, the participants experienced sexual abuse by a family member before the age of fourteen. The median age at the start of sexual abuse was seven to eight years, and the median duration of abuse was two years. The group consisted of eighty-four abused children and a comparison group of eighty-two children. Two yearly interviews followed the first assessment of the group. A fourth interview was conducted four to five years after the third interview.

Noll et al. noted that this study was the first to provide information about the revictimization of child sexual abuse survivors not long after their abuse (seven years after the abuse when the participants were in their adolescence and early adulthood). The study found that participants who had been sexually abused during childhood were twice as likely as the comparison group to have experienced sexual revictimization, such as rape or sexual assault, and almost four times as likely to harm themselves through suicide attempts or self-mutilation. They also suffered about 1.6 times more physical victimization, such as domestic violence. Compared to the nonabused group, the abused group reported 20% more significant lifetime traumas subsequent to being sexually abused. Significant lifetime traumas reported by the participants included separation and losses (for example, having family or friends move away or die), emotional abuse and/or rejection by family, natural disasters, and witnessing violence.

The researchers observed that childhood sexual abuse is the "strongest predictor of self-harm" even when other types of abuse are present. They surmised that the victims may have negative feelings toward their own body and want to hurt it. They wrote that some researchers believe victims may want to reveal internal pains through outward manifestation of self-harm. Others wish to re-experience feelings of shame.

Jeremy Coid, Ann Petruckevitch, Gene Feder, Wai-Shan Chung, Jo Richardson, and Stirling Moorey surveyed a large sample of women to determine whether childhood sexual and physical abuse increases the risk of revictimization ("Relation between Childhood Sexual Abuse and Physical Abuse and Risk of Revictimization in Women: A Cross-Sectional Survey," *The Lancet,* vol. 358, no. 9280, August 11, 2001). A survey involving more than 1,200 women ages sixteen to eighty-five was conducted in primary care practices in London, England. Fifty-four percent of the respondents were white.

The researchers found that women who had a history of unwanted sexual intercourse before age sixteen were more likely to experience intimate partner violence and rape. Those who had been severely beaten before age sixteen by their parents or caregivers reported adult abuse in the form of intimate partner violence, rape, and other traumatic experiences. The women also reported a co-occurrence of sexual and physical abuse both during childhood and adulthood.

CHAPTER 7
CHILD ABUSE AND THE LAW

JUVENILE COURTS

As early as the mid-seventeenth century in colonial America, adults accused of child abandonment, of excessive physical abuse, and of depriving their children of basic necessities faced criminal trials. In 1899 Cook County, Illinois, established the first juvenile court system, not so much to protect abused and neglected children but mainly to keep the abandoned children and runaways off the streets. Then in 1944 the U.S. Supreme Court held, in *Prince v. Massachusetts* (321 U.S. 158), that the government has the authority to protect children from child labor. (In this case, a Jehovah's Witness guardian of a nine-year-old girl was found in violation of state child labor law for furnishing the child with periodicals to sell in the streets.)

Today all fifty states have authorized juvenile family courts to intervene in child abuse cases, and all fifty states consider child abuse of any kind to be a felony and a civil crime. A felony could result in a prison term; a loss of a civil suit could result in the payment of a fine or in losing custody of the child. (While many states have distinct and separate juvenile courts, some states try juvenile or family cases in courts of general jurisdiction, where child protection cases are given priority over other cases on the court's docket.)

Government child protective services (CPS) initiates a civil court proceeding (after consultation with CPS lawyers) if it seeks to remove the child from the home, provide in-home protective services, or require the abuser to get treatment. Criminal proceedings are initiated by a government prosecutor if the abuser is to be charged with a crime, such as sexual abuse.

In civil child protection cases, the accused has the right to a closed trial (a hearing with no jury and closed to the public) in which court records are kept confidential, although a few states permit jury trials. In criminal child protection cases, however, the person charged with abuse is entitled to the Sixth Amendment right to an open trial (a jury trial opened to the public), which can be waived only by the defendant.

In 1967 *In re Gault* (387 U.S.1) substantially changed the nature of juvenile courts. Initially, children were not subject to constitutional due process rights or legal representation, and judges presiding over these courts were given unlimited power to protect children from criminal harm. The U.S. Supreme Court decided *In re Gault* that children—whether they have committed a crime or are the victims of a crime—are entitled to due process and legal representation. These rights, however, are interpreted differently among the states.

Court-Appointed Special Advocate

In the past, for many abused and neglected children who could not be reunited with their families, foster care became a permanent placement. In the 1970s David W. Soukup, presiding judge of the King County Superior Court in Seattle, Washington, realized that judges did not always have enough information to make the right decision to serve the best interests of the child.

Traditionally the child's advocate in court had been the guardian *ad litem* (literally, for the lawsuit). In other words, the guardian *ad litem* is an attorney appointed by the court for the lawsuit being prosecuted. The lawyers, however, usually did not have the time or training to conduct a thorough review of each child's case. Consequently, Judge Soukup recruited and trained community volunteers to serve as the children's long-term guardians *ad litem*. The role of the court-appointed special advocate (CASA) was born on January 1, 1977, and Seattle's program has since been adopted nationwide.

In 1984 the National CASA Association was formed in Seattle, Washington. Congress passed the Victims of

Child Abuse Act of 1990 (Public Law 101-647) to require that a CASA volunteer be provided to every child maltreatment victim who needs such an advocate. More than nine hundred CASA programs, with more than seventy thousand volunteers, have been established in all fifty states and the District of Columbia and the U.S. Virgin Islands (National CASA Association, http://www.nationalcasa.org [accessed November 20, 2004]).

Typically the judge appoints a CASA volunteer, who then reviews all records pertaining to the maltreated child, including CPS reports and medical and school records. The volunteer also meets with the child, parents and family members, social workers, health care providers, school officials, and other people who may know of the child's history. The research compiled by the CASA volunteer helps the child's lawyer in presenting the case. It also helps the court in deciding what is best for the child. Each trained volunteer works with one or two children at a time, enabling the volunteer to research and monitor each case thoroughly.

PROBLEMS FOR THE PROSECUTOR

For the prosecutor's office, child abuse can present many problems. The foremost is that the victim is a child. This becomes an even greater problem when the victim is very young (from birth to age six), since the question of competency arises. More and more studies have examined children's reliability in recalling and retelling past events. Researchers have found that different settings and interview techniques may result in children remembering different details at different times.

The prosecutor may also worry about the possible harm the child may suffer in having to relive the abuse and in being interrogated by adversarial defense attorneys. If the child is an adolescent making accusations of sexual abuse, the defendant's attorney may accuse the teenage victim of seducing the defendant or having willingly taken part in the acts.

Other factors that prosecutors must consider include the slowness of the court process and the possibility that the case may be delayed, not just once, but several times. This is hard enough for adults to tolerate, but it is particularly difficult for children. The delay prolongs the child's pain. Children may become more reluctant to testify or may no longer be able to retell their stories accurately. There is a far greater difference between a thirty-one-year-old testifying about something that happened when he or she was twenty-six and an eleven-year-old retelling an event that happened at six years of age. Prosecutors are also obliged to keep the child's best interests in mind and to try and preserve the family.

Prosecuting Child Sexual Abuse

Prosecuting a child sexual abuse case is particularly challenging. A child who has been physically abused will often display unmistakable signs of the abuse, such as broken bones. Sexual abuse does not necessarily leave such visible marks. So the abuse is less likely to have been noticed by others and is more difficult to verify once an accusation has been made.

Many other difficulties exist. For example, physical abusers will sometimes admit to having "disciplined" their children by striking them, or have actually been seen committing abusive acts in public. Sexual abusers almost never admit to their actions when confronted, and their abuse always takes place in secret. Another major difficulty is that young children who have little or no knowledge of sex may have trouble understanding, let alone explaining in a courtroom, what was done to them.

DISCLOSURE

What should parents do when their children claim to have been abused? It may come as an offhand remark, as if the child is testing to see what a parent's reaction will be. Perhaps the child is engaged in sexual behavior, a common symptom of sexual abuse. For example, the child may go through the motions of sexual intercourse and then say that this is what a parent, stepparent, relative, or a teacher at school has done. A major preschool sexual abuse case against Margaret Kelly Michaels, a teacher at the Wee Care Day Nursery in Maplewood, New Jersey, began when a boy who was having his temperature taken rectally at the pediatrician's office remarked that his teacher had been doing the same thing to him while he napped at school. The remark ultimately led to Michaels being charged with various forms of sexual abuse, and a nine-month trial at which several children testified. (The case, discussed in more detail later in this chapter, was dropped by the prosecution in 1994.)

Sometimes a parent realizes that something is wrong when the child's behavior changes. Some young children have an especially hard time expressing themselves verbally and may instead begin having sleep difficulties, such as nightmares and night terrors; eating problems; a fear of going to school (if that is the site of the abuse); regression; acting out, such as biting, masturbating, or sexually attacking other family members; and withdrawing. These behavior changes, however, do not necessarily mean that the child is being sexually abused. Children may also express themselves in their drawings.

The abuse may have occurred for a long time before children tell. Why do children keep the abuse a secret? Children who reveal their abuse through the nonverbal ways listed above may be afraid to speak out because they believe the threats of death or punishment made by their abusers. Child Abuse Listening and Mediation (CALM), a Santa Barbara, California, counseling organization, lists some of the reasons children do not tell:

- Children feel responsible for what has happened to them.

- Children fear adults will not believe them.

- Children believe threats from the offender.

- Children do not know how to describe what has happened to them.

- Children are taught to be respectful of adults.

- Children fear getting an adult in trouble or disobeying an adult who has requested secrecy.

According to CALM, children tell:

- when they come in contact with someone who appears to already know

- when they come in contact with someone who does not appear to be judgmental, critical, or threatening

- when they believe a continuation of the abuse will be unbearable

- when physical injury occurs

- when they receive sexual abuse prevention information

- if pregnancy is a threat

- when they come into contact with someone who may protect them

If parents believe their child, particularly if the abuser is not a family member, their first reaction may be to file charges against the alleged perpetrator. Parents rarely realize how difficult and painful the process can be. Some experts claim that children psychologically need to see their abuser punished, while others feel children are victimized by the court process, only this time by the very people who are supposed to protect them.

THE CHILD'S STORY

Some experts believe children do not lie about abuse. They point out that children cannot describe events unfamiliar to them. For example, the average six-year-old has no concept of how forced penetration feels or how semen tastes. Experts also note that children lie to get themselves out of trouble, not into trouble, and reporting sexual abuse is definitely trouble. Children sometimes recant, or deny that any abuse has happened, after they have disclosed it. Perhaps the reaction to the disclosure was unfavorable, or the pain and fear of talking about the experience were too great. The child's recanting under interrogation in a court of law may prove damaging to the case and may encourage claims that the child has made false accusations.

Not a Lie but Not the Truth Either

Kenneth V. Lanning, a supervisory special agent at the Behavioral Science Unit at the National Center for the Analysis of Violent Crime of the Federal Bureau of Investigation Academy, Quantico, Virginia, claimed that children rarely lie about sexual abuse ("Criminal Investigation of Sexual Victimization of Children," *The APSAC Handbook on Child Maltreatment,* 2nd ed., Thousand Oaks, CA: Sage Publications, Inc., 2002). Some children, however, may recount what they believe in their minds to be the truth, although their accounts may turn out to be inaccurate. Lanning gave the following explanations for these inaccuracies:

- The child may be experiencing distorted memory due to trauma.

- The child's story might be a reflection of normal childhood fears and fantasy.

- The child may have been confused by the abuser's use of trickery or drugs.

- The child's testimony may be influenced by the suggestive questions of investigators.

- The child's account might reflect urban legends and cultural mythology.

The Pressure of the Judicial System

Once the child becomes enmeshed in the courts, his or her testimony may become muddled. Children, by definition, are immature in their physical, reasoning, and emotional development. Therapists who believe children do not invent abuse feel that if a child's story changes, then psychological progress is being made because the child is dealing with the emotional trauma. For the courts, however, changing stories raise doubts.

Often, the goals of the therapist and the judicial system are at odds. The therapist's goal is to protect the best interests of the child. If, to encourage the child to speak out, a therapist asks leading questions (questions that suggest a specific answer—"Did daddy take his clothes off?"—rather than, "What did daddy look like? What was he wearing?"), the purpose is to help the child remember painful events that need to be expressed. The courts, however, look at such questions as leading the witness. Cases have fallen apart when it appeared that therapists put words in the children's mouths. Critics charge that an alleged abuse may go to trial because an overzealous therapist or investigator has implanted the occurrence of abuse into the child's impressionable mind.

By the time a case makes it to the courtroom, most children are under a great deal of stress. Many will have undergone a thorough genital/rectal examination by a physician and relentless interrogations by innumerable strangers. A child may have been interviewed many times by therapists, lawyers, the police, CPS workers, and the parents. Some of these people may have experience with sexual abuse cases; many may not, and their goals will be very different. How can a child possibly handle all this?

Nonetheless, the U.S. legal system demands this process in order to give every accused person a fair trial and a chance to be cleared of the charges.

Sexual abuse cases are different from most trials in that the question is not just who did it, but did it actually happen? In cases where there is frequently no physical evidence of the crime, it is crucial for the jury to hear the children testify. Many people, however, feel that children are not able to present credible evidence to a jury. Testimony by others, such as the parents, is often excluded by hearsay rules (rules that prevent a witness from repeating in court those statements someone else has made about the case).

THE CHILD AS A COMPETENT WITNESS

Traditionally, judges protected juries from incompetent witnesses, which in early America were considered to include women, slaves, and children. Children in particular were believed to live in a fantasy world, and their inability to understand such terms as "oath," "testify," and "solemnly swear" denied them the right to appear in court. In 1895 the U.S. Supreme Court, in *Wheeler v. United States* (159 U.S. 523), established the rights of child witnesses. The court explained:

> There is no precise age which determines the question of competency. This depends on the capacity and intelligence of the child, his appreciation of the difference between truth and falsehood, as well as of his duty to tell the former. The decision of this question rests primarily with the trial judge, who sees the proposed witness, notices his manner, his apparent possession or lack of intelligence, and may resort to any examination which will tend to disclose his capacity and intelligence as well as his understanding of the obligation of an oath. To exclude [a child] from the witness stand would sometimes result in staying the hand of justice.

As a result of this ruling, the courts formalized the *Wheeler* decision, requiring judges to interview all children to determine their competency. It was not until 1974 that the revised Federal Rules of Evidence abolished the competency rule so that children may testify at trial in federal courts regardless of competence.

In state courts, judges sometimes still apply the competency rule regardless of state laws that may have banned it. In the 1987 Margaret Kelly Michaels case, the judge chatted with each child witness before he or she testified, holding a red crayon and asking questions like, "If I said this was a green crayon, would I be telling the truth?"

Children Can Be Unreliable Witnesses If Subjected to Suggested Events

A study by psychologists Debra Ann Poole and D. Stephen Lindsay showed that children may not be able to distinguish fact from fiction when subjected to suggested events prior to formal interviews. Poole and Lindsay examined children's eyewitness reports after the children were given misinformation by their parents ("Children's Eyewitness Reports after Exposure to Misinformation from Parents," *Journal of Experimental Psychology: Applied,* vol. 7, no. 1, March 2001).

A total of 114 children ages three to eight participated, on a one-to-one basis, in four science activities with a man called "Mr. Science." Three interviews were conducted afterward. The first interview occurred right after the science activities in which an interviewer asked each child nonsuggestive questions about the activities. About three and a half months later the children's parents read them a story, in three instances, about their science experience. The story included two science activities they had experienced and two others that they had not experienced. The story also included an event in which the child experienced unpleasant touching by Mr. Science. In reality this event did not happen. The children were then interviewed. The final step in the interview consisted of a source-monitoring procedure, in which the children were reminded of their actual experiences, as well as the story, to help them distinguish fact from fiction. A final interview was conducted after another month. This time the children were not given any misinformation.

The interview conducted soon after the science activities showed that the children recalled their experiences, with the amount of events reported increasing with the age of the child. When prompted for more information, the amount of new information reported also increased with age. The reports resulting from the promptings remained accurate.

In the interview that occurred soon after the children were read the storybook with misleading suggestions, 35% (forty of the 114 children) reported fifty-eight suggested events in free recall (without prompting from the interviewer), including seventeen events relating to the unpleasant touching by Mr. Science. In the last interview a month later, with no additional misinformation given the children, 21% (twenty-four children) reported twenty-seven suggested events, including nine suggested events that involved unpleasant touching. Even when the children were prompted to provide more information about their experiences, they continued to report false events. The researchers concluded that, since children's credibility as eyewitnesses depends on their ability to distinguish their memories from other sources, interviewers will have to develop better procedures to help them do so.

INNOVATIONS IN THE COURT

Anatomically Detailed Dolls

Many legal professionals use dolls with sexual organs made to represent the human anatomy to help children explain what has happened to them in court. Advocates of the use of dolls report that they make it easier to get a child to talk about things that can be very difficult to discuss. Even when children know the words, they may be too embarrassed to say them out loud to strangers. The dolls allow these children to point out and show things difficult or even impossible for them to say. Some experts claim dolls work because children find them easier to use, as they are age-appropriate and familiar to them.

Lori S. Holmes, training coordinator for CornerHouse, a child abuse evaluation and training center in Minneapolis, Minnesota, noted that the use of anatomical dolls helps the child demonstrate internal consistency. A child who has made allegations of abuse can show the interviewer exactly what happened to him or her, thus confirming the oral disclosure ("Using Anatomical Dolls in Child Sexual Abuse Forensic Interviews," *American Prosecutors Research Institute Update,* vol. 13, no. 8, 2000).

Potential problems, however, exist in using dolls. Critics of this method believe that dolls suggest fantasy to children, and the exaggerated sexual organs on a doll (they are proportionately larger than life-size) may suggest improper sexual activity. Since most children's dolls do not have such sexual parts, the appearance of such parts on a doll might bring to a child's mind things he or she might not have thought of otherwise. According to the "affordance phenomenon," children will experiment with any opportunities provided by a new experience. Some experts believe that what might appear to be sexual behavior, like putting a finger in a hole in the doll, may have no more significance than a child putting a finger through the hole in a doughnut. Such exploratory play can have disastrous effects when it is misinterpreted as the re-creation of a sexual act.

Videotaped Testimony and Closed-Circuit Television Testimony

It is difficult for children to deal with the fear and intimidation of testifying in open court. The person who has allegedly abused and threatened them may be sitting before them, while the serious nature of the court can be intimidating to them. Videotaped testimony and closed-circuit television testimony have become common methods used to relieve the pressure on the child who must testify. The federal government and thirty-seven states allow the use of closed-circuit television testimony instead of in-court testimony for children under age eighteen ("Legislation Regarding the Use of Closed-Circuit Television Testimony in Criminal Child Abuse Proceedings," National Center for Prosecution of Child Abuse, http://www.ndaa-apri.org/pdf/closed_circuit_tv_testimony.pdf [accessed November 20, 2004]). States vary in their requirements regarding the use of closed-circuit television testimony. In some states the jury stays in the courtroom while the child, the judge, the prosecutor, the

defendant, and the defense attorney are in a different room. In some states the child alone is in a room separate from the jury and other participants.

The federal government and seventeen states recognize the right to use videotaped testimony taken at a preliminary hearing or deposition (testimony given under oath to be used in court at a later date) for children under age eighteen ("Legislation Regarding the Admissibility of Videotaped Interviews/Statements in Criminal Child Abuse Proceedings," National Center for Prosecution of Child Abuse, http://www.ndaa-apri.org/pdf/statute_admissibility_videotaped_interviews_statements.pdf [accessed November 20, 2004]). A videotape of the pretrial interviews shows the jury how the child behaved and whether the interviewer prompted the child. Often prepared soon after the abuse, videotaped interviews preserve the child's memory and emotions when they are still fresh. Because a videotaped interview presents an out-of-court statement, which the alleged abuser cannot refute face to face, it can be admitted only as a hearsay exception.

Whereas the videotapes generally pertain to oral statements by the child victims, Missouri allows both verbal and nonverbal statements. Nonverbal assertions include the child's actions, facial expressions, or demonstrations of the abuse using anatomical dolls or other visual aids. In Rhode Island and Wisconsin, child witnesses are required to swear under oath regarding their statements. Prior to taking the oath, the significance of the oath is explained to the child—that is, false statements are punishable under the law and that it is important to tell the truth. Some state laws also say that, even with the videotaped testimony, the child may still be called to testify and be cross-examined.

Videotaping can cut down on the number of interviews the child must undergo, and prosecutors indicate that this method encourages guilty pleas. Videotapes can be powerful tools to deal with the problem of the child who recants his or her testimony when put on the witness stand. The case can still be prosecuted, with the jury witnessing the child's opposing statements. Experts believe that a videotape statement containing sufficient details from the child and elicited through nonleading questions makes for very compelling evidence.

Depositions, however, can be as demanding and difficult as a trial. They often take place in small rooms, forcing the child and defendant closer together than they might have been in a courtroom. The judge might not be there to control the behavior of the defendant or his or her attorney. Individuals who might offer the child support, such as victim advocates, may not be permitted to attend.

Furthermore, if the prosecutor claims the child is unable to handle the emotional trauma of the witness stand, the child may have to undergo medical or psychiatric tests by the state or defense attorney in order to permit videotaped testimony. This could be as traumatic as going through with a personal appearance at the trial. Some states permit the child to sit behind a one-way mirror so that the defendant can see the child and communicate with the defense attorney, but the child is shielded from direct confrontation with the defendant.

Critics of videotaping have suggested other possible problems:

- It is possible that people "perform" for the camera instead of communicating.

- Victims are placed under subjective scrutiny by juries when every gesture, change in voice or speech pattern, and eye movement are judged.

- There is no accountability for the videotapes. Multiple copies of tapes are sometimes made and given to various attorneys and witnesses. Some tapes are used at training sessions, often without concealing the victims' names.

THE CONFRONTATION CLAUSE

Use of closed-circuit television testimony or videotape testimony has been challenged on the grounds that the defendant's Sixth Amendment constitutional right permits him or her to confront an accuser face to face. The Confrontation Clause of the Sixth Amendment states, "In all criminal prosecutions, the accused shall enjoy the right . . . to be confronted with the witnesses against him."

Several court rulings in the 1990s have upheld the introduction of closed-circuit television, but only when it was used carefully and with full recognition of the rights of the accused. Those who disagree with these rulings claim that this method unfairly influences the jury to think that the accused is guilty simply because the procedure is permitted, and, worse, it deprives the defendant of his or her constitutional right to confront the accuser face to face.

State Rulings on the Confrontation Clause

STATE V. LOMPREY. In 1992 Mark Lomprey appealed a conviction for sexually abusing his niece (*State of Wisconsin v. Lomprey,* 496 N.W.2d 172 [Wis.App. 1992]). The defendant maintained that his right to cross-examine the child in a videotaped interview that was shown to the court was denied because when he entered the room, she curled herself up into a ball ("withdrew into her shell") and refused to speak. The trial court made two more efforts to provide both sides with opportunities to interrogate the child, but she would not respond. She was so withdrawn that the defendant's attorney did not even attempt to question her. The appeals court found that the child's behavior was "in fact, a statement." A statement includes "nonverbal conduct of a person if it is intended by him as an asser-

tion." The court found that the child asserted through her conduct that she feared the defendant.

COMMONWEALTH V. WILLIS. Leslie Willis, who was indicted for the sexual abuse of a five-year-old child, claimed that the child was an incompetent witness and should not therefore be allowed to testify in his trial. The trial judge conducted a private hearing to determine the child's competency, but the child was unresponsive.

The prosecution proposed that, pursuant to the Kentucky statute allowing a child abuse victim age twelve or younger to testify by videotape or closed-circuit television, the trial should proceed using such method. The state statute permits such testimony if there is "substantial probability that the child would be unable to reasonably communicate because of serious emotional distress produced by the defendant's presence." The trial judge ruled to exclude the child's testimony because he was of the opinion that the provisions of the Kentucky statute allowing such testimony were unconstitutional. He held that the statute not only violated the Sixth Amendment Confrontation Clause and Section Eleven of the Kentucky Constitution "to meet the witnesses face to face," but also the separation of powers doctrine of the state constitution.

Without the testimony of the child witness to the alleged crime, the case could not go to trial. Therefore, the prosecution appealed the case. The Kentucky Supreme Court, in *Commonwealth v. Willis* (Ky., 716 S.W.2d 224 [1986]), upheld the state law permitting the child to testify by videotape or closed-circuit television. It ruled that the law did not violate the defendant's state and federal rights of confronting his witness. The court pointed out that the defendant's right to hear and see the witness testify remained intact. He could "object to and seek exclusion of all portions of a tape which he consider[ed] unfair or unduly prejudicial." He also had the right of cross-examination through consultation with his lawyer. Moreover, the jury could assess the credibility of the witness.

The court also ruled that the state law did not violate the separation of powers doctrine of the Kentucky Constitution, because the law left it up to the judge to use his discretion in applying the law. The court concluded:

The strength of the State and Federal Constitutions lies in the fact that they are flexible documents which are able to grow and develop as our society progresses. The purpose of any criminal or civil proceeding is to determine the truth. [The law] provides such a statutory plan while protecting the fundamental interests of the accused as well as the victim.

Federal Rulings on the Confrontation Clause

COY V. IOWA. In June 1988 the U.S. Supreme Court ruled on a case similar to *Commonwealth v. Willis.* An Iowa trial court, pursuant to a state law enacted to protect child victims of sexual abuse, allowed a screen to be placed between the two child witnesses and the alleged abuser. The lighting in the courtroom was adjusted so that the children could not see the defendant, Coy, through the screen. Coy, however, was able to see the children dimly and hear them testify. The trial judge cautioned the jury that the presence of the screen was not an indication of guilt. Coy was convicted.

In *Coy v. Iowa* (397 N.W.2d 730 [1986]) Coy appealed to the Iowa Supreme Court, arguing that the screen denied him the right to confront his accusers face to face as provided by the Sixth Amendment. In addition, he claimed that due process was denied because the presence of the screen implied guilt. The Iowa Supreme Court, however, upheld the conviction of the trial court, ruling that the screen had not hurt Coy's right to cross-examine the child witnesses, nor did its presence necessarily imply guilt.

The U.S. Supreme Court, however, in a 6–2 decision, reversed the ruling of the Iowa Supreme Court and remanded the case to the trial court for further proceedings. In *Coy v. Iowa* (487 U.S. 1012 [1988]) the high court maintained that the right to face-to-face confrontation was the essential element of the Sixth Amendment's Confrontation Clause. It held that any exceptions to that guarantee would be allowed only if needed to further an important public policy. The Court found no specific evidence in this case that these witnesses needed special protection that would require a screen.

The two dissenters, Justice Harry A. Blackmun and Chief Justice William Rehnquist, argued that the use of the screen is only a limited departure from the face-to-face confrontation, justified by a substantially important state interest that does not require a case-by-case scrutiny.

MARYLAND V. CRAIG. In June 1990, in a 5–4 decision, the U.S. Supreme Court upheld the use of one-way closed-circuit television. In *Maryland v. Craig* (497 U.S. 836), a six-year-old child alleged that Sandra Craig had committed perverted sexual practices and assault and battery on her in the prekindergarten run by Craig. In support of its motion to permit the child to testify through closed-circuit television, the state presented expert testimony that the child "wouldn't be able to communicate effectively, would probably stop talking and would withdraw, and would become extremely timid and unwilling to talk."

The Supreme Court decision, written by Justice Sandra Day O'Connor, noted that the Sixth Amendment Confrontation Clause does not guarantee *absolute* right to a face-to-face meeting with the witness. The closed-circuit television does permit cross-examination and observation of the witness's demeanor. "We are therefore confident," Justice O'Connor declared, "that use of the one-way closed-circuit television procedure, where necessary to further an important state interest, does not impinge upon

the truth-seeking or symbolic purposes of the Confrontation Clause."

Justice Antonin Scalia, dissenting, felt that the Constitution had been juggled to fit a perceived need when the Constitution explicitly forbade it. He stated, "The Court today has applied 'interest-balancing' analysis where the text of the Constitution simply does not permit it. We are not free to conduct a cost-benefit analysis [comparison of the benefits] of clear and explicit constitutional guarantees and then to adjust their meaning to comport [agree] with our findings."

HEARSAY EVIDENCE

The Hearsay Rule

Together with the Sixth Amendment Confrontation Clause, the hearsay rule is intended to prevent the conviction of defendants by reports of evidence offered by someone other than the witness. With a few exceptions, hearsay is inadmissible as testimony because the actual witness cannot be cross-examined and his or her demeanor cannot be assessed for credibility of testimony. Whether or not to accept the hearsay evidence from a child's reports of abuse to a parent has been frequently debated.

Some Exceptions to the Hearsay Rule

Some courts consider spontaneous declarations or excited utterances made by a person right after a stressful experience as reliable hearsay. Courts also allow statements individuals have made to physicians and other medical personnel for purposes of medical treatment or diagnosis. In this case, it is generally assumed that people who consult with physicians are seeking treatment and, therefore, tell the physicians the truth about their illness.

Hearsay evidence is especially important in cases of child sexual abuse. Cases often take years to come to trial, by which time a child may have forgotten the details of the abuse or may have made psychological progress in dealing with the trauma. The parents may be reluctant to plunge the child back into the anxious situation suffered earlier. Hearsay evidence can be crucial in determining the validity of sexual abuse charges in custody cases. In these cases juries need to know when the child first alleged abuse, to whom, under what circumstances, and whether the child ever recanted.

The Supreme Court Rules on Hearsay Evidence: *Ohio v. Roberts*

In 1980 the U.S. Supreme Court, in a case that was not about child abuse, established the basis for permitting hearsay evidence: the actual witness has to be unavailable and his or her statement has to be reliable enough to permit another person to repeat it to the jury (*Ohio v. Roberts*, 448 U.S. 56 [1980]). Many judges have chosen to interpret unavailability on physical standards rather than the emotional unavailability that children who are afraid to testify may exhibit. Furthermore, legal experts insist that the reliability of a statement does not refer to whether the statement appears to be truthful, but only that it has sufficient reliability for the jury to decide whether it is true.

WHITE V. ILLINOIS. In *White v. Illinois* (502 U.S. 346 [1992]), the U.S. Supreme Court dealt with both the hearsay rules and the Confrontation Clause of the Sixth Amendment. Randall White was charged with sexually assaulting a four-year-old girl, S. G., in the course of a residential burglary. The child's screams attracted the attention of her babysitter, who witnessed White leaving the house. S. G. related essentially the same version of her experience to her babysitter, her mother (who returned home shortly after the attack), a police officer, an emergency room nurse, and a doctor. All of these adults testified at the trial. S. G. did not testify, being too emotional each time she was brought to the courtroom.

White was found guilty and appealed on the grounds that, because the defendant had not been able to face the witness who had made the charges of sexual assault, her hearsay testimony was invalid under the Confrontation Clause. The high court, in a unanimous decision, rejected linking the Confrontation Clause and the admissibility of hearsay testimony.

S. G.'s statements fulfilled the hearsay requirements in that they were either spontaneous declarations or made for medical treatment and, therefore, in the eyes of the Supreme Court, "may justifiably carry more weight with a [court] than a similar statement offered in the relative calm of a courtroom." The Supreme Court concluded that whether the witness appeared to testify had no bearing on the validity of the hearsay evidence. Furthermore, because the hearsay statements in this case fit the "medical evidence" and "spontaneous declaration" exceptions, its decision upheld hearsay evidence as valid.

BUGH V. MITCHELL. Richard Bugh was convicted of sexually molesting his four-year-old daughter in 1989. He was convicted based on hearsay testimony. The girl had told four people in out-of-court statements about the sexual abuse: her mother, a counselor, a county social services supervisor, and a medical doctor. Fourteen years later, having gone through a series of appeals, Bugh petitioned the U.S. Court of Appeals for the Sixth Circuit, challenging the hearsay testimony. Bugh claimed that the trial court's admission of hearsay testimony violated his Sixth Amendment confrontation rights.

On May 13, 2003, in *Bugh v. Mitchell* (No. 01-3417), the appeals court ruled that the hearsay testimonies were admissible. The court added that the defendant's confrontation rights had not been violated because he had the chance to cross-examine the child and the four witnesses. The court rejected Bugh's argument that the child's state-

ments to her mother were not excited utterances because when she told her mother of the alleged molestation "there was no startling event which would have produced nervous excitement." The court noted that the hearsay exception applied in this case, relying on *State v. Wagner* (508 N.E.2d 164, 167, Ohio Ct. App. [1986]), "in which the Ohio appeals court noted the 'limited reflective powers' of a three-year-old and the lack of motive or reflective capacities to prevaricate the circumstances of an attack, as supporting the trustworthiness of a child's communications to others."

The Court Rejects Hearsay Evidence

In 2003 the Indiana Supreme Court heard an appeal by William Carpenter, who had been found guilty of sexually molesting his three-year-old daughter, A. C., in 2000 (*Carpenter v. State,* 786 N.E.2d 696). Among the evidence presented at the 2000 trial were out-of-court statements made by the child to her mother and grandfather. Relying on its decision in *Pierce v. State* (677 N.E.2d 39, Ind. [1997]), the state supreme court noted that in *Pierce,* the child's statements were spontaneous and took place soon after the alleged molestation. On the other hand, in Carpenter's case, the state could not establish the precise time of alleged molestation or whether the child's statements occurred immediately after the alleged molestation. The court observed:

> We find that the testimony recounting A. C.'s statements to her mother and grandfather and her videotape interview failed to exhibit sufficient indications of reliability as the protected person statute requires because of the combination of the following circumstances: there was no indication that A. C.'s statements were made close in time to the alleged molestations, the statements themselves were not sufficiently close in time to each other to prevent implantation or cleansing, and A. C. was unable to distinguish between truth and falsehood.

Crawford v. Washington Overrules *Ohio v. Roberts*

On March 8, 2004, the U.S. Supreme Court, in *Crawford v. Washington* (No. 02-9410), overturned its 1980 ruling in *Ohio v. Roberts,* which held that the Sixth Amendment right of confrontation does not prohibit hearsay evidence if a judge deems that evidence reliable and trustworthy. *Crawford* was not a child abuse case. In 1999 Michael Crawford stabbed a man who allegedly attempted to rape his wife. During the trial the state introduced an out-of-court, tape-recorded statement to police by his wife, who was present during the assault. The state wanted to show that Crawford did not stab the man in self-defense as he had told police. His wife did not testify during the trial because of Washington's spousal privilege, which prohibits one spouse from testifying against the other without the other's consent. The trial court found the wife's statement to be reliable and trustworthy and accepted it as evidence. Crawford was convicted of assault with a deadly weapon.

Upon Crawford's appeal, the Washington Court of Appeals reversed the trial court ruling. The Washington Supreme Court subsequently reinstated the conviction. The U.S. Supreme Court agreed to hear the case to determine whether the state's use of the wife's statement violated the Confrontation Clause. In reversing the judgment of the Washington Supreme Court, the U.S. Supreme Court held that when a hearsay statement is "testimonial," the Confrontation Clause bars the state from using that statement against a criminal defendant unless the person who made the statement is available to testify at trial, or the defendant had a prior opportunity to cross-examine that person.

Although the U.S. Supreme Court stated, "We leave for another day any effort to spell out a comprehensive definition of 'testimonial,'" it gave as an example of a testimonial statement that which is made during police interrogations (for example, the pretrial statement of Crawford's wife). The Supreme Court added that their *Crawford* ruling holds regardless of whether or not the statement is a hearsay exception or is judged reliable, thus overruling *Ohio v. Roberts*. The case was sent back to the Washington Supreme Court for further proceedings. Although *Crawford* was not a child abuse case, some experts believe it will have implications in child abuse cases.

A CALIFORNIA COURT INTERPRETS *CRAWFORD V. WASHINGTON*. In a California case defendant Seum Sisavath was convicted, among other things, of several child sexual abuse charges involving two sisters, ages four and eight. The younger child was not at trial because she was found incompetent to testify. Based on the hearsay testimonies of an officer who responded to the mother's call to police and of an investigator from the district attorney's office who attended a videotaped interview of the younger child, the court admitted the statements. Sisavath was found guilty of most of the sexual charges and sentenced to thirty-two years to life. The defendant petitioned the California Court of Appeals.

While the appeal was pending, the U.S. Supreme Court decided *Crawford v. Washington*. Consequently, the appeals court ruled that the "testimonial" hearsay statements against the defendant were inadmissible under *Crawford* because they violated the Confrontation Clause of the Sixth Amendment. Since the U.S. Supreme Court did not define "testimonial," the appeals court observed,

> It is more likely that the Supreme Court meant simply that if the statement was given under circumstances in which its use in a prosecution is reasonably foreseeable by an objective observer, then the statement is testimonial . . . . We have no occasion here to hold, and do not hold, that statements made in every MDIC [Multidisciplinary Interview Center] interview are testimonial

under *Crawford*. We hold only that Victim 2's [younger victim's] statements in the MDIC interview in this case were testimonial. [The MDIC is a facility specially designed and staffed for interviewing children suspected of being victims of abuse.]

EXPERT WITNESSES

Videotaping and closed-circuit television permit juries to see and hear child witnesses, but it does not mean that the juries will understand or believe them. Prosecutors often request permission to bring in an expert witness to clarify an abused child's behavior, particularly to explain why a child might have waited so long to make an accusation or why the child might withdraw an accusation made earlier.

The danger of bringing in an expert witness is that the expert often lends an unwarranted stamp of authenticity to the child's truthfulness. If an expert states that children rarely lie about sex abuse, that expert might be understood by the jury to be saying that the defendant must be guilty, when the expert has no way of knowing if that is the case. In some highly contested cases, expert witnesses swayed the jurors in their decision. In the Margaret Kelly Michaels case (discussed at the end of the chapter), an expert witness explained how the children's problems were symptomatic of their abuse. In the Eileen Franklin case in Chapter 8, the expert witness convinced the jury of the validity of repressed memory and explained that inconsistencies in Eileen Franklin's story were symptoms of her trauma.

Rules Governing the Use of Expert Testimony

The states have their own rules when it comes to expert testimony. Federal courts, however, follow the Federal Rules of Evidence. On December 1, 2000, the Federal Rules of Evidence were amended because of concerns that experts in the past had lacked the proper qualifications. The new rule requires that before the jury can hear expert testimony, the trial judge first has to determine that the expert has the proper "knowledge, skill, experience, training, or education" to help the jury understand the evidence.

For expert testimony to be acceptable in court, the statements made must be very general and explain only psychological tendencies, never referring specifically to the child witness. The U.S. Court of Appeals for the Eight Circuit, in *United States v. Azure* (801 F.2d 336 [1986]), reversed the conviction of the defendant because an expert's testimony was too specific. During trial an expert witness had testified that the alleged victim was believable. According to the court, "By putting his stamp of believability on [the young girl's] entire story, [the expert] essentially told the jury that [the child] was truthful in saying that [the defendant] was the person who sexually abused her. No reliable test for truthfulness exists and [the expert witness] was not qualified to judge the truthfulness of that part of [the child's] story."

FALSE ACCUSATIONS OF CHILD SEXUAL ABUSE

The willingness of people to believe children's accusations of sexual abuse has varied greatly since the mid-twentieth century. At one time, people were simply unwilling to believe that sexual abuse of children was happening or happening with any frequency. Once society accepted the fact that child sexual abuse was occurring, responses to accusations of child sexual abuse went from disbelief to almost total acceptance by the public. In the 1980s and 1990s, when daycare workers were prosecuted for alleged child and ritual abuses, some experts, claiming children do not lie about these things, further contributed to the belief that predators were everywhere. In the aftermath of the numerous convictions of abusers, some of which have been overturned and others have not been resolved, medical and legal experts have learned many things. They acknowledge that child sexual abuse indeed occurs and children may not tell for various reasons. Experts have also found that some child witnesses are reliable, while others are not. Authorities have since developed better interviewing techniques of child witnesses.

Child Molestation Conviction Overturned after Twenty Years

On May 4, 2004, John Stoll of Bakersfield, California, was exonerated after serving twenty years for alleged child molestation. Stoll, two men, and a woman were accused of operating a sex ring involving sodomy, group sex, and pornography in 1984. The group was accused of sexually molesting six boys, ages six to eight. The children were never medically examined, and authorities did not find child pornography or any physical evidence to support the charges. During the trial the defense was not allowed to bring up the fact that the investigators asked the children leading and suggestive questions. In court the children gave conflicting testimony. Nonetheless, the defendants were convicted.

In dismissing the case against Stoll, Judge Lee P. Felice of the Superior Court of California (Kern County) stated that the investigators used manipulative questioning of the children, forcing them to give false testimony. Four of the six accusers, all adults in 2004, testified that the investigators' persistence during interviews caused them to recount false stories of molestation. A fifth witness indicated he could not remember the interviews. Stoll's son, six years old at the time he testified, still insisted his father molested him. Stoll claimed his ex-wife influenced the boy's testimony because of a bitter divorce. In the 1980s in Bakersfield, authorities prosecuted eight alleged sex rings, consisting of thirty people, for child molestation. Twenty-two convictions have since been overturned.

Suing Child Protective Services

In June 2000 the Washington Supreme Court, in *Tyner v. the State of Washington Department of Social and Health Services, CPS,* ruled that CPS could be sued for negligent handling of investigations (No. 67602, Supreme Court of Washington). In 1993 David Tyner III was accused by his wife of sexually abusing their four-year-old daughter. The couple was in the process of a divorce. CPS did not uncover any abuse but continued to prohibit the father from seeing his children. Tyner sued CPS for mishandling the investigation. The court held that "CPS owes a duty of care to a child's parents, even those suspected of abusing their own children, when investigating allegations of child abuse." The court reinstated a jury verdict of more than $200,000 against the department.

Suing the Police

In September 2000 the Washington Supreme Court, in the first court ruling of its kind, unanimously ruled that the police can be held financially liable for negligence in child abuse investigations (*Rodriguez v. City of Wenatchee,* No. 69614-4, Supreme Court of Washington). The ruling stemmed from a lawsuit filed by Pastor Robert Roberson, his wife, and others accused of child molestation in Wenatchee, Washington. The Washington Supreme Court reinstated the $30 million lawsuit brought by the defendants.

The case started in 1994 when a nine-year-old foster child was placed in the home of Bob Perez, chief sex-crimes investigator of Wenatchee, Washington. The following year the girl told her foster father about being sexually abused by her parents. After the parents were convicted, the child made allegations of a sex ring involving the Robersons and forty-three adults since 1988. Based on the girl's testimony and that of her thirteen-year-old friend and a former member of Roberson's church, the pastor, his wife, and nineteen others were arrested on 27,726 counts of sexual abuse against sixty children. In December 1995 the Robersons were acquitted. In 1996 Perez's foster daughter recanted, denying her sexual abuse allegations and saying that Perez had pressured her. Her friend had also recanted her testimony.

On August 3, 2004, approximately ten years after the Wenatchee sexual abuse cases first surfaced, another civil lawsuit filed by those falsely accused reached the Court of Appeals of Washington. In *Roberson v. Wenatchee* (No. 21777-9-III), the appeals court unanimously upheld a lower court ruling, directing the city of Wenatchee to pay a fine of $718,000 for withholding information about investigator Robert Perez from persons who had sued the city after they were acquitted.

THE REGISTRATION OF SEX OFFENDERS

At a national conference on sex offender registries in 1998, Director Jan M. Chaiken of the Bureau of Justice

Statistics of the U.S. Justice Department reported that nearly two-thirds of the 95,000 sex offenders in state prisons that year committed their violent sex crimes against children under age eighteen. The victims of the majority of the violent sex offenders were children younger than twelve. The number of sex offenders in state prisons has since risen to 118,500 in 2002 (Paige M. Harrison and Allen J. Beck, *Prisoners in 2002*, U.S. Department of Justice, Bureau of Justice Statistics, July 2003). Three federal laws have been enacted to track sex offenders after their release from prison:

The Jacob Wetterling Act

The Jacob Wetterling Crimes against Children and Sexually Violent Offender Registration Act, also known as the Jacob Wetterling Act, was signed into federal law on September 13, 1994, as part of the Violent Crime Control and Law Enforcement Act of 1994 (Public Law 103-322). The act provides funding to states to establish registration systems for sex offenders. States must require abusers who have committed a criminal offense against a minor to register every year for ten years after release from prison, parole, or probation. Sexually violent predators must report their addresses to the state every ninety days until it is determined they are no longer threats to public safety. Sexually violent predators include those who have committed sexually violent crimes, as well as those who may not have committed sexual crimes but suffer from mental abnormalities or personality disorders that may predispose them to commit predatory or violent sex offenses.

Jacob Wetterling was an eleven-year-old boy kidnapped near his home in St. Joseph, Minnesota, by an armed, masked man on October 22, 1989. His abduction was similar to a case involving a boy from a nearby town who was kidnapped and sexually assaulted earlier that year. Jacob was never found, but police believed the cases were linked and encouraged the creation of a database so that police departments could share information.

Megan's Law

"Megan's Law" (Public Law 104-145), signed May 17, 1996, amended the Jacob Wetterling Act by requiring states to release information on registered sex offenders if needed to protect the public. In 1994 the nation's first notification law was enacted in New Jersey after seven-year-old Megan Kanka was raped and murdered by a convicted sex offender who lived across the street from her family. Since then many states have enacted legislation ("Ashley's Law" in Texas and "Polly's Law" in California, for instance) that requires the registration and tracking of sex offenders.

The Pam Lychner Act

The Pam Lychner Sexual Offender Tracking and Identification Act (Public Law 104-236), signed on October 3, 1996, also amended the Jacob Wetterling Act by requiring the Federal Bureau of Investigation (FBI) to establish a National Sex Offender Registry to help state-to-state tracking and management of released sex offenders. It further allows the FBI to conduct sex offender registration and community notification in states that do not have "minimally sufficient" systems in place for such purposes. The Pam Lychner Act was named after a victim's rights activist who was killed in an airplane crash in 1988.

The Lychner Act also requires a registered sex offender moving to a new state or establishing residence upon release from prison or being placed on parole, supervised release, or probation to notify the FBI and state authorities within ten days of the move. Failure to do so the first time is a misdemeanor punishable by up to one year in prison and a fine of not more than $100,000. A second offense is a felony punishable by up to ten years in prison and a fine of not more than $100,000.

State Sex Offender Registries

As of February 2004 all fifty states and the District of Columbia had centralized sex offender registries. The states, the District of Columbia, and the U.S. territories of Guam, Puerto Rico, and the Virgin Islands submitted records on nearly 300,000 convicted sex offenders to the FBI National Sex Offender Registry. As of September 15, 2004, thirty-five states and the District of Columbia had Internet sites where the public could access information about the offenders.

Supreme Court Upholds Megan's Law

In its first review of Megan's Law, in 2003, the U.S. Supreme Court heard two cases challenging state sex-offender registry laws. In the first case two sex offenders argued that the registration requirement is a retroactive punishment prohibited by the Due Process Clause of the Fourteenth Amendment and by the *Ex Post Facto* Clause of the U.S. Constitution, which bans a law that applies retroactively.

Under Alaska's law a person convicted of an aggravated sex offense or of two or more sex offenses must register for life and verify the information every three months. Both the registration and notification requirements are retroactive. John Doe et al. were released from prison in 1990 and completed rehabilitation programs for sex offenders. They claimed they already served time and that they were being punished a second time by the registration law. In a 6–3 vote, in *Smith et al. v. John Doe et al.* (No. 01-729 [2003]), the Supreme Court held that the intent of the Alaska sex-registration law was not to punish. Delivering the opinion of the Court, Justice Anthony Kennedy noted:

> The fact that Alaska posts the information on the Internet does not alter our conclusion. It must be acknowledged that notice of a criminal conviction subjects the

offender to public shame, the humiliation increasing in proportion to the extent of the publicity. And the geographic reach of the Internet is greater than anything which could have been designed in colonial times. These facts do not render Internet notification punitive [inflicting punishment]. The purpose and the principal effect of notification are to inform the public for its own safety, not to humiliate the offender. Widespread public access is necessary for the efficacy of the scheme, and the attendant humiliation is but a collateral consequence of a valid regulation.

The second case was brought before the U.S. Supreme Court by state personnel responsible for compiling the state's sex-offender registry and for posting it on the Internet. John Doe, a convicted sex offender, filed a lawsuit on behalf of himself and similarly situated sex offenders, claiming that Connecticut's sex-offender registration law violates, among other things, the Fourteenth Amendment's Due Process Clause. John Doe claimed that the state did not hold a hearing to determine whether or not he was likely to be currently dangerous. The U.S. District Court and the U.S. Court Appeals for the Second Circuit agreed with John Doe, prohibiting the public disclosure of registered sex offenders. In *Connecticut Department of Public Safety v. John Doe,* the U.S. Supreme Court voted 9–0, reversing the appellate court ruling. The Court stated that "due process does not require the opportunity to prove a fact that is not material to the State's statutory scheme."

CHILD PORNOGRAPHY LAWS

Although the First Amendment protects pornography, it does not protect child pornography. Under the definition established in *Miller v. California* (413 U.S. 15 [1973]), pornography may be banned if it is deemed legally obscene. To be considered obscene, material "taken as a whole" must:

- appeal to a prurient interest in sex;

- be patently offensive in light of community standards; and

- lack serious literary, artistic, political, or scientific value.

Since 1982 child pornography has been banned by the U.S. Supreme Court ruling *New York v. Ferber* (458 U.S. 747), which held that pornography depicting children engaged in sexually explicit acts can be banned, whether or not it is obscene, because of the state's interest in protecting children from sexual exploitation. In other words, such images are not protected by the First Amendment. The Child Pornography Prevention Act of 1996 (Public Law 104-208) added a definition of child pornography, stating that an actual minor need not be used in creating a depiction in order for the depiction to constitute child pornography.

In October 1998, in an effort to further protect children from sexual predators who target minors through the Internet, Congress enacted the Protection of Children from Sexual Predators Act (Public Law 105-314). The legislation provides punishment for any individual who knowingly contacts, or tries to contact, children under eighteen in order to engage in criminal sexual activity, or who knowingly transfers obscene material to children.

Protecting Children from Pornography on the Internet

Congressional debate continues on how the government should enforce obscenity standards in cyberspace. Some policy makers believe any obscenity standards could interfere with free speech and would be difficult to enforce, while others believe this is an issue relating to child protection, not to the First Amendment.

COMMUNICATIONS DECENCY ACT (CDA). In 1996 Congress first attempted to protect minors from Internet material that, judged under contemporary community standards, would be considered "obscene or indecent" for them. Congress passed the Communications Decency Act (CDA), or Title V of the Telecommunications Act (Public Law 104-104), which makes it a federal crime to use any facility or means of interstate or foreign commerce to entice or force any person under age eighteen to engage in prostitution or any sexual act.

On June 26, 1997, the U.S. Supreme Court, in *Reno v. American Civil Liberties Union* (521 U.S. 844), held by a 7–2 decision that the Communications Decency Act "abridges the freedom of speech protected by the First Amendment" because "in order to deny minors access to potentially harmful speech, the CDA effectively suppresses a large amount of speech that adults have a constitutional right to receive and to address to one another."

CHILD ONLINE PROTECTION ACT (COPA). In October 1998 Congress enacted the Child Online Protection Act (COPA; Public Law 105-277). In light of the U.S. Supreme Court's ruling on the CDA, Congress narrowed the scope of COPA to include just the material published on the World Wide Web. In comparison, the CDA included all communications over the Internet. COPA applied only to persons who are in the business of distributing pictures, articles, images, and video and audio recordings for the purpose of making a profit. In addition, COPA limited the materials to those that are considered harmful to children, unlike the CDA, which bans all "indecent" and "patently offensive" communications.

Persons liable to COPA violations include all those who place such obscene material on the Internet in order to earn a profit (although it is not necessary that they make a profit). The person may be a Web site administrator who creates and maintains a Web site, a content provider such as an online bookstore or magazine, or a content contributor who writes or creates graphics for communications media. COPA requires all commercial sites on the Internet to obtain credit card numbers or adult identification numbers from users. Violation of COPA entails heavy fines ($50,000–$150,000 per day) and up to six months in jail.

COPA, however, exempts the following persons from liability:

• a telecommunications carrier who provides telecommunications services

• a person who provides an Internet access service

• a person who provides an Internet information location tool

• a person engaged in the transmission, storage, retrieval, hosting, formatting, or translation (or any combination of these functions) of a communication made by another person, without alteration or deletion of some parts of the communication content

COPA was set to be put into effect on November 29, 1998, but on October 22, 1998, plaintiffs, including the American Civil Liberties Union (ACLU), commercial World Wide Web providers, and Web site users who used the materials described by COPA, filed a complaint with the U.S. District Court for the Eastern District of Pennsylvania, challenging the constitutionality of COPA under the First and Fifth Amendments. The plaintiffs argued that they would be forced to either establish age-verification barriers or delete materials from their Web sites that may be perceived to violate COPA. The plaintiffs asked the court to issue a temporary restraining order prohibiting the U.S. attorney general from enforcing COPA. U.S. District Judge Lowell A. Reed Jr. issued a temporary restraining order against the enforcement of COPA.

On February 1, 1999, in *American Civil Liberties Union v. Reno* (31 F.†Supp. 2d 473, 476 [E.D. Pa. 1999]), U.S. District Judge Reed, Jr., issued a preliminary injunction against the enforcement of COPA. Judge Reed ruled:

> The Supreme Court has repeatedly stated that the free speech rights of adults may not be reduced to allow them to read only what is acceptable for children. . . . While the public certainly has an interest in protecting its minors, the public interest is not served by the enforcement of an unconstitutional law. Indeed, to the extent that other members of the public who are not parties to this lawsuit may be affected by the statute, the interest of the public is served by preservation of the status quo until such time that this Court may ultimately rule on the merits of plaintiffs' claims at trial.

On June 22, 2000, the U.S. Court of Appeals for the Third Circuit, in *American Civil Liberties Union v. Reno* (217 F.3d 162 [3d Cir. 2000]), affirmed Judge Reed's ruling. Upon appeal by the U.S. attorney general in 2001, the U.S. Court of Appeals ruled in *Ashcroft v. American Civil Liberties Union et al.* that COPA violates the First

Amendment because it relies, in part, on "contemporary community standards" (per *Roth v. United States*, 354 U.S. 476 [1957]) to determine whether or not certain materials are harmful to children. According to the appeals court, the *Roth* decision could not be applied to the Internet or the World Wide Web because juries across the country would have different community standards. Some juries might apply the "most puritan" community standards, which would put too much burden on First Amendment freedoms. The court also found it unnecessary to review the rest of the law.

Subsequently, the government appealed its case to the U.S. Supreme Court. On May 13, 2002, in *Ashcroft v. American Civil Liberties Union et al.* (535 U.S. 564), the Supreme Court limited its decision to ruling that COPA's use of community standards to identify material harmful to children does not necessarily make it unconstitutional as far as First Amendment freedoms are concerned. It further found the appeals court decision incomplete and sent the case back for further proceedings. The Court did not lift the injunction against the COPA enforcement.

On remand, the U.S. Court of Appeals of the Third Circuit again affirmed the U.S. District Court issuance of a preliminary injunction against COPA. On March 6, 2003, the appellate court, in *American Civil Liberties Union v. Ashcroft* (322 F.3d 240 [2003]), held that, among other things, "COPA is clearly a content-based restriction on speech." The court stated:

> We conclude that the statute is substantially overbroad in that it places significant burdens on Web publishers' communication of speech that is constitutionally protected as to adults and adults' ability to access such speech. In so doing, COPA encroaches upon a significant amount of protected speech beyond that which the Government may target constitutionally in preventing children's exposure to material that is obscene for minors.

After the 2003 Third Circuit Court ruling, the federal government again sought review by the U.S. Supreme Court. On June 29, 2004, over five years after COPA was enacted, the U.S. Supreme Court, by a vote of 5–4, upheld the U.S. District Court's 1999 injunction against the enforcement of COPA. In *Ashcroft v. American Civil Liberties Union et al.* (No. 03-218), the Supreme Court returned the case to the District Court, saying that the government failed to show that there are no "less restrictive alternatives" to COPA. The high court wrote:

> Content-based prohibitions, enforced by severe criminal penalties, have the constant potential to be a repressive force in the lives and thoughts of a free people. To guard against that threat the Constitution demands that content-based restrictions on speech be presumed invalid . . . and that the Government bear the burden of showing their constitutionality.

CHILD PORNOGRAPHY PREVENTION ACT (CPPA). On April 16, 2002, the U.S. Supreme Court resolved the question of whether another 1996 law, the Child Pornography Prevention Act (CPPA; Public Law 104-208), is unconstitutional because it prohibits free speech that is not obscene based on *Miller* nor child pornography based on *Ferber*. The CPPA, in part, bans any visual depiction that "is, or appears to be, of a minor engaging in sexually explicit conduct." Such depiction, called virtual child pornography, includes computer-generated images and images using youthful-looking adults. The CPPA also prohibits the advertisement or promotion of any sexually explicit image that "conveys the impression" that children are performing sexual acts.

The Supreme Court, in *Ashcroft v. Free Speech Coalition et al.* (535 U.S. 234), ruled 6–3 that banning virtual child pornography is unconstitutional because, unlike *Ferber*, actual children are not used in its production. Moreover, the high court claimed that the government cannot prohibit material fit for adults just because children might get hold of it. The court also struck down the government's argument that child pornography whets the appetites of pedophiles and encourages them to commit unlawful acts. As to that part of the law that bans material that "conveys the impression" it contains children performing sexual acts, the justices noted that anyone found in possession of such "mislabeled" material could be prosecuted.

CHILDREN'S INTERNET PROTECTION ACT (CIPA). The Children's Internet Protection Act (CIPA; Public Law 106-554), enacted by Congress in 2000, requires all public libraries receiving federal funds to install software that blocks visual depictions of obscenity, child pornography, and material harmful to children. Libraries, library associations, library patrons, and some Web sites filed lawsuits challenging the law.

Two lawsuits in Philadelphia, which were consolidated, were tried on May 31, 2002, and, as required by law, were decided by a special three-judge federal panel. In *American Library Association v. United States* (Civil Action No. 01-1303) and *Multnomah County Public Library v. United States* (201 F.†Supp. 2d 401), the panel unanimously ruled that CIPA abridges the First Amendment rights of library patrons. The court found that limitations in filtering programs might also block access to other material protected by First Amendment speech.

The government filed an appeal to the U.S. Supreme Court, which delivered its ruling on June 23, 2003. In *United States v. American Library Association, Inc., et al.* (No. 02-361), by a 6–3 vote, the high court reversed the lower court decision, saying that Congress can require public libraries receiving federal funds to install computer software that blocks access to Internet pornography. Chief Justice Rehnquist delivered the opinion and was joined by Justices O'Connor, Scalia, and Thomas. Justices Breyer and Kennedy, joining in the judgment of the plurality but not with its opinion, added that CIPA allows libraries to let any adult access a blocked Web site if the adult asks a librarian to unblock a specific site or to disable the entire computer filter.

CLOSING THE LEGAL LOOPHOLE OF THE "INCEST EXCEPTION" IN SOME STATE LAWS

In about forty states an "incest exception" is found in criminal codes and sentencing guidelines. This means that a person who commits incest (sexual abuse of a family member) gets off with a lighter sentence, if any at all, compared to a person who sexually abuses another's child. In some states, a family member who commits incest with a child is charged with a misdemeanor. In other states the molester can get off with probation and therapy. Children's lawyer and author Andrew Vachss first brought up the incest exception issue in a *Parade* magazine article, "Our Endangered Species: A Hard Look at How We Treat Children" (March 29, 1998). Vachss is an advisory board member of the National Association to Protect Children, which is an organization working to change incest laws in different states.

In 1999 a bill was introduced in the U.S. Congress that would have banned states from treating rape committed by a biological relative as a lesser crime than the rape of a stranger. That legislation was not enacted, and, as of 2004, no such federal law had been passed. In the meantime, the National Association to Protect Children decided to fight the incest exception one state at a time. In 2002 the association was instrumental in North Carolina in changing its archaic incest law of 1879. House Bill 1276 closed "the legal loophole that exist[ed] under the state's incest laws by equalizing punishments for crimes committed against children without regard to familial status." Prior to the new legislation, a father who raped his child was found guilty of minor felony, punishable by probation, and an uncle who raped his niece was required to perform forty-five days of community service for the misdemeanor offense of incest. In April and May of 2003 Arkansas and Illinois, respectively, reformed their incest laws. Under Arkansas' old incest laws an adult who raped a child in his or her own family was considered guilty of incest and was either fined or put under probation. In Illinois the old incest laws imposed a punishment of probation or two years of counseling.

DRUG-EXPOSED INFANTS

In November 1997 the South Carolina Supreme Court, in *Whitner v. South Carolina* (492 S.E.2d 777 [S.C. 1997]), held that pregnant women who use drugs can be criminally prosecuted for child maltreatment. The court found that a viable (potentially capable of surviving outside the womb) fetus is a person covered by the state's child abuse and neglect laws. The ruling was handed down in a case appealed by Cornelia Whitner, who was sentenced to eight years in prison in 1992 for pleading guilty to child neglect. This was the first time the highest court of any state upheld the criminal conviction of a woman charged with such an offense. Whitner's newborn tested positive for cocaine.

In March 1998 Malissa Ann Crawley, charged with the same criminal offense, began serving a five-year prison sentence in South Carolina. In June 1998 the U.S. Supreme Court refused to hear appeals by Whitner and Crawley.

Whitner's lawyer had argued that if a woman could be prosecuted for child abuse for having used drugs while pregnant, what was to keep the law from prosecuting her for smoking or drinking alcohol or even for failing to obtain prenatal care? Other critics claimed that women who are substance abusers, fearing prosecution, might not seek prenatal care and counseling for their drug problems, which would further endanger the child.

Cases similar to *Whitner v. South Carolina* had been brought before other state courts, but none had convicted a substance-ingesting pregnant woman. These included Florida, Kentucky, Michigan, Nevada, Ohio, Washington, and Wyoming.

First Case of Homicide by Child Abuse for Illegal Drug Use During Pregnancy

In another South Carolina case Regina McKnight, a crack addict, was arrested in 1999 after giving birth to a stillborn. In 2001 she was convicted of homicide by child abuse and was sentenced to twelve years in prison. The jury found her guilty of killing a viable fetus, considered a child under South Carolina law. In January 2003 the South Carolina Supreme Court ruled against McKnight (*State v. Regina D. McKnight,* Opinion No. 25585). The court pointed out that the state legislature amended the homicide by child abuse statute in 2000, about three years after the court held in *Whitner v. South Carolina* that the term "child" includes a viable fetus. The court added, "The fact that the legislature was well aware of this Court's opinion in *Whitner,* yet failed to omit "viable fetus" from the statute's applicability, is persuasive evidence that the legislature did not intend to exempt fetuses from the statute's operation." In October 2003 the U.S. Supreme Court refused to hear McKnight's case.

Mandatory Reporting of Child Abuse by Pregnant Women

As of June 2004 the District of Columbia and twenty-three states had laws requiring the mandatory reporting of drug-exposed infants. (See Table 7.1.) After receiving a report of a drug-exposed infant, CPS typically comes to the mother's aid, sometimes removing the infant from her custody on a temporary or permanent basis. As of Sep-

TABLE 7.1

States with reporting laws regarding drug-exposed infants, 2003

Arizona	Minnesota
California	Missouri
Colorado	North Dakota
District of Columbia	Oklahoma
Florida	South Carolina
Hawaii	South Dakota
Illinois	Tennessee
Indiana	Texas
Iowa	Utah
Kentucky	Virginia
Massachusetts	Washington
Michigan	Wisconsin

SOURCE: "States That Have Reporting Laws Regarding Drug-Exposed Infants," *2003 Child Abuse and Neglect State Statutes Series Ready Reference, Reporting Laws: Drug-Exposed Infants*, U.S. Department of Health and Human Services, National Clearinghouse on Child Abuse and Neglect Information, June 2003

tember 2004 South Dakota alone mandated the reporting of substance-ingesting pregnant women for "child abuse" to law enforcement instead of to social services. Failure to report such cases of child abuse would constitute a crime punishable by up to six months in prison.

In 1989 a public hospital in Charleston, South Carolina, run by the Medical University of South Carolina (MUSC), offered to work with the city officials and police to test pregnant women suspected of drug use. The women were not told they were being screened for drugs and would be turned over to police if they tested positive. Many of the women were prosecuted and subsequently imprisoned for child abuse.

In 1993 ten women who had been subjected to the "Search and Arrest" policy of the hospital and police filed a lawsuit, charging that "warrantless and nonconsensual drug tests conducted for criminal investigatory purposes were unconstitutional searches" prohibited by the Fourth Amendment. In 1997, in *Ferguson v. City of Charleston,* the U.S. District Court upheld the policy. In 1999 upon appeal, the U.S. Court of Appeals for the Fourth Circuit, in *Ferguson v. City of Charleston* (186 F.†3d 469), affirmed the judgment of the district court, saying that the searches constitute a "special needs" exception to the Fourth Amendment, which justifies searches done for non-law-enforcement ends, in this case, the medical interests of the mothers and infants, even though law-enforcement means were used.

The U.S. Supreme Court reviewed the ruling by the Fourth Circuit Court to determine whether the MUSC policy involved searches justified by "special needs." On March 21, 2001, the Court ruled 6–3 that MUSC's policy was unconstitutional (*Ferguson v. City of Charleston,* 532 U.S. 67). The Court noted:

> While the ultimate goal of the program may well have been to get the women in question into substance abuse

treatment and off drugs, the immediate objective of the searches was to generate evidence for law enforcement purposes in order to reach that goal. Given that purpose and given the extensive involvement of law enforcement officials at every stage of the policy, this case simply does not fit within the closely guarded category of "special needs."

The Supreme Court remanded the case to the U.S. Court of Appeals for the Fourth Circuit to determine whether or not the women gave informed consent to the hospital to test them for drugs. On October 17, 2002, the appellate court, in *Ferguson v. City of Charleston* (No. 97-2512), noted that eight of the women did not provide informed consent to the drug testing; therefore, the "Search and Arrest" policy violated their Fourth Amendment rights. The City of Charleston appealed to the U.S. Supreme Court, but the Court declined to rehear the case.

CHILD ABUSE LAWS RELATING TO DOMESTIC VIOLENCE

Some local laws that have been passed impose penalties for domestic violence when children are present. For example, Salt Lake County, Utah, and Houston County, Georgia, enacted statutes creating a new crime of child maltreatment when domestic violence is witnessed by a child. Multnomah County, Oregon, passed legislation upgrading some assault offenses to felonies (serious crimes) when a child is present during domestic violence. Debra Whitcomb conducted a study involving a survey of prosecutors to determine their responses to cases where children witness domestic violence ("Prosecutors, Kids, and Domestic Violence Cases," *National Institute of Justice Journal,* no. 248, March 2002).

The survey asked 128 prosecutors across the country how they would respond to three domestic violence cases in which children were present. A majority of prosecutors (94%) would report a battered mother to CPS if she were found abusing the child. All indicated they would prosecute the abusing mother. Prosecutors would more likely report a battered mother if she failed to protect her child from abuse (63%) than if she failed to protect the child from witnessing the domestic violence (40%). More than three times as many prosecutors would charge the mother with a crime for the child's abuse (77.5%) than for exposure to family violence (25%). (See Table 7.2.)

Court Sides with Battered Women Whose Children Are Removed

Battered women with children are often further penalized by CPS's removal of their children. On December 21, 2001, Jack B. Weinstein, a federal judge, ruled that New York City's Administration for Children's Services (ACS) violated the constitutional rights of mothers and their children by removing the children simply because the mothers were victims of domestic violence. In this first case of

TABLE 7.2

Prosecutors' responses to scenarios involving children and abuse

Scenario	Would Report At Least Sometimes	Would Prosecute At Least Sometimes
Mom Abuses Children	94% (n=90)	100% (n=82)
Mom Fails to Protect from Abuse	63% (n=87)	77.5% (n=80)
Mom Fails to Protect from Exposure	40% (n=86)	25% (n=73)

SOURCE: Debra Whitcomb, "Table 1: Prosecutors' Responses to Scenarios Involving Children and Abuse," in "Prosecutors, Kids, and Domestic Violence Cases," *National Institute of Justice Journal,* Issue 248, March 2002

its kind, fifteen battered women had brought the class action suit *Nicholson v. Scoppetta.*

On January 3, 2002, the judge issued an injunction ordering ACS to stop separating a child from his or her battered mother unless the child "is in such imminent danger." The injunction asserts, "The government may not penalize a mother, not otherwise unfit, who is battered by her partner, by separating her from her children; nor may children be separated from the mother, in effect visiting upon them the sins of their mother's batterer."

THE STATUTE OF LIMITATIONS

A statute of limitations is a law that sets the time within which criminal charges or civil claims can be filed and after which one loses the right to sue or make a claim. Most states provide for extensions of the statute of limitations, either through state law or judicial tolling doctrines. A tolling doctrine is a rule that suspends the date from which a statutory period starts to run. An example is the minority tolling doctrine, which provides that a statutory period does not begin to run until the child becomes an adult. For instance, in 2003, in response to revelations of clergy abuse, Illinois extended the statute of limitations in cases of childhood sexual abuse, allowing prosecutors twenty years from the time the victim turns eighteen to bring criminal charges. Victims wishing to bring a civil suit have up to ten years from the time they discover abuse and its connection to their injuries.

Exception to Statute of Limitations in Cases of Repressed Memory

One of the legal issues contested in cases of childhood sexual abuse of repressed memory is how long the statute of limitations should run, since typically the victim has allegedly repressed the memories for many years. In 1991 Paula Hearndon sued her stepfather, Kenneth Graham, for sexually abusing her from 1968 to 1975 (when she was between the ages of eight and fifteen). According to Hearndon, the traumatic amnesia she experienced because of the abuse lasted until 1988. Because of Florida's four-year statute of limitations, the lawsuit did not proceed.

In September 2000, however, the Florida Supreme Court, in a 5–2 decision, ruled that memory loss resulting from the trauma of childhood sexual abuse should be considered an exception to the statute of limitations (*Hearndon v. Graham*, No. SC92665, Supreme Court of Florida [2000]).

The court, while observing that disagreements about recovered memory exist, stated:

> It is widely recognized that the shock and confusion resultant from childhood molestation, often coupled with authoritative adult demands and threats for secrecy, may lead a child to deny or suppress such abuse from his or her consciousness.

U.S. Supreme Court Rules on California's Retroactive Change of Statute of Limitations

In 2003 the U.S. Supreme Court heard arguments in a case that involved California's statute of limitations. In 1998 Marion Stogner was charged with the alleged sexual molestation of his two daughters between 1955 and 1973. Although the statute of limitations had expired, prosecutors brought criminal charges under a 1994 state law that had removed the statute of limitations for the time the crime was committed. In the trial court Stogner claimed that the *Ex Post Facto* Clause of the U.S. Constitution forbids revival of prosecution that was previously time-barred. The trial court agreed, but the California Court of Appeals reversed the ruling (*People v. Stogner v. California*, A084772 [1999]), saying that the 1994 law is not unconstitutional as an *ex post facto* law. (Article 1 of the U.S. Constitution forbids the passing of an *ex post facto* law, or a law that applies retroactively).

Upon the defendant's second appeal, the California Court of Appeals, in *Stogner v. Superior Court* (93 Cal. App. 4th 1229, 114 Cal. Rptr. 2d 37, [2001]), held that the 1994 law allows the prosecution of Stogner's alleged crimes committed between 1955 and 1973. On June 26, 2003, the U.S. Supreme Court ruled on *Stogner v. California* (01-1757). By a 5–4 vote, the high court reversed the appeals court decision, concluding that "a law enacted after expiration of a previously applicable limitations period violates the *Ex Post Facto* Clause when it is applied to revive a previously time-barred prosecution."

MAJOR PRESCHOOL ABUSE CASES

In the 1980s and early 1990s alleged incidents of mass molestation of preschool children in the United States triggered hysteria not only among the parents of the children involved in the cases but also among the public. Some of these cases continued to be appealed into the early 2000s. Some had not been resolved. Many demon-

strate the typical issues and problems that the legal system faces in dealing with child abuse cases.

The McMartin Preschool Case

The McMartin Preschool case is often considered the case that started a string of prosecutions involving preschool sexual abuse. In 1983 Judy Johnson, the mother of a two-and-a-half-year-old child enrolled at the McMartin Preschool in Manhattan Beach, California, told police that her son had been molested by Raymond Buckey, the adult grandson of the preschool director, Virginia McMartin. Police sent letters to two hundred parents of current and former students, informing them of the molestation investigation. Soon other parents claimed to remember strange happenings, such as their children sometimes coming home in underwear and clothes that were not their own. The parents also reported behavior changes for which they could find no explanation.

Raymond Buckey was arrested, but charges of sexual abuse were later dropped for lack of evidence. In 1984 he was rearrested. His grandmother, Virginia; his mother, Peggy McMartin Buckey; his sister, Peggy Ann; and three other female teachers were also arrested. In 1986 Virginia, Peggy Ann, and the teachers were released for lack of evidence.

The prosecution's primary investigator was Kee MacFarlane, director of the Children's Sexual Abuse Diagnostic Center of the Children's Institute International (CII; Los Angeles), an organization that dealt with maltreated children. CII personnel interviewed the children who had allegedly been abused. The children began to tell stories about being drugged, sodomized, penetrated with sharp objects, and used in a game called "Naked Movie Star." The interviewers used anatomically correct dolls to help the children explain what happened. The interviews were videotaped.

When the case finally went to trial in 1986, the children were ages eight to twelve and were recounting events that occurred when they were three to five years old. Defense attorneys used the videotapes to show how the interviewers elicited the desired replies from the children by asking leading questions. They also claimed that the use of anatomically correct dolls put ideas into the children's heads.

As the trial wore on, the allegations grew more fantastic (drinking blood in a church, riding in a van with a half-dead baby). The children turned out to be unreliable witnesses and many recanted their earlier statements. On January 18, 1990, the trial involving Raymond and his mother, Peggy, ended with acquittals on some counts. The jury deadlocked on other charges. Pressured by the parents, however, the prosecutor immediately retried Raymond Buckey on the deadlocked charges. The hung jury voted for acquittal. The prosecutor decided not to retry him. Raymond had already spent five years in jail and Peggy had spent two years.

Some people observe that the McMartin case is an example of how a case can be mishandled by everyone involved. They argue that MacFarlane, the child sex abuse expert who headed the investigation, was not licensed to practice therapy in California. Critics point out that the children's testimonies were the result of events suggested to them by their parents who were caught up in the mass hysteria and by the therapists who conducted the interviews. It was later discovered that Judy Johnson, the mother who made the initial allegations of child molestation, was suffering from paranoid schizophrenia. She was also drinking alcohol frequently. After her first accusation, she continued to recount bizarre stories to investigators about her son's behavior, such as his having also been molested by a Los Angeles School Board member. The prosecution did not share this information with the defense for nearly a year. Johnson died of alcohol poisoning in 1986.

The Fells Acres Case

In 1984 a five-year-old boy told his uncle that Gerald Amirault, the son of the owner of the Fells Acres Day School in Malden, Massachusetts, had touched his private parts. He also told his mother of other incidents of abuse. Police notified parents about the situation, instructing them to question their children and watch for behaviors related to sexual abuse. Forty-one children, ages three to six, eventually told stories of being raped by a clown, of being forced to watch animals being killed, and of having their pictures taken naked. Although the children testified about a "secret" or "magic" room they visited daily, no child could show the police the location of the room, nor could the police find it. Violet Amirault and her children, Cheryl Amirault LeFave and Gerald Amirault, were convicted of sexual abuse. The mother and daughter received a sentence of eight to twenty years, and Gerald was sentenced to thirty to forty years.

Violet and Cheryl were released in 1995 after the Massachusetts Superior Court overturned their convictions because the seating arrangement of the child witnesses (facing the jury but not the defendants) violated their right to "face-to-face" confrontations with their accusers as guaranteed by Article 12 of the Massachusetts Declaration of Rights. Two years later the state's highest court reinstated their convictions, claiming that the accused had not offered sufficient proof that justice had been miscarried. Violet Amirault died of cancer later that year.

In June 1998 a Superior Court judge overturned Cheryl's conviction, noting that the accusers, then teenagers, who had never recanted their allegations of abuse, could not testify. The judge claimed that, due to investigators' leading interview methods, it could not be

determined if the accusers were telling the truth. In October 1999, after eight years in prison, Cheryl Amirault LeFave was set free. Her conviction for child molestation stood, but the court commuted her sentence to time served.

On July 6, 2001, the Massachusetts Parole Board voted 5–0, recommending that Gerald's sentence be commuted. On February 20, 2002, Governor Jane Swift rejected the board's recommendation. On April 30, 2004, Gerald Amirault was finally released from prison after serving eighteen years. Authorities said they could not keep him in prison indefinitely due to lack of evidence that he was a sexually dangerous person. The accusers, even as young adults, stuck to their allegations.

The Margaret Kelly Michaels Case

In 1985 a four-year-old boy was being examined at a pediatrician's office. When the nurse took his temperature rectally, the boy remarked that his teacher had done the same thing to him while he napped. The mother went to the authorities. Police charged Margaret Kelly Michaels, the boy's teacher at the Wee Care Day Nursery in Maplewood, New Jersey, with child molestation. A child sexual abuse expert advised the parents of the preschool children to look for changes in their children's behavior as evidence of abuse.

In 1988 Michaels was found guilty of 115 counts of sexual abuse against nineteen children and sentenced to forty-seven years in prison. She was charged with inserting objects, including serrated eating utensils, into the children's genital organs, forcing them to eat a cake made of feces, and playing the piano naked. The state's evidence consisted of the children's allegations during the pretrial period. No medical evidence was found, and none of the other teachers noticed the alleged abuse that supposedly went on for seven months.

In 1993 the New Jersey Appellate Division reversed the conviction, remanding the case for a retrial. The court concluded:

> Certain questions [by investigators] planted sexual information in the children's minds and supplied the children with knowledge and vocabulary which might be considered inappropriate for children of their age group. Children were encouraged to help the police "bust this case wide open." Peer pressure and even threats of disclosing to the other children that the child being questioned was uncooperative were used.

The New Jersey Supreme Court affirmed the appeals court's ruling and ordered a hearing to determine if the children's testimony was tainted. According to the court:

> The interrogations of the child sex abuse victims were improper and there is a substantial likelihood that the evidence derived from them is unreliable. Therefore, if the State seeks to reprosecute Margaret Kelly Michaels, a pretrial hearing must be held in which the State must

prove by clear and convincing evidence that the statements and testimony elicited by the improper interview techniques nonetheless retain a sufficient degree of reliability to warrant admission at trial.

The prosecution decided to drop the case. In 1994 Michaels was released after serving five years in prison.

CHAPTER 8
REPRESSED MEMORY VERSUS FALSE MEMORY

In the early 1900s Austrian psychoanalyst Sigmund Freud first proposed the theory of repression, which hypothesizes that the mind can reject unpleasant ideas, desires, and memories by banishing them into the unconscious. Some clinicians believe that memory repression explains why a victim of a traumatic experience, such as childhood sexual abuse, may forget the horrible incident. Some also believe that forgotten traumatic experiences can be recovered later.

In 1988 Ellen Bass and Laura Davis wrote *The Courage to Heal: A Guide for Women Survivors of Child Sexual Abuse* (New York, NY: HarperCollins, 1988). It has been described as the "bible" of the recovered-memory movement. The authors claimed that Freud was right about his theory that the physical symptoms of hysteria in his patients were indicative of childhood sexual abuse. They listed such symptoms as feeling powerless and having trouble feeling motivated as signs that a person had experienced childhood sexual abuse.

Proponents of recovered-memory therapy are convinced their patients cannot heal until they confront their memories. Some clinical therapists believe that memories rediscovered through hypnosis and other recovery techniques are true and that they must be acknowledged in order for treatment to be successful. Some have been known to recommend that patients cut off all ties with their families to speed up recovery.

Some memory researchers do not agree, saying that children who have suffered serious psychological trauma do not repress the memory; rather, they can never forget it. They cite the examples of survivors of concentration camps or children who have witnessed the murder of a parent who never forget. These researchers believe that memory is inaccurate and that it can be manipulated to "remember" events that never happened. Many mental health professionals warn the public about believing per-

sons who have no training in mental health. For example, they note that authors Bass and Davis were not licensed therapists. Bass was a creative writing teacher, and Davis was a student in one of her writing workshops.

THE FALSE MEMORY SYNDROME FOUNDATION

In the early 1990s many adult patients (mostly women) who sought the help of psychotherapists for emotional problems were told that they may have been sexually abused as children and had no memory of the abuse. Through recovered memory therapy (hypnosis, dream interpretations, joining survivor groups, etc.), women were encouraged to remember the abuse so that they could get rid of their emotional complaints. In response to the growing cases of recovered repressed memories of childhood sexual abuse, an organization of parents claiming to have been falsely accused was formed in 1992. The False Memory Syndrome Foundation (FMSF) was founded by Pamela Freyd, whose adult daughter had accused her father of childhood abuse. The daughter, Jennifer J. Freyd, is a professor of psychology who specializes in memory.

Some mental health professionals have dismissed the FMSF as an extreme organization. The foundation has been accused of protecting child abusers and attempting to discredit the psychiatric profession. Opponents of the FMSF claim that rather than work toward improving therapy, the FMSF sides with those people considered extreme on its scientific board. The board includes experts such as Dr. Elizabeth Loftus (a memory specialist who has challenged the truth of repressed memories), Dr. Richard Ofshe (who specializes in memory related to social coercion and police interrogation, such as in cases of confessing to a crime one did not commit), and Paul McHugh (who disputes the existence of multiple personality disorder). Nevertheless, families who claim they have been torn apart by what they insist are false memories consider the FMSF a lifeline to others suffering the same accusations. FMSF affiliations are found in other countries.

The Debate Continues

Although allegations of recovered repressed memories have declined since their peak in the early 1990s, the controversy over the validity of repressed memories of childhood sexual abuse has not abated. For many, there is no room for the possibility that perhaps the other side might be right. Nonetheless, there are clinicians and memory researchers who believe that the workings of the mind have yet to be fully understood. They agree that, while it is possible for a trauma victim to forget and then remember a horrible experience, it is also possible for a person to have false memories.

STUDIES ON FALSE MEMORIES

Psychologist Elizabeth F. Loftus, a leading opponent of the recovered-memory movement, claims that repression is not normal memory and that it is empirically unproven. She does not believe that the mind could block out experiences of recurrent traumas, with the person unaware of them, and then recover them years later (*The Myth of Repressed Memory: False Memories and Allegations of Sexual Abuse,* New York, NY: St. Martin's Press, 1994).

Memory researchers such as Loftus have shown that false memories can be implanted fairly easily in the laboratory. In *The Myth of Repressed Memory,* Loftus recounted assigning a term project to students in her cognitive psychology class. The project involved implanting a false memory in someone's mind. One of the students chose his fourteen-year-old brother as his test subject. The student wrote about four events his brother had supposedly experienced. Three of the experiences really happened, but the fourth one was a fake event of the boy getting lost at the mall at age five. For the next five days the younger brother was asked to read about his experiences (written by his older brother) and then write down details that he could remember about them. The younger brother "remembered" his shopping-mall experience quite well, describing details elaborately.

In "Make-Believe Memories" (*American Psychologist,* November 2003), Loftus noted that memories can be influenced by imagination. "Imagination not only can make people believe they have done simple things that they have not done but also can lead people to believe that they have experienced more complex events," wrote Loftus. She described a study in which participants were told to imagine performing a common task with certain objects, such as flipping a coin. The second meeting consisted of imagining doing a task without using any object. In a subsequent meeting, participants were tested on their memory of the first day's task performance. Some participants "remembered" not only tasks they had not done but also unusual ones they had not performed.

Being Lost in a Mall Is Not the Same as Being Abused in Childhood

Heidi Sivers, Jonathan Schooler, and Jennifer J. Freyd noted that one should be as cautious in interpreting findings that support recovered memories as in interpreting those that support false memories ("Recovered Memories," *Encyclopedia of the Human Brain,* San Diego, CA: Academic Press, 2002). According to the authors, questions have been raised about generalizing experiences of "benign" false memories, such as remembering being lost in a mall, to recalling being abused by one's parents. False memory studies are limited by the fact that researchers cannot experiment with implanting sexual abuse memories due to obvious ethical considerations and possible repercussions.

The authors added that in false memory research, such as Loftus's "lost in a mall" study, one cannot be certain that the allegedly false event did not actually happen to the subject. Although the subject's relative who was recruited to help plant the false memory was sure the subject had never had such an experience, the findings could have been interpreted as cases in which the relatives were the ones who had forgotten the incident.

IMPLANTING A FALSE MEMORY TO PROVE A CASE: THE PAUL INGRAM CASE. In an unusual situation, Richard Ofshe, social psychologist, expert on cults, and a member of the FMSF Scientific and Professional Advisory Board, implanted a false memory of abuse in the mind of Paul Ingram who was accused of sexually abusing his two daughters. In 1988 after returning home from a religious retreat, Ingram's two daughters accused him and several men in the community of extensive sexual and satanic abuse. After months of interrogations and pressure from a psychologist and police detectives, Ingram began to confess to all kinds of horrific behavior. As his children brought up new charges, he would search his memory until he finally "remembered" and could even supply details of the events. The daughters' accusations included the murder of infants, abortions, and satanic orgies, even involving their mother.

Dr. Ofshe, who had been hired by the prosecution, did not believe Ingram's memories were genuine. Dr. Ofshe told Ingram he had spoken to one of Ingram's sons and one of his daughters, and they related the time Ingram forced them to have sex in front of him. This was one of the few charges that had not been brought against Ingram, and never was, but within a day Ingram submitted a written confession with details of the memory of the event. When Dr. Ofshe informed Ingram he was mistaken, Ingram protested, saying that the event was as real as anything else.

Although he was not sure about his memories, Ingram, a very religious man, was convinced that his daughters would never lie and that he had a dark side he had not known. His pastor, who was counseling the daughters, told Ingram that the abuse had indeed happened. The pastor exorcised him and admonished him to pray to God to bring back memories of his evil acts. Later on Ingram claimed remembering the abuse. Before Dr. Ofshe could submit his report to the prosecution, Ingram pleaded guilty to the charges of rape.

Richard Ofshe reported to the prosecution, "My analysis of this interrogation is that it is quite likely that most of what Mr. Ingram reports as recollections of events are products of social influence rather than reports based on his memory of events." Ingram later realized his false recollections and withdrew his guilty plea. The Washington State Supreme Court rejected his appeal. Ingram received a twenty-year prison sentence. In 1996 Ingram, having exhausted all of his appeals, applied for pardon from then-governor Mike Lowry through the Washington pardons board. Memory experts Elizabeth Loftus and Richard Ofshe, as well as the county prosecutor, sheriff, and Ingram's son, testified on his behalf. The board denied Ingram's request for pardon. On April 8, 2003, Paul Ingram was released from prison after serving fourteen years of his sentence. He was required to register as a sex offender.

TRAUMA AND DISSOCIATION

Some psychologists believe sexual abuse can be so psychologically traumatic that the victim dissociates from full awareness of the horrible experience. In other words, dissociation is the mind's defense mechanism against the trauma. Other scientists disagree, however. For example, Daniel L. Schacter (*Searching for Memory: The Brain, the Mind, and the Past,* New York, NY: Basic Books, 1996) questioned how a patient could dissociate so much of her past, and yet function in society for years without her problems being obvious in her behavior before she consults a therapist. Schacter argued that patients who have really experienced many episodes of dissociation should also have a documented history of the manifestations of such disorder before ever having recovered repressed memories of long-term abuse.

Dissociative Amnesia for Childhood Abuse Memories

According to James A. Chu, Lisa M. Frey, Barbara L. Ganzel, and Julia A. Matthews, although research has shown that memories can be inaccurate and can be influenced by outside factors such as overt suggestions, most studies show that memory tends to be accurate when it comes to remembering the core elements of important events ("Memories of Childhood Abuse: Dissociation, Amnesia, and Corroboration," *American Journal of Psychiatry,* vol. 156, no. 5, May 1999). The authors conducted a study of ninety female patients ages eighteen to sixty who were undergoing treatment in a psychiatric hospital. Dissociative amnesia, discussed in this study, is a type of dissociation, or dissociative disorder.

A large proportion of patients reported childhood abuse: 83% experienced physical abuse, 82% were victims of sexual abuse, and 71% witnessed domestic violence. Those who had a history of any kind of abuse reported experiencing partial or complete amnesia. The occurrence of physical and sexual abuse at an early age accounted for a higher level of amnesia.

Contrary to the popular belief that recovered memory of childhood abuse typically occurs under psychotherapy or hypnosis, most of the patients who suffered complete amnesia for their physical and sexual abuse indicated first recalling the abuse when they were at home and alone. Most patients did not recover memory of childhood abuse as a result of suggestions during therapy. Just one or two participants (for each of the three types of abuse) reported first memory of abuse while in a therapy session. Nearly half (48% for physical abuse and 45% for sexual abuse) were not undergoing psychological counseling or treatment when they first remembered the abuse.

Critics of recovered memories have noted the lack of corroboration (confirmation that the abuse really occurred) in many instances of recovered memories. In this study, the researchers found that, among patients who tried to corroborate their abuse, more than half found physical evidence such as medical records. Nearly nine of ten of those who suffered sexual abuse found verbal validation of such abuse.

BETRAYAL TRAUMA THEORY

Psychologist and professor Jennifer J. Freyd proposed the betrayal trauma theory to explain how children who had experienced abuse may process that betrayal of trust by mentally blocking information about it (*Betrayal Trauma: The Logic of Forgetting Childhood Abuse,* Cambridge, MA: Harvard University Press, 1997). Freyd explained that people typically respond to betrayal by distancing themselves from the betrayer. Children, however, who have suffered abuse at the hands of a parent or a caregiver might not be able to distance themselves from the betrayer. Children need the caregiver for their survival so they "cannot afford *not* to trust" the betrayer. Consequently, the children develop a "blindness" to the betrayal.

In 2001 Jennifer J. Freyd, Anne P. DePrince, and Eileen L. Zurbriggen reported on their preliminary findings relating to the betrayal trauma theory ("Self-Reported Memory for Abuse Depends upon Victim-Perpetrator Relationship," *Journal of Trauma & Dissociation,* vol. 2, no. 3). The researchers found that persons who had been abused by a trusted caregiver reported greater amnesia, compared with those whose abusers were not their caregivers. Greater amnesia was also more likely to be associated with the fact that the perpetrator was a caregiver than with the repeated trauma of abuse.

A LONGITUDINAL STUDY OF MEMORY AND CHILDHOOD SEXUAL ABUSE

Between 1986 and 1998 Catherine Cameron conducted a long-term study of child sexual abuse survivors

(*Resolving Childhood Trauma*, Thousand Oaks, CA: Sage Publications, Inc., 2000). The researcher interviewed seventy-two women, ages twenty-five to sixty-four, during a twelve-year period. The women comprised a group of sexual abuse survivors who sought therapy for the first time in the 1980s. On average, it had been thirty years since their first abuse occurred (thirty-six years for those who suffered amnesia). The women were in private therapy, were better educated, and were more financially well off than most survivors. Twelve imprisoned women were included in the survey. They came from a low socioeconomic background, were serving long sentences, and had participated only in brief group therapy sessions, lasting less than a year.

Cameron sought to study amnesia as both an effect and a cause—what was it about the abuse that resulted in amnesia, and how did the amnesia affect the victim later on in life? Twenty-five women were amnesic, having no awareness of the abuse until recently. Twenty-one were nonamnesic, unable to forget their abuse, and fourteen were partially amnesic about their abuse. The imprisoned women were not assigned a specific category because they were part of a therapy group.

About eight of ten of the amnesic and partially amnesic women believed that they did not remember the sexual abuse because the memories were too painful to live with (82%) and they felt a sense of guilt or shame (79%). More than half of each group believed the amnesia served as a defense mechanism resulting from their desire to protect the family (58%) and love for, or dependence on, the perpetrator (53%). About three-quarters (74%) thought the amnesia occurred because they felt no one would believe them or help them. More than one-third (37%) thought the amnesia had come about because they needed to believe in a "safe" world.

During the years between the abuse and the recall of the abuse, the amnesics reported experiencing the same problems as the nonamnesics, including problems with relationships, revictimization, self-abuse, and dependency on alcohol. Because the amnesics, however, had no conscious knowledge of their childhood abuse, they could not find an explanation for their problems. The author claimed that the conflict between the amnesia and memories that needed release left the amnesic victims depressed and confused.

Cameron addressed the allegations that some therapists implant false memories of sexual abuse in their clients. She noted that 72% of the amnesic women in her study had begun to recall their abuse prior to seeking therapy. Once the survivors in her study confronted their traumatic past, they took charge of how they wanted their therapy handled. Cameron also observed that, since it is evident that recovered memories of childhood abuse are common, they should not be labeled as "false memories"

nor accepted as "flawless truth," but should instead be explored by proponents of the opposing views.

SCIENTIFIC PROOF OF REPRESSED MEMORY?

While some repressed memory experts such as Lenore Terr, a clinical professor of psychiatry, dismiss all laboratory experiments on memory as invalid, others have tried to prove scientifically that memories can be forgotten. Linda Meyer Williams, of the Family Research Laboratory of the University of New Hampshire in Durham, studied the recall of women who had been abused in childhood, for whom there were medical records proving the abuse ("Recall of Childhood Trauma: A Prospective Study of Women's Memories of Child Sexual Abuse," *Journal of Consulting and Clinical Psychology,* vol. 62, no. 6, 1994).

Williams used data gathered between 1973 and 1975 on 206 girls (ages ten months to twelve years) who had been examined for sexual abuse in a city hospital emergency room. In 1990 and 1991 129 of these women were included in a study that was, they were told, a follow-up on the lives and health of women who had received health care as children at the hospital. The women, between the ages of eighteen and thirty-one at the time of the study, were not told of their history of child sexual abuse, although some women suspected the reason for their hospital visit.

Of the 129 women, 38% failed to report the sexual abuse documented by the hospital; of this group, however, 68% reported other childhood sexual abuses. Williams doubted that the women were simply unwilling to discuss the abuse because other personal subjects—such as abortions, prostitution, or having sexually transmitted diseases—were not withheld.

Twelve percent (fifteen respondents) of the total sample reported that they were never abused in childhood. Williams suggested that this was an undercount of the likely number of women who had forgotten childhood abuse. Because the abuse these women suffered was known to at least one other person (the person who brought the child to the hospital), it was less likely to have been repressed than abuse that was always kept a secret.

Williams concluded that if it is possible that victims do not remember having been abused, their recovery of repressed memory later on in life should not come as a surprise. In fact, 16% of the women who recalled the sexual victimization that brought them to the hospital reported there were periods when they "forgot" the abuse.

In a second paper on the same research ("Recovered Memories of Abuse in Women with Documented Child Sexual Victimization Histories," *Journal of Traumatic Stress,* October 1995), Williams described the interviews with some of the women who had forgotten. It is not clear whether the women were truly amnesic or whether the abuse was simply not a part of their conscious lives for a time.

Most reported that they recalled the abuse when a television movie or some other event jogged their memories. None had sought therapy to uncover repressed memories. Williams suggested that these women (inner-city, mainly black, women) did not have the financial resources or knowledge to get professional help.

A Rebuttal

Critics of Williams's conclusions pointed out that one of the reasons women in the study had forgotten their abuse was that the trauma had occurred in infancy. (Experts contend that events that happen before the acquisition of language at two to three years of age are forgotten because there is no way to express the event.) Williams disagreed, noting that, while 55% of those who had been abused at three years or younger had no memory of the occurrence, 62% of those who were four to six years old also did not remember.

In addition, critics questioned how Williams could be certain that those who claimed not to remember were actually telling the truth. The researchers never confronted the women who did not report abuse by showing them their hospital records.

VICTIMS' PERCEPTION OF THEIR FORGETTING EXPERIENCES

Michelle A. Epstein and Bette L. Bottoms investigated the temporary forgetting of past abuse and trauma to determine victims' own explanations for their forgetting experiences ("Explaining the Forgetting and Recovery of Abuse and Trauma Memories: Possible Mechanisms," *Child Maltreatment,* vol. 7, no. 3, August 2002). The researchers observed that many studies of forgetting experiences involve mainly childhood sexual abuse. In this study Epstein and Bottoms added other childhood traumatic experiences, including being in a serious car accident, experiencing other severe accidents, being at a fire, being a victim of a major crime, emotional or verbal abuse, severe neglect, and surgery/hospitalization.

Study participants were 1,411 college women, consisting of 37% whites, 22% Asian Americans, 21% African-Americans, 14% Hispanics, and 6% other ethnic/racial groups. The women ranged in age from eighteen to sixty years, with a median age of twenty-one (half were younger than twenty-one and half were older than twenty-one).

About one-quarter (26%) of the women reported at least one incident of childhood sexual abuse, 27% reported childhood physical abuse, and 54% reported one or more other traumatic experiences. The authors found no statistical difference in women who reported experiencing "a time when they could not remember" sexual abuse (14%) and physical abuse (11%). Compared to women who temporarily "forgot" having experienced other types of trauma (6%), those who reported sexual abuse and multiple traumas experienced temporary forgetting at much higher rates, 14% and 17%, respectively.

A majority of participants attributed their temporary forgetting to mechanisms other than the "classic Freudian repression" (complete lack of conscious memories and forgetting these memories, followed by memory recovery of the abuse or trauma). These mechanisms included active cognitive avoidance (actively not thinking of abuse or trauma), retrieval failure (simple forgetting), and relabeling (looking at an experience in a different light "because its negative implications are less likely to be understood during childhood"). Epstein and Bottoms concluded that, when they counted only women who reported classic Freudian repression, just 4%, or two sexual abuse victims; 10%, or three physical abuse victims; and 11%, or four victims of other traumas, represented such repression. Nevertheless, the authors pointed out that they were not claiming that repression does not occur.

GOING TO COURT

Suing Alleged Abusers

According to the False Memory Syndrome Foundation (FMSF), between 1983 and 1998 many individuals who had "recovered" memories of childhood sexual abuse sued their alleged abusers, many at the instigation of their therapists. During those years a total of 589 lawsuits based on repressed memory were filed, of which 506 were civil and 83 were criminal. Following a sharp rise in 1992, the year the FMSF was created, the number of lawsuits dropped rapidly after 1994.

While the courts readily accepted some early cases of child sexual abuse, courts in more and more states are becoming increasingly suspicious of accounts of outrageous abuse. Therapists are being held liable for malpractice not only by their patients, but often by third parties (usually the accused parents of someone who has allegedly recovered memories of sexual abuse).

The Case of Eileen Franklin

In 1990 George Franklin was convicted of killing his daughter Eileen's friend twenty years earlier. Eileen claimed to have recovered memories of her father's murderous act as she was gazing into her own daughter's eyes. She told her secret to her therapist. She then told police she suddenly remembered herself as a nine-year-old watching her father kill her friend. Later on Eileen changed her account of how she recalled the murder, at one point telling police that the details of the killing became clearer to her after she underwent therapy.

Lenore Terr was an influential expert witness at this first criminal trial in the United States involving recovered memory. Terr, who supports the idea of repressed memory, later wrote about Eileen's story in the book *Unchained Memories: True Stories of Traumatic Memories, Lost and Found* (New York, NY: Basic Books, 1994).

Harry MacLean, who reported on the case in his book *Once upon a Time: A True Story of Memory, Murder, and the Law* (New York, NY: HarperCollins, 1993), claimed that Professor Terr had repeatedly distorted the facts to suit her purpose. Terr claimed to offer a dramatic proof of Eileen's truthful testimony when she described the "body memory" (a physical manifestation of trauma that the conscious mind has forgotten) of Eileen's repressed trauma. According to Terr, Eileen had a habit of pulling her hair out, resulting in a balding spot on her scalp. Eileen had allegedly seen her father murder her friend with a blow to the head using a large rock.

According to MacLean, in his interviews with Eileen's mother, sisters, school friends, and teachers, no one could remember Eileen's pulling out her hair or having a bleeding spot on her scalp. Dr. Ofshe and Ethan Watters (*Making Monsters: False Memories, Psychotherapy, and Sexual Hysteria,* New York, NY: Scribners, 1994) found more than forty photos taken of Eileen during the relevant period that were wrongly withheld from the defense and that showed no trace of a bald spot.

In November 1995 a federal appeals court overturned George Franklin's murder conviction. By this time Franklin had served almost seven years of a life sentence. The court ruled that the trial had been tainted by the improper allegation that Franklin had confessed and by the exclusion of crucial evidence: Eileen had been hypnotized by her therapist, Kirk Barrett, prior to the first trial, making her testimony unreliable. The court ordered a retrial. On July 2, 1996, the prosecution dropped the charges, citing the problem of Eileen's hypnosis that, by California law, would probably prevent her from testifying. In addition, new DNA evidence showed that it was impossible for Franklin to have committed the second murder his daughter had accused him of, which she claimed happened when she was fifteen.

In June 1997 George Franklin filed a civil suit in federal court against his daughter, her therapist, Barrett, and county officials, claiming violation of his civil rights. The suit alleged, among other things, that Eileen, Barrett, and county officials conspired to deny George Franklin the due process of law and violated his Fifth, Sixth, and Fourteenth Amendment rights to confront witnesses against him. He also sued Professor Terr for conspiring with Eileen to give false testimony.

In 2000 the court dismissed Franklin's suit against the county officials. The judge for the Ninth Circuit Court of Appeals also threw out the claims against Professor Terr, writing in his opinion, "Terr is absolutely immune . . . for civil damages based on the allegation that she conspired to present her own and another witness's perjured testimony at Franklin's criminal trial. . . . Absolute witness immunity is based on the policy of protecting the judicial process" (*Franklin v. Terr,* No. 98-16843 [2000]). The court dismissed the suit against Barrett because George Franklin failed to state the right claim that the therapist had conspired with a state official to deny him his constitutional rights. Franklin had sought a token $1 award from his daughter, but that, too, was thrown out.

Suing the Therapist

In February 2004 Elizabeth Gale settled a lawsuit against three therapists and the Rush-Presbyterian-St. Luke's Medical Center and Tush North Shore Medical Center in Chicago, Illinois, for $7.5 million. In 1986 Dr. Bennett Braun, a psychiatrist, first diagnosed Gale as having multiple personality disorder when the patient sought treatment for mild depression. Gale was hospitalized for five and a half years and was treated by two other therapists, Doctors Roberta Sachs and Corydon Hammond. Under hypnosis, Gale believed that she was involved in a secret cult that sacrificed children. She was told she had repressed memories of her participation in the cult. She had a tubal ligation, with Braun's approval, so that she would not bear any more children for the cult.

Dr. Bennett Braun settled a similar repressed-memory malpractice suit in 1997, with co-defendants Dr. Elva Poznanski and the Rush-Presbyterian-St. Luke's Medical Center, for $1.6 million. The plaintiff, Patricia Burgus, consulted Braun for postpartum depression in 1986. For the next six years, using hypnosis and medication, Braun convinced his patient that she had developed more than three hundred multiple personalities as a result of child abuse. She believed that she was horribly tortured by her family and had participated in ritual murders, cannibalism, and devil worship. Braun also convinced Burgus and her husband that their two sons, ages four and five, might be predisposed to multiple personality disorder like their mother and should be committed to the hospital psychiatric ward. Doctors Braun and Poznanski helped the children "remember" abuse perpetrated by their mother, exposing them to guns and handcuffs for "therapeutic" purposes.

Third-Party Suits

The courts now often hold therapists liable to a third party, usually the patient's accused parent, when they implant or reinforce false memories in their patients. Social worker Susan L. Jones, while treating Joel Hungerford's daughter Laura, convinced her that her anxiety attacks were the result of sexual abuse by her father. Jones not only advised Laura to cease contact with her father but also convinced the patient to file a complaint of aggravated felonious sexual assault against Joel. In addition Jones contacted the police regarding the alleged assault and aided the prosecution in indicting Joel Hungerford.

Hungerford sued Jones for the misdiagnosis and negligent treatment of his daughter's condition. Jones claimed that she owed Hungerford no duty of care, meaning that since she had treated Laura Hungerford, not Joel Hungerford, Joel Hungerford could not claim that her treatment had hurt him. On December 18, 1998, in *Joel Hungerford v. Susan L. Jones* (No. 97-657 [1998]), the New Hampshire Supreme Court, in this case of "first impression" (with no existing precedent), ruled:

> We hold that a therapist owes an accused parent a duty of care in the diagnosis and treatment of an adult patient for sexual abuse where the therapist or the patient, acting on the encouragement, recommendation, or instruction of the therapist, takes public action concerning the accusation. In such instances, the social utility of detecting and punishing sexual abusers and maintaining the breadth of treatment choices for patients is outweighed by the substantial risk of severe harm to falsely accused parents, the family unit, and society.

IMPORTANT NAMES AND ADDRESSES

American Bar Association
Center on Children and the Law
740 15th St. NW
Washington, DC 20005
(202) 662-1720
FAX: (202) 662-1755
E-mail: ctrchildlaw@abanet.org
URL: http://www.abanet.org/child

American Humane Association
Children's Division
63 Inverness Dr. E
Englewood, CO 80112-5117
(303) 792-9900
Toll-free: 1-800-227-4645
FAX: (303) 792-5333
E-mail: children@americanhumane.org
URL: http://www.americanhumane.org

Center for Effective Discipline
155 West Main St.
Suite 1603
Columbus, OH 43215
(614) 221-8829
FAX: (614) 221-2110
E-mail: info@stophitting.org
URL: http://www.stophitting.com

Child Welfare League of America
440 First St. NW, 3rd Fl.
Washington, DC 20001-2085
(202) 638-2952
FAX: (202) 638-4004
URL: http://www.cwla.org

Childhelp USA
15757 North 75th St.
Scottsdale, AZ 85260
(480) 922-8212
Toll-free: 1-800-4-A-CHILD
FAX: (480) 922-7061
URL: http://www.childhelpusa.org

Children's Bureau
U.S. Department of Health and
Human Services

330 C St. SW
Washington, DC 20447
URL: http://www.acf.dhhs.gov/programs/cb

Children's Defense Fund
25 E St. NW
Washington, DC 20001
(202) 628-8787
FAX: (202) 662-3540
E-mail: cdfinfo@childrensdefense.org
URL: http://www.childrensdefense.org

**Children's Healthcare Is a Legal Duty,
Inc. (CHILD, Inc.)**
P.O. Box 2604
Sioux City, IA 51106
(712) 948-3500
FAX: (712) 948-3704
E-mail: childinc@netins.net
URL: http://www.childrenshealthcare.org

Crimes against Children Research Center
University of New Hampshire
20 College Rd.
126 Horton Social Science Center
Durham, NH 03824-3586
(603) 862-1888
FAX: (603) 862-1122
E-mail: kelly.foster@unh.edu
URL: http://www.unh.edu/ccrc

False Memory Syndrome Foundation
1955 Locust St.
Philadelphia, PA 19103-5766
(215) 940-1040
FAX: (215) 940-1042
E-mail: mail@fmsfonline.org
URL: http://www.fmsfonline.org

Family Research Laboratory
University of New Hampshire
20 College Rd.
126 Horton Social Science Center
Durham, NH 03824-3586
(603) 862-1888

FAX: (603) 862-1122
E-mail: doreen.cole@unh.edu
URL: http://www.unh.edu/frl

**Family Violence and Sexual
Assault Institute**
6160 Cornerstone Ct. E
San Diego, CA 92121
(858) 623-2777
FAX: (858) 646-0761
E-mail: fvsai@alliant.edu
URL: http://www.fvsai.org

Family Violence Prevention Fund
383 Rhode Island St.
Suite 304
San Francisco, CA 94103-5133
(415) 252-8900
FAX: (415) 252-8991
E-mail: info@endabuse.org
URL: http://www.endabuse.org

**International Society for Prevention of
Child Abuse and Neglect**
25 West 560 Geneva Rd.
Suite L2C
Carol Stream, IL 60188
(630) 221-1311
FAX: (630) 221-1313
E-mail: ispcan@ispcan.org
URL: http://www.ispcan.org

**Minnesota Center against
Violence & Abuse**
School of Social Work, University of Minnesota
105 Peters Hall
1404 Gortner Ave.
St. Paul, MN 55108-6142
(612) 624-0721
FAX: (612) 625-4288
URL: http://www.mincava.umn.edu

**National Association of Counsel
for Children**
1825 Marion St.

Suite 242
Denver, CO 80218
Toll-free: 1-888-828-6222
E-mail: advocate@NACCchildlaw.org
URL: http://NACCchildlaw.org

National Association to Protect Children
46 Haywood St.
Suite 315
Asheville, NC 28801
(828) 350-9350
E-mail: info@protect.org
URL: http://www.protect.org

National CASA Association
100 West Harrison St.
North Tower, Suite 500
Seattle, WA 98119
Toll-free: 1-800-628-3233
Fax: (206) 270-0078
E-mail: inquiry@nationalcasa.org
URL: http://www.nationalcasa.org

National Center for Missing & Exploited Children
Charles B. Wang International Children's Building
699 Prince St.
Alexandria, VA 22314-3175
(703) 274-3900
Toll-free: 1-800-843-5678
Fax: (703) 274-2220
URL: http://www.missingkids.org

National Center for the Prosecution of Child Abuse
American Prosecutors Research Institute (APRI)
99 Canal Center Plaza
Suite 510
Alexandria, VA 22314
(703) 549-4253
FAX: (703) 836-3195
E-mail: ncpca@ndaa-apri.org
URL: http://www.ndaa-apri.org/apri/
programs/ncpca/ncpca_home.html

National Center for Victims of Crime
2000 M St. NW
Suite 480
Washington, DC 20036
(202) 467-8700
FAX: (202) 467-8701
E-mail: webmaster@ncvc.org
URL: http://www.ncvc.org

National Child Abuse Defense & Resource Center
P.O. Box 638
Holland, OH 43528
(419) 865-0513
FAX: (419) 865-0526
E-mail: NCADRC@aol.com
URL: http://www.falseallegation.org

National Clearinghouse on Child Abuse and Neglect Information
330 C St. SW
Washington, DC 20447
(703) 385-7565
Toll-free: 1-800-394-3366
FAX: (703) 385-3206
E-mail: nccanch@caliber.com
URL: http://nccanch.acf.hhs.gov

National Coalition for Child Protection Reform
53 Skyhill Rd.
Suite 202
Alexandria, VA 22314
(703) 212-2006
FAX: (703) 212-2006
E-mail: info@nccpr.org
URL: http://www.nccpr.org

National Council of Juvenile and Family Court Judges
P.O. Box 8970
Reno, NV 89507
(775) 784-6012
FAX: (775) 784-6628
E-mail: admin@ncjfcj.org
URL: http://www.ncjfcj.org

National Council on Child Abuse and Family Violence
1025 Connecticut Ave. NW
Suite 1012
Washington, DC 20036
(202) 429-6695
Toll-free: 1-800-799-7233
FAX: (831) 655-3930
E-mail: info@nccafv.org
URL: http://www.nccafv.org

National Criminal Justice Reference Service (NCJRS)
P.O. Box 6000
Rockville, MD 20849-6000
(301) 519-5500
Toll-free: 1-800-851-3420

FAX: (301) 519-5212
E-mail: askncjrs@ncjrs.org
URL: http://www.ncjrs.org

National Domestic Violence Hotline
P.O. Box 161810
Austin, TX 78716
Toll-free: 1-800-799-7233
Fax: (512) 453-8541
E-mail: ndvh@ndvh.org
URL: http://www.ndvh.org

National Runaway Switchboard
3080 North Lincoln Ave.
Chicago, IL 60657
(773) 880-9860
Toll-free: 1-800-621-4000
FAX: (773) 929-5150
E-mail: info@nrscrisisline.org
URL: http://www.nrscrisisline.org

Office on Violence against Women
810 Seventh St. NW
Washington, DC 20531
(202) 307-6026
FAX: (202) 307-3911
URL: http://www.ojp.usdoj.gov/vawo

Prevent Child Abuse America
200 South Michigan Ave., 17th Fl.
Chicago, IL 60604-2404
(312) 663-3520
FAX: (312) 939-8962
E-mail: mailbox@preventchildabuse.org
URL: http://www.preventchildabuse.org

silentlambs
Toll-free: 1-877-WTABUSE
URL: http://www.silentlambs.org

Survivors Network of Those Abused by Priests (SNAP)
P.O. Box 6416
Chicago, IL 60680-6416
Toll-free: 1-877-762-7432
URL: http://www.snapnetwork.org

UNICEF
333 East 38th St.
New York, NY 10016
(212) 686-5522
Toll-free: 1-800-4UNICEF
FAX: (212) 779-1670
URL: http://www.unicefusa.org

RESOURCES

The National Child Abuse and Neglect Data System (NCANDS) of the U.S. Department of Health and Human Services (HHS; Washington, DC) is the primary source of national information on child maltreatment known to state child protective services (CPS) agencies. The latest findings from NCANDS are published in *Child Maltreatment 2002* (2004). The most recent national incidence study, *The Third National Incidence Study of Child Abuse and Neglect* (NIS-3; 1996), is the single most comprehensive source of information about the incidence of child maltreatment in the United States. The NIS-3 findings are based on data collected not only from CPS but also from community institutions (such as day care centers, schools, and hospitals) and investigating agencies (such as public health departments, police, and courts). Other HHS publications used include *The NSDUH Report: Pregnancy and Substance Use* (2004), *The Child Abuse Prevention and Treatment Act as Amended by The Keeping Children and Families Safe Act of 2003* (2004), *Child Welfare Outcomes 2001: Annual Report* (2004), *Major Federal Legislation Concerned with Child Protection, Child Welfare, and Adoption* (2003), *The NHSDA Report: Children Living with Substance-Abusing or Substance-Dependent Parents* (2003), and *Children of Color in the Child Welfare System: Perspectives from the Child Welfare Community* (2003).

The National Clearinghouse on Child Abuse and Neglect Information of the HHS provided an assortment of helpful publications used in the preparation of this book, including *The Child Welfare System* (2004), *Child Abuse and Neglect Fatalities: Statistics and Interventions* (2004), *2003 Child Abuse and Neglect State Statute Series Statutes-at-a-Glance: Mandatory Reporters of Child Abuse and Neglect* (2003), *2003 Child Abuse and Neglect State Statutes Series Ready Reference—Reporting Laws: Drug-Exposed Infants* (2003), *Understanding the Effects of Maltreatment on Early Brain Development* (2001), and *In Harm's Way: Domestic Violence and Child Maltreatment* (undated).

Other federal government publications used for this book include *2004 Trafficking in Persons Report* (U.S. Department of State, 2004), *Educator Sexual Misconduct: A Synthesis of Existing Literature* (U.S. Department of Education, 2004), *Child Welfare: HHS Could Play a Greater Role in Helping Child Welfare Agencies Recruit and Retain Staff* (U.S. General Accounting Office, 2003), and *A Nation Online: How Americans Are Expanding Their Use of the Internet* (U.S. Department of Commerce, 2002).

Different offices of the U.S. Department of Justice produce publications relating to child maltreatment. The Bureau of Justice Statistics published *Profile of Jail Inmates, 2002* (2004), *Intimate Partner Violence, 1993–2001* (2003), *Prisoners in 2002* (2003), *Prisoners in 2001* (2002), *Sexual Assault of Young Children as Reported to Law Enforcement: Victim, Incident, and Offender Characteristics* (2000), and *Intimate Partner Violence* (2000). The Office for Victims of Crime published the *OVC Bulletin: Children at Clandestine Methamphetamine Labs: Helping Meth's Youngest Victims* (2003), *Internet Crimes against Children* (2001), and *Sexual Assault Nurse Examiner (SANE) Programs: Improving the Community Response to Sexual Assault Victims* (2001). The Office of Juvenile Justice and Delinquency Prevention published *Explanations for the Decline in Child Sexual Abuse Cases* (2004), *Nonfamily Abducted Children: National Estimates and Characteristics* (2002), *The Decline in Child Sexual Abuse* (2001), and *Crimes against Children by Babysitters* (2001). The National Institute of Justice published *Prosecutors, Kids, and Domestic Violence Cases* (2002), *An Update on the "Cycle of Violence"* (2001), *Childhood Victimization: Early Adversity, Later Psychopathology* (2000), and *Research on Women and Girls in the Justice System* (2000).

Online Victimization: A Report on the Nation's Youth (Crimes against Children Research Center, University of New Hampshire, NH, and National Center for Missing &

Exploited Children, Alexandria, VA, 2000) discussed the findings of the first *Youth Internet Safety Survey. Teenage Life Online: The Rise of the Instant-Message Generation and the Internet's Impact on Friendships and Family Relationships* by the Pew Internet & American Life Project (Washington, DC, 2001) found that adolescents who have Internet access do communicate with strangers they meet online.

The Family Research Laboratory (FRL) at the University of New Hampshire, Durham, is a major source of studies on domestic violence. Murray A. Straus, David Finkelhor, Linda Meyer Williams, Kathleen Kendall-Tackett, Lisa Jones, Richard K. Ormrod, and many others associated with the laboratory have done some of the most scientifically rigorous research in the field of abuse. Studies released by the FRL investigate all forms of domestic violence, many based on its two major surveys: the *National Family Violence Survey* (1975) and the *National Family Violence Resurvey* (1985). Much of the research from these two surveys has been gathered into *Physical Violence in American Families: Risk Factors and Adaptations to Violence in 8,145 Families* (Murray A. Straus and Richard J. Gelles; Christine Smith, ed., Somerset, NJ: Transaction Publishers, 1990). Dr. Murray A. Straus is also widely known for his studies on corporal punishment. Several of Dr. Straus's journal articles, his book *Beating the Devil Out of Them: Corporal Punishment in American Families and Its Effects on Children* (2nd. ed, New Brunswick, NJ: Transaction Publishers, 2003), and papers presented at meetings on domestic violence in various countries were helpful in the preparation of this book.

Many journals published useful articles on child maltreatment that were used in the preparation of this book. They include the *American Journal of Drug and Alcohol Abuse, American Journal of Psychiatry, American Psychologist, Archives of Pediatrics & Adolescent Medicine, BMC Medicine, British Medical Journal, Child Abuse & Neglect, Child Maltreatment, Clinical Psychology: Science and Practice, Family Forum, Journal of Child Sexual Abuse, Journal of Consulting and Clinical Psychology, Journal of Experimental Psychology: Applied, Journal of Family Violence, Journal of Interpersonal Violence, Journal of Instructional Psychology, Journal of the American Academy of Child & Adolescent Psychiatry, Journal of the American Medical Association, Journal of Trauma & Dissociation, Journal of Traumatic Stress, The Lancet, National Institute of Justice Journal, Neuron, New England Law Review, Pediatrics, Psychoneuroendocrinology,* and *State Legislatures.*

Several reports were used in the preparation of this book. They include *Child Maltreatment in the United Kingdom—A Study of the Prevalence of Child Abuse and Neglect* (National Society for the Prevention of Cruelty to Children, London, England, 2000), *The Nature and Scope of the Problem of Sexual Abuse of Minors by Catholic Priests and Deacons in the United States* (United States Conference of Catholic Bishops, Washington, DC, 2004), *A Call to Action: Ending Crimes of Violence Against Children and Adults with Disabilities: A Report to the Nation* (State University of New York, Upstate Medical University, Department of Physical Medicine and Rehabilitation, Syracuse, NY, 2003), *The Sexual Abuse of Children in the Roman Catholic Archdiocese of Boston: A Report by the Attorney General* (2003) by Massachusetts Attorney General Thomas F. Reilly, and *The Police Chief* (Julian Fantino, "Child Pornography on the Internet: New Challenges Require New Ideas," International Association of Chiefs of Police, Alexandria, VA, 2003). Issue papers on foster care and family preservation by the National Coalition for Child Protection Reform (Alexandria, VA) were also used in the preparation of this book.

The American Professional Society on the Abuse of Children (APSAC), in *The APSAC Handbook on Child Maltreatment* (Thousand Oaks, CA: Sage Publications, Inc., 2002), brought together a variety of child abuse experts to discuss ongoing controversies in their fields, as well as to challenge long-held assumptions and conclusions. The National Center for Children in Poverty discussed *Depression, Substance Abuse, and Domestic Violence: Little Is Known about Co-Occurrence and Combined Effects on Low-Income Families* (Columbia University, Mailman School of Public Health, New York, NY, 2004). The David and Lucile Packard Foundation publication *The Future of Children,* published by the Woodrow Wilson School of Public and International Affairs of Princeton University (Princeton, NJ) in collaboration with the Brookings Institute (Washington, DC), provides information on major issues related to the well-being of children. Information from *The Future of Children: Domestic Violence and Children* (1999), *The Future of Children: Protecting Children from Abuse and Neglect* (1998), and *The Future of Children: Sexual Abuse of Children* (1994) was used in this publication.

Helpful books used for this publication include *What Parents Need to Know about Sibling Abuse: Breaking the Cycle of Violence,* by Vernon R. Wiehe (Springville, UT: Bonneville Books, 2002); *Confronting Chronic Neglect: The Education and Training of Health Professionals on Family Violence* (Washington, DC: National Academy Press, 2002); *The Epidemic of Rape and Child Sexual Abuse in the United States,* by Diana E. H. Russell and Rebecca M. Bolen (Thousand Oaks, CA: Sage Publications, Inc., 2000); *Neglected Children: Research, Practice, and Policy* (Howard Dubowitz, ed., Thousand Oaks, CA: Sage Publications, Inc., 1999); *Understanding Family Violence: Treating and Preventing Partner, Child, Sibling, and Elder Abuse,* by Vernon R. Wiehe (Thousand Oaks, CA: Sage Publications, Inc., 1998); *Issues in Inti-*

mate Violence (Raquel Kennedy Bergen, ed., Thousand Oaks, CA: Sage Publications, Inc., 1998); *The Book of David: How Preserving Families Can Cost Children's Lives,* by Richard J. Gelles (New York, NY: Basic Books, 1996); *Wounded Innocents: The Real Victims of the War Against Child Abuse,* by Richard Wexler (Buffalo, NY: Prometheus Books, 1990); and *The Secret Trauma: Incest in the Lives of Girls and Women,* by Diana E. H. Russell (New York, NY Basic Books, 1986).

Books used for information on recovered memory include *Encyclopedia of the Human Brain,* vol. 4 (V.S. Ramachandran, ed., San Diego, CA: Academic Press, 2002); *Resolving Childhood Trauma: A Long-Term Study of Abuse Survivors,* by Catherine Cameron (Thousand Oaks, CA: Sage Publications, Inc., 2000); *Searching for Memory: The Brain, the Mind, and the Past,* by Daniel Schacter (New York, NY: Basic Books, 1996); *Betrayal Trauma: The Logic of Forgetting Childhood Abuse,* by Jennifer J. Freyd (Cambridge, MA: Harvard University Press, 1996); *The Myth of Repressed Memory: False Memories and Allegations of Sexual Abuse,* by Elizabeth F. Loftus (New York, NY: St. Martin's Press, 1994); *Making Monsters: False Memories, Psychotherapy, and Sexual Hysteria,* by Richard Ofshe and Ethan Watters (New York, NY: Scribner's, 1994); *Unchained Memories: True Stories of Traumatic Memories, Lost and Found,* by

Lenore Terr (New York, NY: Basic Books, 1994); *Once upon a Time: A True Story of Memory, Murder, and the Law,* by Harry MacLean (New York, NY: HarperCollins, 1993); and *The Courage to Heal: A Guide for Women Survivors of Child Sexual Abuse,* by Ellen Bass and Laura Davis (New York, NY: HarperCollins, 1988).

Thomson Gale thanks the International Labour Organization (ILO) for granting us permission to use graphics from *Investing in Every Child: An International Labour Organization Economic Study of the Costs and Benefits of Eliminating Child Labour* (Geneva, Switzerland, 2004). The ILO also published *Helping Hands or Shackled Lives? Understanding Child Domestic Labour and Responses to It,* by June Kane (2004). The Gallup Organization granted permission to use graphics from the *Gallup Youth Survey,* "One-Third of Teens Know of Abuse among Peers," by Steve Crabtree (2003).

Other international organizations publish literature relating to children. Human Rights Watch and the Coalition to Stop the Use of Child Soldiers reported on the numbers and status of child soldiers all over the world in *Human Rights Watch World Report 2004: Human Rights and Armed Conflict* (2004) and *Child Soldier Use 2003: A Briefing for the Fourth UN Security Council Open Debate on Children and Armed Conflict* (2004), respectively.

INDEX